MY BROTHER, ERNEST HEMINGWAY

LEICESTER HEMINGWAY

My Brother,
Ernest Hemingway

THE WORLD PUBLISHING COMPANY

CLEVELAND AND NEW YORK

Published by The World Publishing Company
2231 West 110th Street, Cleveland 2, Ohio

Published simultaneously in Canada by
Nelson, Foster & Scott Ltd.

Library of Congress Catalog Card Number: 62-9043

FIRST EDITION

FOR DORIS

A NOTE AND ACKNOWLEDGMENTS

The conversations recorded in this biography are as accurate as I could make them. I did not have a tape recorder, and I do not possess total recall. But my own notes, ship's log, and memory enabled me to reproduce many conversations. In writing dialogue, Ernest polished, edited, and was the supreme master of this art. In talking, he sometimes tried out ideas, phrases, and sounds in uncommon speech patterns, and was occasionally addicted to the use of so-called Indian talk. His speech was free-flowing and he used language that was uninhibited and sometimes unprintable. In presenting Ernest's conversations, I have been mindful of the obligations of a brother, a friend, and a biographer. Ernest did not favor the publication of his letters so they have not been reproduced here. He regarded all biographies as unlucky during the subject's lifetime. Yet at the end of the last letter I had from him, he wished me luck with this book.

I am indebted to the following persons:

Earl Adams, Arturo Barea, Tyley Hancock Bayley, Thomas Browne Bennett, Mr. and Mrs. Harvey Breit, George Brown, Mr. and Mrs. Otto Bruce, James Cannon, Robert Capa, Mr. and Mrs. Canby Chambers, Mrs. Grenville Davis, Jean Decamp, Mr. and Mrs. Paul de Kruif, Marlene Dietrich, James Dilworth, Wesley

7

Dilworth, John Dos Passos, Coert duBois, Alfred Dudek, Marcel Duhamel, William Dwyer, Charles Fenton, John Ferno, Sidney Franklin, Donald Friede, Capt. Gregorio Fuentes, Mrs. John Gardner, Capt. Tommy Gifford, Mr. and Mrs. Arnold Gingrich, John Groth, Henry Grund, Carlos Gutierrez, Anson Tyler Hemingway, Dr. Clarence Edmunds Hemingway, Grace Hall Hemingway, Gregory Hemingway, John Hadley Nicanor Hemingway, Martha Gellhorn Hemingway, Mary Welsh Hemingway, Patrick Hemingway, Pauline Pfeiffer Hemingway, Josephine Herbst, John Herrmann, William Dodge Horne, Ralph Ingersoll, Howell G. Jenkins, Mrs. Jasper J. Jepson, Capt. Jakie Key, Dr. Carlos Kohly, Francesca LaMonte, Maj. Gen. Charles Truman Lanham, Michael Lerner, Leonard Lyons, Archibald MacLeish, Dr. Meyer Maskin, Antony Mason, Grant Mason, Jr., Herbert L. Matthews, Rose McConnell, Ruth Arnold Meehan, Mrs. Ernest J. Miller, Mrs. Paul Scott Mowrer, Joseph O'Keefe, Edwin Pailthorpe, Archer Pelkey, Virginia Pfeiffer, Pablo Picasso, Mr. and Mrs. Luis Quintanilla, Alfred Rice, Dr. Harold Rome, Capt. Josey Russell, Arnold Samuelson, Mrs. Sterling S. Sanford, Capt. Bra Saunders, Irwin Shaw, Mr. and Mrs. William Smith, Maurice Speiser, Frederick Spiegel, Mrs. William C. Stanfield, Jr., James Sullivan, Mrs. William Targ, Col. John W. Thomason, Jr., Mr. and Mrs. Charles Thompson, William Walton, John Wheeler, Earl Wilson, and Ira Wolfert.

L. H.

ILLUSTRATIONS

MY BROTHER, ERNEST HEMINGWAY

Prologue

This is a book about Ernest Hemingway the writer, the soldier of fortune, the big-game hunter, deep-sea fisherman, and bullfight buff. Ernest was all of these things. He was also my only brother. In the early years after I was born he changed my diapers with amusement and called me "the bipehouse." Later he changed my nickname to "the Baron." He taught me even more than my father did about shooting, fishing, and fighting.

One calm evening after World War II while we watched the sun setting beyond Havana, Ernest talked about life and the things that made a good one. We laughed together over some of the observations on his own life that had been made by people outside the family.

"Jeezus, Baron," he said finally, "someday I'd like to have somebody who really knew me write a book about me. Maybe you'll be the one. After all, the Huxleys made out all right, and the James brothers—Frank and Jesse especially."

A good deal of time has passed since then. But Ernest never took back anything he said. In the time that has gone by, some of the material written about Ernest by scholars, columnists, reviewers, and indignant custodians of public virtue has been so heinously and hilariously inaccurate that it does not merit consideration. A few of the writers have been just and accurate.

Ernest was one of those rare humans who was truly original. That he has a secure position in world literature as a gifted writer is certain. That he also possessed absolute integrity, both emotional and aesthetic, is clear to the people who have read his books and to those who knew him well. But the fact that he was a child of God besieged by a welter of familial and personal problems is either forgotten or overlooked by most students of his work and life.

As Ernest's brother, I have many times been asked for insights into his life and character. These glimpses might well be called notes for a biography, since his life was so abundant that a definitive account would be almost impossible. As Ernest once pungently observed, "The true story of a man's life should really cover everything that happened to him and around him every twenty-four hours for fifty years."

Ernest lived as he died—violently. He had a tremendous respect for courage. During his own lifetime he traded in it, developed it, and taught other people a great deal about it. And his own courage never deserted him. What finally failed him was his body. This can happen to anyone.

The morning of that last July 2, when he took the final action of his life and for the last time fondled his silver-inlaid 12-gauge double-barreled Richardson shotgun, there was no one to witness the exact manner of his death. It may indeed have been "in some way an incredible accident," as his widow Mary told reporters after the news of Ernest's death was released.

In the circumstances of his death Ernest created a mystery, a thing he had never done in his lifetime of writing—a lifetime concerned with death and violence, tenderness and humanity, the comic and the true.

When news of Ernest's death reached the radio and television stations across the country about noon of that final Sunday, Ernest's three sons were engaged in varied pursuits. John was trout fishing in Oregon, Patrick was on a safari with a client in British East Africa, and Gregory was in and out of a medical library studying for a midsummer exam in Miami. I was being splashed on a beach in the Florida Keys, teaching my young daughter to swim. None of us received the news until late in the afternoon when friends, relatives, and communications finally caught up with us. Our older sister Marcelline was in Detroit, Ursula was in Honolulu, Madelaine at Walloon Lake, Michigan, and Carol out on Long Island. They all had the word by evening, and preparations were soon under way, with the assistance of his friend Pop Arnold in Ketchum, Idaho, for attending the funeral, first scheduled for the following Wednesday. When it was discovered that Patrick couldn't arrive before Wednesday evening, even with the best jet connections from Africa and Europe, the funeral was rescheduled for Thursday.

The day following Ernest's death, statements were issued by the Vatican, the White House, and the Kremlin, as at the passing of a world statesman. Never before had an author been given such news coverage following his death. The entire world was realizing with a sense of shock that the loss of this man would be felt by all mankind.

In midsummer the Sawtooth Mountains of Idaho are their greenest. In the higher ranges the snow stays through the warm season. But down in Sun Valley there is a fine crop of hay by July, and the Wood River runs trout-cold down one edge of the winding fold in these old, smooth foothills of the Rockies.

Between Hailey and Ketchum, a dozen miles away, the valley narrows from two miles to less than half a mile. Along its western edge the mountains feel closer and a steady line of trees marks the course of the river. Just outside Ketchum sits the two-story house where Ernest Hemingway lived and worked during the last years of his life. The house has a natural wood color like so many of the houses in this winter sports area. But Ernest's house on the west side of the Wood River has an unusual view. Instead of catching sunsets, like most dwellings in Ketchum, it faces the rising sun.

By the morning of July 6, those members of the Hemingway family who could attend the services had arrived in Idaho. Of the more than a dozen honorary pallbearers, only half were able to

attend. Many other friends from far away had flown in to honor
the man who had spent a lifetime writing about what he had
learned of life, writing so simply and well that all men could
understand some of what he said and be moved by it.

Early that morning the mountain air was chill, and you could
see your breath. The sun was up well before six, and fine clouds
far overhead moved slowly eastward over the valley. There was
an insistent smell of sage in the air as though great quantities of
it lay somewhere upwind just over the horizon. In the lower
meadow the Wood River gurgled over the pebbled bed and fish
occasionally darted out of the shadows to feed.

By midmorning the chill had vanished. The sun made small
heat waves shimmer above the tops of the cars as they pulled in
beyond the State Police barricade at the cemetery entrance.

The cemetery lay on a gentle slope, around a small hill north
of town. A galvanized wire fence enclosed it. And beyond this,
less than thirty yards from the freshly dug grave, waited a group
of photographers and technicians with tape recorders.

Ernest's grave was beside that of Taylor Williams, an old
hunting friend. For years Taylor, called "Beartracks," was a
shooting instructor at Sun Valley. He died two years ago, and
Ernest had been a pallbearer at his funeral. Plots in the cemetery
at Ketchum are twenty-five dollars each, so the Hemingway
family bought six. Ernest always liked space.

The burial ceremony began at 10:30 A.M., on schedule. A small
gathering of townspeople and curious strangers had collected
around the fence. First to arrive were the pallbearers, all local
friends, including the undertaker. To enter the area, everyone
needed a plain white envelope with Ernest's address on it, containing a single sheet asking that the bearer be admitted to the
graveside service. The envelopes had been distributed the day before, and each one was checked.

After the relatives, honorary pallbearers, and friends had
gathered, Mary Hemingway approached, escorted by Ernest's
sons. She wore a simple black dress and a black hat with a wide
brim. She crossed herself before sitting down. Then the priest,
Father Robert J. Waldmann, looking unused to so much com-

motion, walked to the front of the group. He was followed by two altar boys.

". . . that's Jack Hemingway, the author's oldest son, sitting down now," a voice from beyond the fence intoned into a microphone. "And beyond him is . . ." The voice faded as the priest began the graveside service in Latin.

Then lapsing into English, Father Waldmann began a meditation on death, and since he had been requested to read verses 3, 4, and 5 of the first chapter of Ecclesiastes, he began, "What profit hath a man of all his labour which he taketh under the sun? One generation passeth away, and another generation cometh: but the earth abideth for ever." He paused. Then he passed on to a new thought, omitting the next verse which contains the passage "The sun also riseth."

Mary looked up quickly. Later she told friends, "I wanted to stand up right then and say, 'Stop the ceremony.'"

Father Waldmann continued in English, "Our Father, we beseech Thee to forgive Thy servant Ernest . . ." Behind the fence, the tape recorders continued to receive a play-by-play account of the service as though it were a sporting spectacle. In mood the scene was curiously theatrical. To the eye it had a clearly etched quality.

Suddenly there came a resounding "Ka-whomp." Everyone in the burial party remained motionless, barely turning to see what had happened. Just behind Father Waldmann, near the upper end of the coffin and close to the fence with its gathering of newsmen and photographers, lay a form dressed in white. At its lower end a pair of new brown shoes pointed heavenward.

The group stood in stunned fixity. The priest retraced his words, and then continued. Silently the funeral director circled the group, bent down, lifted the fainting altar boy to his feet, and held him as he rocked unsteadily, making small convulsive sobs. Then he quietly led him away.

"What was the name of the one who fainted?" The whisper carried clearly from behind the fence into the service area. The large cross of white flowers at the grave's upper end stood wildly askew. It had been disturbed as the altar boy fell. No one touched it during the remainder of the ceremony. It seemed to me that Ernest would have approved of it all. Ave Marias and Pater Nosters were said three times. Then the casket was covered with a bronze shield, lowered into the grave, and sprinkled with the soil of the land in which it would rest.

It would have been difficult for anyone present, knowing Ernest had seen the valley from that vantage countless times, to look around without thinking, "I will lift up mine eyes unto the hills." At the foot of Ernest's grave there is a simple marker. Beneath it rests the body of a Basque shepherd.

Chapter 1

Ernest came straight out of the Midwestern Victorian era of the nineties. Our parents were an unusual pair for that middle-class society. But our grandparents were far more typical in their decorum—and in their unquestioning harking to that vast ground swell known even then as Public Opinion.

Grandfather Ernest Miller "Abba" Hall was a kindly, well-read English gentleman who manufactured and sold cutlery through Randall, Hall and Company on West Lake Street, Chicago. Grandmother Caroline Hancock Hall was an intense, poetic little firebrand with a strong will and serious artistic talent. She calmly dictated the lives of her husband and two children. Though they lived in Chicago, she favored Nantucket for vacations, so the family went there during the summer.

Grandfather Anson Tyler Hemingway was an easygoing real estate man with much more interest in outdoor living than in making money. He had come to Chicago from Connecticut in a covered wagon at the age of ten. Grandmother Adelaide Edmunds Hemingway was another dedicated, intense woman who absolutely ruled her family of six children. Vacation was just a word to her. But in the summer, the family took trips to

Lake Delavan in Wisconsin and to Oregon and Starved Rock
in western Illinois.

These were the people who molded our parents, Grace Ernestine
Hall and Clarence Edmunds Hemingway, in the Victorian tradi-
tion. Both grew up in Chicago, Grace on the South Side during
her early years and later in the Oak Park section where Clarence
spent his entire adult life. But as was common in the vast middle
class of the Middle West, they believed themselves to be members
of the upper class. They prided themselves on their interest in
church missionary work and the fine arts. They aided all sorts of
uplift movements, ranging from the establishment of nature-study
groups—Father founded the local branch of the Agassiz Society—
to Protestant missionary societies dedicated to spreading the Word
all over the world.

Father, the oldest in his family, had three brothers and two
sisters. After high school hours he studied photography and made
wet-plates of early Oak Park scenes. He also played football. But
his real love was nature. "When I was a boy there were plenty of
prairie chickens north of Lake Street," he used to tell us. These
rolling grasslands are now lined with solid miles of houses. During
one summer Father spent three months with the Sioux Indians of
South Dakota, absorbing nature lore and gaining a great admiration
for Indian ways. Another summer, while a student at Rush Medical
College, he worked as cook on a government surveying party in the
Great Smoky Mountains of North Carolina. He loved the outdoor
life, but medicine was his consuming interest.

Our mother's great passion was for music. Having shown an early
interest in piano, she continued studying through her teens and
also cultivated her contralto voice. By the time she finished high
school, she had a solid basic training in music. Her independence
and energy were remarkable. Chaperoned by her younger brother,
Leicester, she rode a high-wheel bicycle on outings which was considered a daring thing to do. She wanted to study voice in Europe,
but Grandmother Hall considered that ambition too bold. Mother
did manage to tour England and France. But for serious music
study, she settled in upper Manhattan. For a year she worked in-
tensively under Madame Capiani there. Then she made her sing-

ing debut under the direction of Anton Seidl, conductor of the New York Philharmonic, and had excellent notices from the critics. But then she returned to Oak Park to marry the promising young physician, Dr. Clarence E. Hemingway. They had met in Oak Park High School—Father had graduated in 1889, Mother in 1890. After finishing his studies at Rush Medical College, Father had interned at the University of Edinburgh. By mail he and Mother compared notes on Europe and their friendship flourished. The Halls encouraged the match. So did the Hemingways. Yet when the young couple married, in the fall of 1896, our mother felt she was sacrificing a great musical career. For most of her life that feeling rankled within her.

Father longed to be a medical missionary like his brother Will. He was offered chances to go to Guam and to Greenland. At another point he was determined to settle in Nevada where he could at least escape city life. Mother, cultural arbiter, dealt firmly with this wanderlust. So our father settled down and built a large, successful practice right where he was, in Oak Park. He was medical examiner for three insurance companies and the Borden Milk Company as well as head of the obstetrical department at the Oak Park Hospital. During his career he delivered more than three thousand babies.

Our parents began married life at 439 North Oak Park Avenue, just across the street from where Grandmother and Grandfather Hemingway still lived. Oak Park, never incorporated into the city of Chicago and now the largest village in the world, was proudly described by its residents as "the place where the saloons end and the churches begin." This twelve-by-twenty-four-block area at the western edge of the city was then considered an ideal community for bringing up a family.

Marcelline, our oldest sister, was born in 1898. When Ernest was born on July 21, 1899, he was a healthy baby. According to Mother he cried a lot. According to family records, he was breast-fed for the first year, began putting on weight after the first ten days of regaining his birth weight, and had reached a hefty seventeen pounds by the time he was three months old. He was early with teething, learned to walk before he was a year old, and indulged in a jabbering lingo of his own during most of his waking hours.

Striving to catch up with Marcelline, Ernest progressed quickly. He had the usual baby words and mispronunciations that were parroted in fun and served only to confuse. But he was shrewdly perceptive.

Years later, Mother admitted, "Marcie was such a darling that Ernie was almost two before he managed to claim his full share of attention. By then he was such a strongly independent child."

One of the early attention-insuring devices Ernest latched onto was the use of what Mother called "naughty words." "Go wash your mouth out with soap" was a common command in the Hemingway family, and the list of words our parents deemed improper was a long one. This punishment emphasized the power of words. Ernest knew the taste of soap from an early age. So did our sisters. So did I. Part of Ernest's later reputation as a realist was gained through his adroit use of these same words, and he once wrote an article for *Esquire* entitled "In Defense of Dirty Words."

From the start there was a succession of nurses and mother's helpers in the Hemingway household. For beyond singing lullabies and breast-feeding, our mother lacked domestic talents. She abhorred didies, deficient manners, stomach upsets, house-cleaning, and cooking. It was necessary for each child to have considerable outside aid in reaching the acceptable stages of walking, talking, and self-reliance. Mother had a lovely voice with great tone control. Father always admitted it was her voice he fell in love with. That was an easy thing to do. Her natural breathing and diaphragm control produced a fine tremolo and she had perfect pitch. She could sing as few other women in the last half century. One of Madame Capiani's other pupils was Galli-Curci. She trained her protégées well.

Father, extremely proud of having produced a scion, did some adroit guiding toward an interest in nature, and in hunting and fishing, the noncompetitive sports he loved so much. Ernest was introduced to fishing before he could say "pish," a bit of bad diction he was never allowed to forget. While walking, whether down by the beach or over fields or in the yard, he was regularly told the names of different things he saw, touched, tasted, and smelled. Our father had a way of explaining even the simplest of things so that they became fascinating.

There is a sixteen-year difference in age between Ernest and me. This time lag is responsible for my inability to report firsthand on a number of early events in Ernest's life. To cover this period, I've had to rely on conversations with our mother, father, sisters, and family friends who were personally involved in these happenings. I wish I had been there earlier.

During the summer of 1900 our parents visited Walloon Lake in northern Michigan and were seized with a strange sense of shared destiny. They bought a tract of land—two acres of shore line more than four miles from the foot of the lake, which was then known as Bear Lake. Nine miles from Petoskey, it was some three hundred miles north of Chicago, and much cooler. Here they built a cottage. Mother's fascination with Sir Walter Scott's novels came into play. The place was christened "Windemere," and remains so to this day.

Built for four hundred dollars, the twenty-by-forty-foot cedar cottage could be heated by the seven-foot fireplace designed by Father. Later a screened porch and separate kitchen building were added. Father sank a well right in the kitchen, tapping an ever-abundant supply of cold spring water. Then he had an annex with another three rooms built back among the large hemlocks.

The best thing about the Windemere location was its beach. The clean sand made it an excellent place to camp, even had there been no house at all. A favorite family picture shows Ernest, one year old, and sister Marcelline splashing in the shallows. Mother had this one printed on post cards to send to relatives and friends.

Walloon is a lake of many moods. Mother was so moved by it she wrote "Lovely Walloona," a cheerful ditty in waltz time that was published by the E. A. Stege Company of Chicago in 1901. She would have Ernest and Marcelline stand at her side while she played and they sang, to the best of their ability, "Oh, lovely Walloon—a, fairest of all the inland seas," and on and on, and on, for three verses. The song was never a hit outside of our family, but it had a catchy melody.

The summer he was two, Ernest went out in the boat whenever Father went trolling or fished around the old sawmill pilings. The following year Ernest had his own sapling rod and went everywhere with a trout creel slung over his shoulder. Our proud parents stuffed the family album with pictures of Ernest in his trout-fishing regalia. There were plenty of pike, large-mouth bass, perch, and bluegills in the lake and Ernest learned to name the catches accurately.

"Daddy, read to me."

"All right. Get the bird book."

By the time he was three, Ernest had been calmed with readings on hundreds of occasions. Our father used books of natural history with good color illustrations. From these Ernest learned the birds of North America. Mother was quick to put him through the paces for any and all visitors.

"Now, Ernie, what's this one?" she would ask.

"*Icterus galbula*," he'd say, or "*Cardinalis*." He had learned more than two hundred and fifty of the Latin names. *Erithacus rubecola* and *Merula migratoria* were as familiar to him as "oriole" and "robin" were to lads years older. Mother, a severe critic, would beam with pride. Ernest must have felt then that to excel was a very satisfying thing.

Ernest began the first grade of school when he was five. Mother decided he could do the same classwork as Marcelline who was a year older, as were most of his other classmates. This spurred his competitive spirit. Throughout his school days he tried not only to equal students older than himself, but to surpass them. By high school years he was getting straight A's, and seldom missed a day's attendance.

When Ernest was three our sister Ursula was born. Two years later, Madelaine, known as Sunny, came squirming along. She was Ernest's favorite from the first. As soon as she was old enough, Ernest permitted her, Tom Sawyer fashion, to help him clean fish and skin game.

"You can carry the snakes and hold the frogs," he'd say when she begged to go hunting with him. To Sunny he gave the honor of burying the fish entrails around the roots of the apple trees Father had planted in the side yard at Windemere. With Sunny, Ernest created a secret language. Marcelline and Ursula scoffed, "That's just pig Latin," but they couldn't unravel it—nor could anyone else. Only the nicknames—Ernest was Oinbones, and Sunny was Nunbones—were known to outsiders.

There were lots of outsiders in those days. Uncle George bought land on Pine Lake at Ironton, about ten miles from Windemere. By road the distance was considerably longer, but George's son and two daughters were frequent visitors. Our grandparents came often. Once Father's brother Will came home on sabbatical leave. He was a Protestant medical missionary in Shensi Province, China. His daughters, with their Oriental costumes and ability to speak Chinese, delighted Ernest. He questioned them constantly, wanting to learn everything about life in another country.

And he learned well. When our sister Ursula visited Ernest in Havana, some forty years later, she asked suddenly, "Hey, do you remember 'Jesus Loves Me'?" And Ernest, then a bearded patriarch, burst into the Chinese version of the hymn he had learned from our cousins while still in grade school. He and Ursula sang together until the tears rolled down their cheeks.

Stoicism was something else Ernest learned early and well at Windemere. Summer vacations were not all hunting and fishing. As soon as a child was old enough to hold a broom or a rake, he was given definite daily tasks to do. The beach needed raking every morning, and the slope down from the cottage toward the beach was a second project. Ernest was given the daily errand of the "milk run," bringing Mason jars of milk from the Bacon farm half a mile away and returning the empty jars.

It was on the milk run that he almost lost his life—the first time. A dark, shaded ravine separates the high ground of Windemere from that of the Bacon farm. A small stream, choked with water cress, flows along the bottom of this ravine. The ground on either side is brown humus, from decomposing hemlock trees.

One morning Ernest ran off to get the milk, carrying a short

stick in his hand. When he reached the ravine, he stumbled in the
loose earth and fell forward, bringing up the hand with the stick
to protect his face. The stick was driven into the back of his
throat, gouging out parts of both tonsils. The blood gushed and
he lost quite a lot before he got back to the cottage. Fortunately
our father was there and stanched the bleeding.

The sight of her young son hemorrhaging as he ran toward the
house was a shocking one to Mother. Years later, when I was a
youngster and picked up a stick or even a sharp piece of candy,
the warning was swift. "Remember Ernest!" someone would always
say.

Ernest's throat was tender for some time after the accident. Our
father told him to concentrate on whistling when he felt like crying as a way to take his mind off the pain. And whistling became
Ernest's stoic reaction to pain from that time on. A picture of the
wounded hero taken in an Italian hospital during World War I
shows him whistling through clenched teeth.

The summer that Ernest was five Grandfather Hall died. He left
Mother enough money to build the kind of house she had wanted
for years. She designed its fifteen rooms, including a thirty-by-
thirty-foot music room two stories high with a balcony—very im-
practical as far as heating went, but fine for recitals and concerts.
Later it was used for painting exhibitions.

The house was the answer to the family's growing space needs.
A two-story, gray stucco structure located at 600 North Kenilworth
Avenue, it fitted in well with that neighborhood of large Oak Park
houses.

Mother was particularly eager to return to Oak Park and the
new house at the end of that summer, so she was more than usually
perturbed about organizing the children for the trip. But our father
was a man of infinite patience. The final morning's packing was
finished when he took in the dock and nailed all the shutters on the
windows so the cottage would be fully protected against the winter
storms.

At last everything seemed squared away. Father led the party
on foot over to the dock at Bacon's farm. From there Heinie

Grund's passenger boat would pick the party up for the trip to Walloon village and the train. Suddenly Father remembered the sick crow Ernest had tried unsuccessfully to nurse back to health. Ernest had insisted on carrying it around with him even after it had died. Everyone had seen Ernest carrying the dead bird while he wandered aimlessly through the morning's bustle and confusion.

"Say, Ernie, what happened to your crow?" Father asked.

"It's all right, Papa. I put it in my dresser drawer with lots of clothes around it so it will keep warm all winter."

Father ran back to Windemere, found the stored tools, reopened one window, and removed the dead bird and nailed the shutter back in place. Then he sprinted back to Bacon's dock just in time to catch the boat. And a good thing too. Mother was in no mood to delay seeing her new house.

That week the family held a small ceremony to light the fire on the hearthstone. Marcelline and Ernest sang two songs. One lit the match and the other placed wood on the flame. The house was then blessed and dedicated to a happy family life.

The new music room was truly a joy to our talented mother. She soon decided that what the family musicales needed most was a cello to provide depth for the violin, piano, and voice she and Marcelline contributed. Ernest's feelings were of minor consideration. He had an ear for music, and a third member was a definite need. So Ernest was started with the cello, a half hour a day at first. Soon he graduated to a full hour's daily practice. This was the system our mother used with each one of us until she was completely convinced the efforts were a waste. And she was very difficult to convince. Malingering was not allowed.

For years Ernest put in his hour a day at the cello. To the everlasting question, "How did you get started writing?" his most truthful answer was often mistaken for a joke by people outside the family. "Part of my success," Ernest used to say, "I owe to the hours when I was alone in the music room and supposed to be practicing. I'd be doing my thinking while playing 'Pop Goes the Weasel' over and over again."

Mother never stopped hoping that one of her six offspring would become a great vocalist. "Ernest was such a disappointment to me—until he was twelve," she used to tell me. She was leader of the vested children's choir at the Third Congregational Church in Chicago in those early days. "I needed good voices and Ernest was a monotone. Marcelline and Ursula both sang beautifully, but every note Ernie tried sounded like the one just before it.

"Then one day when he was twelve, his teacher phoned with the surprising news that he could suddenly carry a tune. That night I had him sing with us in the music room. And in no time at all he was the boy soprano soloist in my vested choir." At this point, Mother would smile wistfully. "All too soon his voice changed. But while he was a soprano, he was really very good."

In these early years Ernest was personally far more fond of shooting than singing. One fall before he was twelve, after Grandfather Hemingway had given Ernest a 20-gauge shotgun as a birthday present, Father took him down to the farm of our Uncle Frank Hines, near Carbondale, Illinois. That was wonderful quail country, but though the trip had been anticipated for months, it was full of upsets that neither father nor son could have foreseen.

Ernest's little gun shot a remarkably close pattern. When his luck was running well he could reach out with it and bring down out of the sky birds that were more than fifty yards away. Father was tremendously proud to have him show off his shooting on the pigeons flying around the barn. They needed thinning out, and this was exhibition work, taking all the hard shots within plain sight of the house where the women and other youngsters were.

Ernest downed more than twenty with a single box of shells. He was told to take a dozen birds down the road to another farm for pigeon pie that night. On the way down the road alone Ernest met a party of country boys coming the other way. They asked him where he got all the birds and he proudly told them.

"I shot 'em around Frank Hines' barn."

"Aw, you're kiddin'. You, a strange kid, shoot those?"

"I certainly did."

"You're a fresh kid. You never killed those—never."

"You're a liar."

"... Take him, Red. Go on. You take him on."

The smallest of the country boys stepped out. Ernest put the birds down and, before he could get off his jacket, felt a stinging wallop. He fought back just as he was then, and was soon flat on his back with the others jeering. Red ran off with the others. Ernest continued down the road with the birds. From that moment on, he was determined to box as well as he could shoot.

Ernest soon realized that the music room he so disliked could be put to a more cheerful use. There were frequent arguments with his classmates.

"Come on over to my house and we can settle it quietly," he used to say.

When the group arrived it would take only a few minutes of scouting to see where Mother and our various sisters were. If the coast were clear, the participants entered the music room by the side door from the back-yard porch. Sunny smuggled in the boxing gloves, water pail, and cloths. These were important for even one-round bouts, but most challenges went three so there was plenty of time for each contestant to show his stuff. Blond, willowy Sunny was timekeeper and sentinel. Her tomboy-type femininity probably helped to keep the fights clean as well as to inspire each contestant to fight his best. When the rugs were rolled out of the way, the waxed hardwood floor was an ideal surface for wiping up any evidence of bloody noses. The lacing from a glove injured one of Ernest's eyes during one such match. Long before the setting sun slanted low through the western windows, the music room would be restored to its previous condition.

Great care was taken to keep these bouts secret from our parents. Father had a horror of physical violence. When only a boy he was once chased into his own kitchen and brutally beaten by a bully right in front of his mother. Grandmother Hemingway would not allow him to strike back, so strictly did she hold to the Biblical admonition about turning the other cheek. During Ernest's high school years our father lost face on at least one occasion ("The Doctor and the Doctor's Wife") by avoiding an honorable stand when physically challenged.

The music room became Ernest's private solution to the problem of bullies and multiple opponents. Our parents must have had some inkling of what was going on. But they wisely chose to ignore it, thereby avoiding edicts that would almost certainly be broken.

Later, when Ernest saw an advertisement for boxing lessons in a Chicago gymnasium, he got Father's permission to sign up. The very first day he got his nose injured by Young A'Hearn. It didn't discourage him. Long after, he told a friend, "I knew he was going to give me the works the minute I saw his eyes."

"Were you scared?" asked the friend.

"Sure. He could hit like hell."

"Why did you go in there with him?"

"I wasn't that scared."

The new house was only five pleasant, elm-shaded blocks from the Scoville Institute, as the Oak Park Public Library was called. Ernest was not an early reader. When learning, he preferred to make up his own stories to go with the pictures in the books. But once he settled down to finding out what the books said he made up for lost time. *St. Nicholas* and *Harper's* magazines were early favorites. The family had made a practice of saving and having them bound as volumes to be kept at Windemere. In them Ernest read Richard Harding Davis and Stephen Crane. He particularly enjoyed reading Kipling, Mark Twain, and R. L. Stevenson. When the *Book of Knowledge* was first published, Father bought a set for Ernest and Marcelline. Those blue volumes did not have full-color illustrations. The more startling drawings were colored orange and green. But the books contained a mass of information on many subjects.

Visits to the library were frequent and valuable. Ernest loved adventure fiction and, next to that, science. Even during grade school—at Oliver Wendell Holmes Elementary, a block from home —he read constantly, though his eyesight was poor. By the time he was ten, he had developed a definite myopia. Our mother's own vision was seriously defective. She realized that the combination of inheritance and eyestrain had poorly equipped him for the paths of scholarship. Yet he absolutely refused to wear glasses. Mother often found him deeply absorbed in reading. "It's a lovely day. Go on outside and pitch some baseball with the boys. Hear them playing down by the school?"

"Aw, Mother, I pitch like a hen," he'd say and go on reading.

Ernest went through the Oak Park and River Forest Township High School without glasses, squinting at far objects and bright lights. After graduation he tried to enlist in the American Expeditionary Forces, but was turned down because of defective sight. Years after the war, after putting in serious time on paper work, he allowed himself to be fitted with glasses. Even then he refused to wear them during social occasions. He continued to squint until the 1930s, when the need to see finally overcame natural vanity.

While they were still in grade school, Mother took both Marcelline and Ernest on trips to Nantucket. Marce went first, and the following year Ernest accompanied Mother.

"Wow, what a surf. What wonderful waves," Mother reported as his reaction to the first day's swimming. Every day spent there meant a delay for the rest of the family in heading for Walloon Lake, so the Nantucket visits were always brief. But Ernest's first taste of salt water was enough to whet his appetite for a lifetime of big-game fishing, when he was finally able to live close to the ocean.

Writing home from Nantucket on September 13, 1910, Ernest said he had sailed up to Great Point, fourteen miles away. He boasted that he had been feeling fine and rough and had gone out in the open ocean where the boat had shipped water grandly. He had purchased the sword of a big swordfish from an old salt named Judas and he planned to present it to Father's Agassiz Society when he got back home.

Mother had taken him along to a meeting on women's suffrage but he had managed to sleep through all of that, he said. He was looking forward to going with Mother to the historical society to see the whaling exhibits after he finished this letter home.

Ernest never joined the Boy Scouts. When he was of scout age it had not yet become a popular movement, though scouting books were well distributed. But he concentrated on learning thoroughly the things Boy Scouts pride themselves on knowing. By the time he was eight he knew the names of all the birds, all the trees, flowers, fish, and animals found in the Middle West, and many more. By the time he reached high school he was an excellent swimmer. He spent hours in the school pool practicing the plunge, a dive in which the swimmer held his breath to see how far he could drift, which helped develop his extreme chest expansion.

Ernest also learned the rudiments of taxidermy from our father who taught Agassiz Society members. Ernest practiced until his knife work in both skinning and fleshing was swift and accurate. He had learned much by dressing out trout and pan fish. This training served him well. He could sharpen a knife until it was scalpel-keen. Much later, he learned to tie salt water baits for big-game fishing—a most difficult achievement. Many veteran charter-boat guides never master the art of tying a marlin bait that does not twirl the trolling line into a kinking snarl.

In the early years, Sunday target practice was the high point of the week at Windemere. Without transportation there was no chance to get to church during those summers. If a missionary were present, a prayer service with singing was held, which was what the children enjoyed. Otherwise Sunday was observed as a day of rest and entertainment.

After Sunday dinner, everyone would wait impatiently until Father finally said, "How about a little target practice?"

"Hurray!" everyone would shout. Shooting meant excitement and the smell of burnt powder. Our father was a really great wing shot. He could hit barn swallows though, as he showed us, they have only about as much meat as the end of your thumb and it would take dozens to make a pie. He never allowed anyone to kill for sport alone. The meat always had to be used. We had clay pigeons for targets. With a hand trap, and later a spring trap, the younger children were allowed to throw the disks toward a nearby hill, well away from the house. Our father was very fond of his first gun, a 12-gauge, lever-action Winchester which shot a close pattern. He had bought it for the surveying trip in North Carolina.

Everyone was allowed to shoot. Our sisters all learned the feel and recoil of a shotgun before they were old enough to hold the weapon alone when firing. Ernest was a good wing shot by the time he was ten. Each child worked up to being allowed to hold and shoot "Daddy's gun." It was a triumph we all shared long before reaching adulthood.

Ernest's first gun was the 20-gauge, single-barrel shotgun given him on his tenth birthday by our Grandfather Hemingway. The gun was fine for both birds and rabbits. As a gift it cemented the fondness between our grandfather and Ernest, who loved to hear his stories about coming West in a covered wagon when he himself was a boy. Grandfather Hemingway also had some fascinating yarns about Civil War battles. He had fought in a volunteer Illinois infantry regiment and had learned and understood a great deal about battle tactics as well as about the unpleasant realities of war.

Grandfather Hemingway's favorite story was about "getting hit in the head by a cannon ball." Having gone through the entire war without a scratch, he was seriously injured when a sharp souvenir section of a cannon ball slipped while he was getting it down from a high shelf. The heavy metal left a gash that required several stitches to close.

The other of Ernest's two early idols was Great-Uncle Tyley Hancock. A wonderful marksman, he had been a gun salesman in the Middle West while market hunting was still legal. He enjoyed drinking whisky, fished wherever conditions were best, lent his fly rods to Ernest, and taught the boy fly-fishing techniques that even our father did not know. Most wonderful of all, he had a walrus mustache and had sailed around the world three times by the age of seven. His older sister, our Grandmother Caroline Hancock Hall, had been along on those voyages, but she died the year before our parents were married. Only Uncle Tyley survived to tell the vivid tales. His father, our Great-Grandfather Hancock (a descendant of John, who had a bigger signature than anybody, the king of England once said) had been master of the bark *Elizabeth*, carrying passengers and freight between England and Australia. Aboard the *Elizabeth*, the *Tropical Times*, the first ship's

newspaper ever printed at sea, was published every few days. And
from her decks, Uncle Tyley Hancock had seen the wonders of the
Pacific and Indian oceans, and other far places. Years later he recalled them to whet the wanderlust of another young boy whose
nautical experiences had so far largely been limited to the waters of
Walloon Lake.

During his teens, Ernest slept out in the open away from the
cottage as often as possible. Since his daily chores had mushroomed
to a full work schedule, he was allowed more freedom with his
nights. Father had purchased Longfield farm across the lake. He
hired a cheerful backwoods farmer named Warren Sumner who
lived nearby to handle the heavy work that required equipment
and mules. Warren and Ernest planted avenues of butternut and
walnut trees, acres of sheepnose, yellow transparents, Jonathan apples, damson plums, and crab apples. These not only had to be
planted and transplanted, but trimmed, pruned, and fertilized. The
hay had to be cut, raked, and gathered. Father believed Ernest
was just the boy for these tasks.

On a still, windless day, a signal blown on the ram's horn could
carry clearly between the farm and Windemere. The distance was
only a mile and a quarter. Rowing across the lake was a pleasant
morning exercise. But at the end of a hard day's work, coming back
with the wind blowing could be less than pleasant.

Ernest loved to "make hay" because it gave him a chance to
develop his muscles and to compete with the other pitchfork
wielders. But the other tasks were painfully monotonous. Early in
his farming career, he was caught several times sprawled in the
shade of a big tree, lost in the fiction of far places and great ad-
ventures. "After that, all I was allowed to take to the other side
were copies of Father's *Journal of the American Medical Association*," he recalled. But he gained some medical knowledge,
strengthened his muscles, and had plenty of time to think during
those long, hot summer days.

One other kind of reading slipped by the family censorship.
Ernest's daily lunch was wrapped in newspaper. While delivering
vegetables to other summer residents in the launch *Sunny*, he

would slowly read and reread the stories of sports, violence, and action that reached him in this way.

Ernest was working over on Longfield farm the day the game wardens came for him. It was his fascination with taxidermy that got him into trouble with the law, one week after his sixteenth birthday. The account Mother wrote to Father on July 30, 1915, states the case and the undercurrents.

Dear Clarence:

I got that special delivery off to you just as the game wardens left, for Leon Ransom called later as it happened, so I sent it by him. This is just how it happened. Two strange men came up to the house and asked the little ones, Sunny, Donald, and Carol, if Dr. was in. They said no, he was back in Chicago but would be back later in the season.

I heard and stepped out on the porch. I said good afternoon, and they immediately asked me if the Dr. wasn't home. I repeated what the children said and asked the older man his name. He said Smith, and grinned at me. I asked if they had called to see the Doctor professionally and they said oh no, with a leer. They had come on business. Then the younger one turns his back and Smith proceeds to sit down on the steps and asked me when I expected the Dr. back and if there were any other men in the family. At this I thought them burglars or fiends of some sort. They had such a beastly, insinuating, sneering way, and would not tell their business. They fired question after question—"How about that young man about eighteen years old, did he stay here nights, where was he now." I told them working on the farm across the Lake. Did he go in a rowboat or a launch? Did he go up to the head of the lake some day between the 20th and 25th of this month and tow a rowboat called the Use-a-lah of Waldemeyer. [Their mauling of the name of the Ursula of Windemere seems to have rankled.] He did. Oh well, then they could identify him. They had two witnesses that he shot a big game bird— had it in his boat, and they were after him. They said he's got a gun, a little rifle, isn't it? And he wears a red sweater. I said if you know so much about my business and that of my family, you don't need to give me any further impudence. This tackling a lone woman and her little children without giving your business or authority and asking impudent questions is not the way to behave yourselves, and just you remember it next time.

He backed off and stood in rather sheepish style and said, "Lady, I've learned a lesson." Oh, but I forgot—he first asked if he could borrow a boat to go over after Ernest, and I said, "No Sir." I'm not lending boats to strangers. As soon as they went, I sent Ruth and Marce to row at top speed to the farm and warn Ernest to go to Dilworths and stay until further notice. They met him just crossing in the launch and gave him the row boat and came back themselves in the launch. After an early supper, Ruth went over and got milk and locked up on the farm, and I went to Bacons to see how the land lay. They knew the men and had directed them here. Mr. Bacon had a talk with them and they said what they were after, but seemed much disappointed that he was under 18 years of age because they would have to try him in the Probate Court. They said to Mr. Bacon that they guessed they'd have to pass it over this time. That is the only ray of hope.

But after that they came here and held the conversation that I quoted at the beginning, so they left angry and said they would get at it from another angle. Now here is what happened. He shot a crane when Weyburns had gone over to Lake Mich. He wrapped it up and left it in the launch, anchored in the lake. When he returned to the launch after the picnic, he found it gone and a young boy who said he was the game warden's son came up to him and asked him about the bird. Ernest said a fellow gave it to him and he was going to take it home and stuff it.

The boy said "all right, but I must take the bird because it's against the law for you to have it in your possession. I was just out drumming up business for my father." Now this is what comes of it. I feel worst over Ernest having declared he did not shoot the bird—but he said he was scared and said the first thing that came to him. I have not acknowledged that I knew anything about the matter, if you don't know you can't talk. Mrs. Hansen and Mrs. Weyburn both declared to Mr. Bacon that they knew nothing about his killing any bird. So you can see the complications. I think I had best send Marce over to Dilworths tomorrow to see him and talk to Mr. Dilworth about it. I don't know whether he had best risk it to come back to Windemere or not.

Mr. Bacon says they are Game and Fish wardens for both counties, Emmet and Charlevoix. Everything else is all right.

Lovingly—G.H.

Ernest, however, had headed for our Uncle George's summer place at Ironton, figuring that in another county he would be safely beyond jurisdiction of local law. Breathing heavily with relief, he told Uncle George all about it. To his dismay, Uncle George showed no trace of sympathy. He advised Ernest to turn himself in and pay the fine. This was done and the whole incident ended. But it aroused high feelings between the two families. And it helped Ernest form his own code of behavior. People who would help you in a jam were of value. All others were worthless.

Though Ernest worked hard at summer farming, he never ran away from home or let his family wonder what had happened to him. Such incidents have been freely reported by biographers and magazine writers. Ernest always sent post cards, telling of birds and game he had seen, even on overnight hikes down the Illinois River and up to Lake Zurich, Wisconsin.

Father was Ernest's most serious backer all during his life. Ernest learned everything he could from him in the early years and loved him deeply. Besides the summer vacations together, the two went hunting every fall when the game season opened. Our father had an extensive gun collection and regarded guns with tremendous respect, having been nearly blinded when a rifle exploded in his face during that surveying summer in the Great Smokies.

Ernest's knowledge of guns served him well while he was still in high school. He took genuine delight in organizing the Boys' Rifle Club. This group got its start while Ernest was editing an issue of the weekly newspaper, the *Trapeze*. "Got to fill this space," he figured. And soon he had dreamed up the new and exclusive society. A similar organization for girls really existed and it always received plenty of space and publicity.

Listing himself and half a dozen friends as members, Ernest proceeded to invent great deeds of prowess. The scores chalked up by the Boys' Rifle Club were high enough to make most amateur marksmen blanch. Members, of course, had the inside story and were all sworn to secrecy. The club's activities were never investigated. There was no problem until the end of the year when the officers were asked to submit pictures for *Tabula*, the school annual. At that point, Ernest pulled his final spoof. He grouped his members, in the fashion of photographs of the day, and took a prominent position himself on the extreme left. Each of the remarkable riflemen held a shotgun—a fact that slipped past the editors and sponsoring teachers and remains to this day a fitting finale to one bit of Hemingway legend.

Ernest took his high school English composition as a challenge and tried to write his best about the things that stimulated him. By his junior year he had written four pieces that the faculty considered material for *Tabula*. He was then a reporter for the *Trapeze*. In his senior year, he was chosen to be one of the six *Trapeze* editors. Another of the paper's editors was his constant competitor, Marcelline.

Ernest originated a high school humor column modeled after the one written by Ring Lardner, then considered the hottest columnist in the Chicago papers. Adopting the Lardner attitude and the slang, he made the basically dull column material seem fresh. Ernest's shrewd eye saw many of the fine points in the comedy of manners that was high school society, complete with high, stiff collars. Marcelline seemed to him the embodiment of the sanctimonious social belle, and Ernest particularly enjoyed aiming barbs at her. He also invented an "anti-prohibition party" and once reported that some family silver belonging to a member of the Trap Shooting Club had changed hands as a result of wagering among the members. In a typical column, headlined: " 'RING LARD-NER JUNIOR' WRITES ABOUT SWIMMING MEET, OAK PARK RIVALS RIVERSIDE," Ernest neatly twitted some of the school dignitaries.

Dear Pashley [that week's editor]:
Well Pash since you have went and ast me to write a story about the swimming meet I will do it because if I didn't you

might fire mee off the paper and then I would want to sling the stuff that Perkins the new air line pilot is named after I would have to go and be a military lecturer or something.

You see Pashley everytime I write anything for your paper a lot of guys want to clean me so this time I will be very careful and only write about myself and about guys what I ain't ascairt of.

Evanston wasn't no meat for us in that swimming meet. If we would have got 20 more points we would have beat them and If I had have gone 15 feet more I would have won the plunge and If Hughes would have carried 4 more states he would have been elected.

But then as the Bible says there ain't no good in crying over split skirts or something I forget what. There was an Evanston guy to the meet by the name of Kohler and he was some plunger. Why that bird would just flap in the water and float on down to glory and fame at the other end. But that guy will never beat us again because Jack Pentecost and I have fixed up a swell scheme.

There is a black line painted on the bottom of the tank running from one end to the other. Well we will put in a running belt along this line and then Kraft and I will plunge and grab the moving line and get towed along clean to the end of the tank. That is a swell scheme, Pash, so keep it dark and don't leave nobody know about it.

But here is another scheme so that we can win swimming meets without Gale being on the team. We will have special events introduced such as

(1) Throwing the Bull (Free Style)
(2) Throwing the Bull (For Time)
(3) Splitting the Infinitive
(4) Rolling the Pills (For Time)
(5) Slinging the Suds (Handicap)

In the first event we could enter R. Harry McNamara, you and me. In the second LeRoy Huxham ought to get first sure. In the third I would bet my last cent that Mickey Kenney would win and in the last two Coxey Muir would start at scratch.

These here extra events would give us a lot of extra points and then we would win the meet sure! But I suppose I had better close now, Pash, because If I revealed any more of our plans you might leave some of the other schools know and besides I

have got to study my Millinery Training for tomorrow because
we must save the country no matter at what cost.

Your Res'y.

Ernest Hemingway

P.S.—Please leave the printer make some extra copies of the paper
because I will want to send them to my friends back in the old
town.

Yours, E.H.

P.P.S.—I interviewed a lot of Prominent men on the meet and
this is what they said.

Coach Reynolds, "_____ _____ _____!!"

Cap White, "_____ _____ _____ __ _____ _____!!!!!"

Stew Standish, "_____ _____ _____ _____ _____ _____!!!!!!!"

Mr. Platt, "On the one hand, Yes. On the other hand, No."

R. Harry McNamara, "I concede the election!"

De Veve George, "Carol brothers carol!"

Marcelline Hemingway, "Yes, he's a very distant relative of
mine!"

Cap Steever, "It's a man's game!"

E.M.H.

During that final year of high school, Ernest wrote more material
for English composition that the faculty advisers thought was
Tabula quality. One *Tabula* sketch described God as "having a
large, flowing beard and looking remarkably like Tolstoy." He
wrote two Indian stories, tales of violence based on his knowledge
of the Ojibways up in Michigan. These were published in *Tabula*
as well.

And he turned out other early writing that had nothing to do
with school assignments. While going through the accumulated
family material after our mother's death, I came upon a notebook
of this early, serious fiction. It was turned over to our sister Sunny,
appointed by Ernest as the official family representative at that
time.

Though the Hemingway family's finances were in solid shape
during Ernest's high school years, his own lack of ready cash was a
social handicap. Our father had been raised frugally. He believed

the path to hell was paved with easy money, so he transferred cash into the hands of his offspring by assigning definite tasks at low, pre-fixed rates. At no time did Ernest's income from the family during his high school years exceed twenty-five cents a week—a tight budget even in those days. It took canny management to afford the occasional date he did have with girls like pretty Caroline Bailey and Lucille Dick.

But Ernest suffered another social handicap which he considered worse than lack of cash. It shouldn't have happened to a country bumpkin, much less to a brilliant young reporter and athlete. In those early years, our parents, with stern Victorian guardianship, forced Ernest to act as social escort for his sister Marcelline, an arrangement distasteful to each of them as an infringement on the right of free choice.

Ernest did manage to save some money from his summer work at Walloon Lake. On the farm, Father arranged all work with Ernest on a contract basis, with plenty of time and perspiration going into the completion of any specific task. He did not insist on unremitting hard labor. He valued vacations too much to be blind on this point. So Ernest had long weekends between tasks and occasional time out for days of trout fishing over on Horton's Creek, a three-mile walk from the farm. There, just at dusk, he caught a record rainbow trout by the old dock on the west side of the bay where Horton's Creek empties into Lake Charlevoix. He entered the fish in competition and learned for the first time the grand feeling of winning a sportsman's prize.

He got to know every foot of the creek, from the marsh where it opened onto Horton's Bay on Pine Lake up through the deep pools and open woods to the dam, and the open fields, the bridge, and finally the very difficult part of the stream in the tamarack swamp where most fishermen get lost for the day within half an hour.

Ernest's friend, Jim Dilworth, lived at Horton's Bay. His home became a convenient second home for Ernest. It was one of several refuges he took when the lively, noisy, but overwhelmingly female domination at Windemere got him down. At that time Marcelline and Ursula were eager campfire girls. Sunny followed their lead later in a round of cooking, sewing, costume-making, and general hilarity. So did Carol, who was four years older than I was. As a completely unplanned-for male child arriving when Ernest was already a junior in high school, I was at first regarded as a further embarrassment, rather than a welcome break in the female tyranny. He was sent on an overnight hike to Lake Zurich when I was born.

Going into the woods and reading, taking long walks, and fishing were distinct pleasures for Ernest between stints of farm work. He camped over on Murphy's Point, a headland less than half a mile from Windemere. There he found time for peaceful reading. Often he returned from camping with books soaked by rain. Our parents were severe about the destruction of any part of the family library. They didn't know he had been mulling over the groundwork for replacements.

Father spent as much time at Walloon as he could, though his practice kept him busy back in Oak Park. During these "vacations" his time was largely filled with cooking, shopping, seeing that the laundry got done and that the children were clean at mealtimes, no matter what they looked like between meals. Even breakfast was a formal affair in that it required proper clothing, dignified manners, and food that was correctly served. Maintaining this decorum in a houseful of growing, headstrong Hemingways would have finished a lesser man than Father.

It was hard for Mother to handle six children. So she delegated the older ones to look after the younger ones and tried to keep to a minimum the number of fractures of etiquette. Whenever there was a serious emotional crisis she rushed to her room, drew the shades, and declared she had a sick headache. Having her wishes crossed always produced a crisis, and there were hundreds of them while we children were growing up. Luckily there were Oberlin College students like Hornell Hart and music students like Ruth Arnold to help take care of the children when our father was not around.

Even at Windemere, Father spent a certain amount of time practicing medicine. He was the only doctor on the lake then. And there was an Ojibway Indian camp at the abandoned sawmill less than two miles away. These Indians were the poor of the area, owning no land and seldom holding jobs for long since all the big timber had been logged out. They had regular emergencies—stabbings, broken bones, serious infections. Ernest often went with Father on these calls. Not only did he admire many of the Ojibways, he learned a lot about emergency medicine under primitive conditions.

One of the first times Ernest tried using his knowledge of emergency medicine, he was the patient. Maybe that was a good thing. Out fishing in the boat with Sunny one day, Ernest got a fishhook caught in his back. "Cut it out," he commanded and began bravely whistling.

"I can't, Oinbones. I just *can't*," Sunny said.

"Cut it out," Ernest insisted grimly. "A small, clean cut is better than a large tear."

Fortunately, Sunny didn't have the heart to use the knife on him. They made it back to Windemere without the hook tearing any flesh out. At the cottage, our father pressed the tip of the hook up through the skin, broke it off, withdrew the rest, and dabbed the puncture with iodine.

Chapter 2

After high school graduation, Ernest wanted to go to war more than anything in the world. But he knew he could not get Father's permission to enlist right away. Father absolutely forbade it. That meant a definite delay. In our family, when something had been forbidden absolutely, it meant anywhere from a few days to possibly months of delay.

All summer, between work and fishing trips, our parents continued urging Ernest to enter Oberlin College where some of the family had gone, or to choose any other college. Ernest used the time to think, to question, and to make plans. After talking it over with personal friends, friends of the family, and finally the family itself, Ernest decided to go to Kansas City. There Father's brother Tyler had married into the White family and was making money in the lumber business. More to the point, Uncle Ty had gone to school with Henry Haskell, prominent on the editorial staff of the *Kansas City Star*. This really good newspaper had already become a recognized training ground for Midwestern writers.

Ernest wanted experience and freedom. The *Star* could provide both, if he could get the chance to show his ability. And Uncle Ty came through. He liked Ernest and wanted to see him working on the *Star*. He did not care about the boy's journalistic career.

But there, at least, the family would know where he was. And Ernest had declared himself dead set on writing and positively against higher formal education.

In Kansas City, Uncle Tyler's introductions gave his job application a push. In those days, everyone hired by the *Star* was on a month's probation. New employees either swiftly mastered the style sheet, wrote as much as was assigned to them, and stayed cheerful about it, or they went skidding out on their backsides. It was an invaluable training ground and stimulated every healthy cub reporter who came near the paper.

"I hit it lucky," Ernest told me years later. "Because the people there liked to see young guys get out and deliver. Things broke my way quickly, like in a ball game. I used to go out with the ambulances, covering the big hospital. It was just police reporting. But it gave me a chance to learn what the help thought, as well as how they did their jobs. My luck was a big fire. Even the firemen were being careful. And I got inside the fire lines where I could see what was going on. It was a swell story . . ." Ernest paused and gave a short laugh. "Sparks fell all over everything. I had on a new brown suit that got burnt full of holes. After I got my information phoned in, I put down fifteen dollars on the expense account for that suit I'd ruined. But the item was turned down. It taught me a hell of a lesson. Never risk anything unless you're prepared to lose it completely—remember that."

The most important benefit of his Kansas City newspaper work was the passage of time. It softened Father's attitude against Ernest's going to war. After his being away from home four months as a self-sufficient young police reporter, Ernest's going off to the war in Europe did not seem a certain way for him to get killed. Soon after Christmas, Father changed his attitude. Ernest was free to go if he could get one of the services to accept him.

By February of 1918, Ernest had learned finally and definitely that his eyesight was not good enough to let him enlist in the American Expeditionary Forces. He had talked with others on the *Star*'s editoral staff, read all the news dispatches, and decided that the American Red Cross Field Service would give the best chance to see the most action.

Ted Brumback, a recent addition to the *Star* staff, had previously been in France for six months with the Red Cross. He was older, less sure of himself physically because of an eye accident, and even more of a romanticist. He wore a beret. Charlie Hopkins, another *Star* man, and Carl Edgar, a friend of Ernest's from Pine Lake who worked in Kansas City, caught the enthusiasm. At the end of April, all four signed up and left Kansas City, heading for New York by way of Michigan so as to get in some trout fishing before leaving for Europe. Then they hurried East, got themselves outfitted with uniforms, and paraded down Fifth Avenue. They were assigned to the Italian sector by the Red Cross.

Three of Ernest's shipboard companions were Frederick W. Spiegel, Bill Horne, and Howell Griffiths Jenkins of Chicago. These young men had just joined the organization and were assigned to the same area. They sailed on the S.S. *Chicago* of the Compagnie Générale Transatlantique. During the ten-day voyage to Bordeaux, Ernest's stateroom was filled with visitors, for on the door he'd placed a large sign reading "Chambre de Chance." Two other roommates were Galinsky and Horchinovitz, a pair of young Poles from Canada who were on their way to fight the Boche. A great many dice were rolled and their numbers noted before the light-hearted group debarked and caught the train for Paris.

Ernest got his first look at Paris while the city was being shelled. Then his group was sent on to Italy where Section Four was soon being used to help the survivors of a munitions plant explosion near Milan. After that there were weeks of frustrating inactivity near the front but well back of it, where Section Four had replaced another unit. Barracks life on the second floor of a former linen mill was frustrating, though Ernest and the others enjoyed having a stream nearby to swim in.

Wangling a chance to operate a Red Cross canteen in the Piave sector where there was more action, Ernest took off. He made friends with the commander in that area and at last got his chance to be actually in the trenches. After nearly a week of nosing around, distributing cigarettes and chocolate, he was learning first-hand how it felt to be under enemy attack.

While he was distributing these supplies up forward, during the early morning hours of July 9, a mortar shell lobbed in very close. Of the four people nearest its point of impact, Ernest was the least seriously hit. One man was killed outright. Another lost his legs. The third was badly injured. Ernest picked the injured man up and carried him to the rear. While doing this, he was hit twice by machine-gun bullets. But Ernest made it back to an aid station with the injured man on his back. Then he fainted.

All of Ernest's wounds, on this occasion, were from the knees down. This is how he told it to the family. All accounts to the contrary are interesting mainly for their elaboration. He was not emasculated by a war wound. He was not hit 237 times in the groin. Nor was he a basket case.

He was certainly hit hard and dangerously and came out of it well. He spent the next three months in hospitals, getting back in shape. More than twenty bits of mortar shell were removed. By the time Ernest actually reached home, more than six months later, it was widely believed that he was one of the most severely wounded Americans in the entire war.

Ernest enjoyed the situation enormously. He was as convinced as anyone that the Great War was the war that would end all wars. And more than most of those daring young veterans, he was determined to make the most of the glory. For the family was still less than reconciled to the fact that he refused to go on to college. But knowing the family attitude about hiding any flicker of light beneath a bushel, his letters home became classics on how to write comical private material for publication.

The October 5, 1918, *Oak Leaves* ran the following story:

> Dr. C. E. Hemingway, whose son, Ernest M. Hemingway, was the hero of a fine Red Cross exploit in Italy, as told in a recent issue of *Oak Leaves*, has received a letter from North Winship, American consul at Milan, Italy, praising the courage of the doctor's son and announcing his intention of keeping an eye on him. And from Ernest, in the hospital, comes the following letter:

> "Dear Folks: Gee, Family, but there must have been a great bubble about my getting shot up. *Oak Leaves* and the opposition came today and I have begun to think, Family, that maybe you

didn't appreciate me when I used to reside in the bosom. It's the next best thing to getting killed and reading your own obituary.

"You know they say there isn't anything funny about this war, and there isn't. I wouldn't say that it was hell, because that's been a bit overworked since General Sherman's time, but there have been about eight times when I would have welcomed hell, just on a chance that it couldn't come up to the phase of war I was experiencing.

"For example, in the trenches, during an attack, when a shell makes a direct hit in a group where you're standing. Shells aren't bad except direct hits; you just take chances on the fragments of the bursts. But when there is a direct hit your pals get spattered all over you; spattered is literal.

"During the six days I was up in the front line trenches only fifty yards from the Austrians I got the 'rep' of having a charmed life. The 'rep' of having one doesn't mean much, but having one does. I hope I have one. That knocking sound is my knuckles striking the wooden bed-tray.

"Well I can now hold up my hand and say that I've been shelled by high explosives, shrapnel and gas; shot at by trench mortars, snipers, and machine guns, and, as an added attraction, an aeroplane machine gunning the line. I've never had a hand grenade thrown at me, but a rifle grenade struck rather close. Maybe I'll get a hand grenade later.

"Now out of all that mess to only get struck by a trench mortar and a machine gun bullet while advancing toward the rear, as the Irish say, was fairly lucky. What, Family?

"The 227 wounds I got from the trench mortar didn't hurt a bit at the time, only my feet felt like I had rubber boots full of water on (hot water), and my knee cap was acting queer. The machine gun bullet just felt like a sharp smack on the leg with an icy snow ball. However, it spilled me. But I got up again and got my wounded into the dugout. I kind of collapsed at the dugout.

"The Italian I had with me had bled all over me and my coat and pants looked like someone had made currant jelly in them and then punched holes to let the pulp out. Well, my captain who was a great pal of mine (it was his dugout) said, 'Poor Hem., he'll be R.I.P. soon.' Rest in peace, that is.

"You see, they thought I was shot thru my chest, because of

my bloody coat. But I made them take my coat and shirt off (I wasn't wearing any undershirt) and the old torso was intact. Then they said that I would probably live. That cheered me up any amount.

"I told them in Italian that I wanted to see my legs, tho I was afraid to look at them. So they took off my trousers and the old limbs were still there, but gee, they were a mess. They couldn't figure out how I had walked a hundred and fifty yards with such a load, with both knees shot thru, and my right shoe punctured in two big places; also over 200 flesh wounds.

" 'Oh,' says I, in Italian, 'my captain it is of nothing. In America they all do it. It is thought well not to allow the enemy to perceive that they have captured our goats.' The goat speech required some masterful lingual ability but I got it across and then went to sleep for a couple of minutes.

"After I came to they carried me on a stretcher three kilometers back to a dressing station. The stretcher bearers had to go over lots, as the road was having the entrails shelled out of it. Whenever a big one would come, whe-e-ee-eeee-whoo-oosh-boom, they would lay me down and get flat.

"My wounds are now hurting like 227 little devils driving nails into the raw. The dressing station had been evacuated during the attack, so I lay for two hours in a stable with its roof shot off, waiting for an ambulance. When it came I ordered it down the road to get the soldiers that had been wounded first. It came back with a load and then they lifted me in.

"The shelling was still pretty thick and our batteries were going off all the time 'way back of us, and the big 350's and 250's going overhead for Austria with a noise like a railway train. Then we'd hear the burst back of the lines. Then shriek would come a big Austrian shell and then the crack of the burst. But we were giving them more and bigger stuff than they sent.

"Then a battery of field guns would go off just back of the shed—boom—boom! Boom—boom! and the 75's and the 149's would go whimpering over to the Austrian lines. And the star shells going up all the time and the machine guns going like riveters—tat-a-tat-tat.

"After a ride of a couple of kilometers in an Italian ambulance they unloaded me at a dressing station, where I had a lot of pals among the medical officers. They gave me a shot of morphine and anti-tetanus serum and shaved my legs and took 28 shell fragments varying in size from [design] to about [design] in size out of my legs.

"Then they did a fine job of bandaging and all shook hands with me and would have kissed me, but I kidded them along. Then I stayed five days at a field hospital and was evacuated to the base hospital here.

"I sent you that cable so you wouldn't worry. I have been in the hospital a month and twelve days and hope to be out in another month. The Italian surgeon did a peach of an operation on my right knee joint and my right foot; took twenty-eight stitches, and assures me that I will be able to walk as well as ever. The wounds all healed up clean and there was no infection. He has my right leg in a plaster splint now, so that will be all right.

"I have some snappy souvenirs, that he took out at the last operation. I wouldn't really be comfortable now unless I had some pain. The surgeon is going to take the plaster off in a week now and will allow me on crutches in ten days. I will have to learn to walk again.

"This is the longest letter I have ever written to anyone and it says the least. Give my love to everybody that asks about me and as Ma Pettingill says, 'Leave us keep the home fires burning.' "

By October 23, the *Chicago Evening Post* had picked up the story, asserting that Ernest had been "shot to pieces," while working in a front-line trench when a shell exploded in it that "buried his companion under a trench mortar." The story ran a full column.

What no one in America knew then was that Ernest had fallen desperately in love for the first time. Shortly after he was transferred to the field hospital outside Milan, a young nurse arrived there. She was on night duty at the American Red Cross Hospital in Milan where Ernest was operated on and recuperated from his wounds. Later she had the forty-patient ward at the American Army Field Hospital where she was sent to help during the flu epidemic in Padua.

She was Agnes H. von Kurowsky, a graduate of Bellevue Hospital. She had joined the American Red Cross in New York but her passport had been held up for a time because her father was German born, though he had become a naturalized American citizen and had since died. This prevented her from sailing for Italy with the main group of Red Cross nurses.

Miss von Kurowsky had poise, a sense of humor, a lithe, graceful carriage, and a wonderfully sensitive nature. In a matter of days she and Ernest developed an emotional bond that grew as the weeks went by. They talked out past incidents in their young lives and reveled in the moments when they could be alone.

"Ernie was an unruly patient in some ways, but he had great popularity with all the other men patients, and drew friends from everywhere," she told me years later. "I was on night duty for quite awhile, and he was there off and on for months while his legs healed. He was often in trouble with the directress, Miss De Long, for his closet was always filling up with empty cognac bottles. Miss Elsie MacDonald, her assistant, was his special friend and always took his part." "Gumshoe MacDonald" as Ernest called her, had been head of the Nurses' Infirmary at Bellevue. He also called her "the Spanish Mackerel."

"Later I was transferred to Padua and, later still, to Torre de Mosta on the Livenza," Miss von Kurowsky said. "In Milan he wrote wonderful letters to me while I was on night duty, and sent them downstairs to the nurses' quarters by one of the other nurses. When he came to see me in Padua he limped in on a cane and was covered with medals. Some of the men I was tending then laughed because, though he had obviously been wounded, he was in Red Cross uniform with no insignia of rank.

"We used to take walks and the countryside was beautiful. An American captain, I think he was Captain Jim Gamble of the Proctor and Gamble firm, wanted Ernie to be his secretary and travel around Europe with him. He had a villa in Sicily and wanted to visit Mallorca regularly. I advised Ernie to go back home and get to work. I was afraid if he stayed over there he'd become a bum.

"I remember that when Ernie was able to go to the races in Milan—his first jaunt away from the hospital—we had to hurry up and sew wound stripes on his uniform jacket before he would appear in public. The races were one of the few places we could go for amusement and the Red Cross were admitted free, so we all went quite often."

Later, when Ernest asked Agnes to marry him she deferred answering, saying she would write him in the coming weeks. When Ernest got her letter he found he had been turned down. Agnes pointed out that she was older and the decision was hers to make. Her refusal hit Ernest like a second mortar shell, and he reacted violently though he'd been given the word as calmly and gently as possible. It was a difficult time for each of them. In bitterness Ernest later wrote to Miss MacDonald that he hoped when Agnes returned to the States she would trip on the gangplank and bust all her goddamn teeth. Agnes later was engaged to an Italian officer, but returned home without marrying the Italian. Ernest confided to a friend, Howell Jenkins, that he felt terrible over her unhappiness but had tried to burn out the memory of her with booze. Several years later, when Ernest and his first wife took a walking tour through northern Italy, Ernest wrote a fond letter to Agnes telling her how much the country reminded him of the happy times they had spent together at the end of the war, and what a truly wonderful person she was. In their separate ways, each of them had made the best recovery possible from that serious early romance. His bitterness gone, Ernest remembered Agnes in the creation of Catherine Barkley of A *Farewell to Arms*.

Ernest was mustered out of the Red Cross while still in Europe. It took nearly a month to get back to Oak Park. His return there was anticipated with much the same excitement that stirred Tennessee as the residents there waited for Sergeant York.

"The night that Ernie came home from the war" was a moment in family history. Our two youngest sisters were allowed to stay up. And at about nine o'clock I was even awakened on purpose— an action unthinkable except in case of disaster and maybe not then. All the lights in the house were on. Out in the dining room, hot chocolate was served and nobody said a word about holding off on the marshmallows. Ernest stood around being kissed and back-slapped while the neighbors came hurrying as the word spread. I was hoisted up onto his shoulders and Carol, the next youngest, insisted on being lifted up too. It was pretty glorious stuff being kid brother to the guy who had personally helped make the world safe for democracy. And I was not the only one who saw him in that light.

By February 1, 1919, the *Oak Parker* had an interview with Ernest, written by Roselle Dean, listing his enemy contact as "wounded three times when he went with a motor truck into the front lines to distribute cigarettes and block chocolate to the soldiers. In No Man's Land, he was at an observation post when a big shell came in and burst, hitting him and killing two Italian soldiers at his side. This felled the young hero, deeply implanting shot in both knees. As soon as he was able to crawl, however, and still under fire, he picked up a wounded man and carried him on his back to the Italian trenches, despite the fact that he was knocked down twice by machine gun fire, which struck him in the left thigh and right foot. In all, Lieutenant Hemingway received thirty-two 45-caliber bullets in his limbs and hands, all of which have been removed except one in the left limb which the young warrior is inclined to foster as a souvenir—if his surgeon-father does not deprive him of this novel keepsake. . . . Lieutenant Hemingway submitted to having twenty-eight bullets extracted without taking an anaesthetic. His only voluntary comment on the war is that it was great sport and he is ready to go on the job if it ever happens again."

Though his voluntary comments may have been limited, Ernest managed to keep a straight face while letting the stories grow. He allowed his modest mask to be lifted from time to time and almost every time some new glory was disclosed. It was a splendid triumph for the young man so recently regarded by his family as an irresponsible gray sheep who would not settle down.

During those first months that he was home, Ernest gave a wonderful party for Sunny and her friends. Old-timers at Oak Park still remember it. He brought a captured Austrian star-shell pistol and more than a half-dozen shells down from his room. A lot of time had passed in the years since the game warden had scared him into running. He seemed as unconcerned about the legality of shooting such a weapon in the heart of Oak Park as he was about the danger of it. Out in the back yard he raised the muzzle of this great pistol with its foot-long barrel and 4-gauge bore.

"Blam!" A thin, fiery line arced into the sky. Five seconds later a great white light burst out and slowly, ever so slowly, it drifted down over on Grove Avenue.

The next shot allowed for more windage. By the time he had fired red, blue, green, and white lights, the still-burning star shells were landing back in our own yard. Two of them that burned small holes in the grass were gleefully stamped out. The neighborhood kids were greatly impressed. So was everyone in our family. For years the pockmarks where the flares had burned into the ground remained in the back yard. Ernest's luck was running so good then that no other fires were started in the area. The empty shells, almost twice the diameter of 12-gauge shotgun shells, smelled deliciously of burned powder for years afterward.

In mid-March, Ernest was still riding the crest. He addressed the assembly of Oak Park High School and gave it all that he had. The front-page story in the *Trapeze*, by editor Edwin Wells, put into the harsh light of print some of what may well have been said in jest.

Lieutenant Ernest M. Hemingway '17, late of the Italian Ambulance Service of the American Red Cross and then of the Italian Army, spoke of his experiences in Italy at assembly last Friday. Caroline Bagley, a classmate of the speaker, introduced him to an audience the greater part of which already knew him.

"Stein," as he has been nicknamed, had lost none of the manner of speech which made his Ring Lardner letters for the *Trapeze* of several years ago so interesting. He told of his experiences first in a quiet sector in the Lower Piave and last in the final big Italian drive.

He seemed especially interested in a division of the Italian Army called "Arditi." "These men," he said, "had been confined in the Italian penal institutions, having committed some slight mistake such as—well—murder or arson, and were released on the condition that they would serve in this division which was used by the government for shock troops.

"Armed only with revolvers, hand grenades, and two-bladed

short swords, they attacked, frequently stripped to the waist.
Their customary loss in an engagement was about two-thirds."

On the day of which Lieutenant Hemingway was speaking,
they came up in camions, the whole regiment singing a song
which from any other body of men would have meant three
months in jail. Hemingway sang the song for the audience in
Italian and then translated it. Several hours after their initial
engagement with the enemy, Lieutenant Hemingway saw a
wounded captain being brought back to a field hospital in an
ambulance.

"He had been shot in the chest but had plugged the holes
with cigarettes and gone on fighting. On his way to the hospital
he amused himself by throwing hand grenades into the ditch
just to see them go off. This illustrates the spirit of these men."

At the time he was wounded Lieutenant Hemingway was assigned to the 69th Regiment of Infantry. He was with several
Italians in an advanced listening post. It was at night but the
enemy had probably noticed them, for he dropped a trench
mortar shell, which consists of a gallon can filled with explosive
and slugs, into the hole in which they were.

"When the thing exploded," Lieutenant Hemingway said, "it
seemed as if I was moving off somewhere in a sort of red din. I
said to myself, 'Gee! Stein, you're dead,' and then I began to feel
myself pulling back to earth. Then I woke up. The sand bags
had caved in on my legs and at first I felt disappointed that I
had not been wounded. The other soldiers had retreated leaving
me and several others for dead. One of these soldiers who was
left started crying. So I knew he was alive and told him to shut
up. The Austrians seemed determined to wipe out this one out-
post. They had star shells out and their trench searchlights were
trying to locate us.

"I picked up the wounded man and started back toward the
trenches. As I got up to walk, my knee cap felt warm and sticky,
so I knew I'd been touched. Just before we reached the trench
their searchlight spotted us and they turned a machine gun on us.
One got me in the thigh. It felt just like a snowball, so hard and
coming with such force it knocked me down. We started on, but
just as we reached the trench and were about to jump in, another
bullet hit me, this time in the foot. It tumbled me and my
wounded man all in a heap in the trench, and when I came to

again I was in a dugout. Two soldiers had just come to the conclusion that I was to 'pass out shortly.' By some arguing I was able to convince them that they were wrong."

So Lieutenant Hemingway told his modest story of the incident for which he was awarded the highest decoration given by the Italian Government. In addition to his medals, one of which was conferred personally by the King of Italy, Lieutenant Hemingway has a captured Austrian automatic revolver, a gas mask, and his punctured trousers. Besides these trophies he has his field equipment which he wore into the assembly hall.

While in Oak Park High he was prominent in the school's activities. He was on the *Trapeze* staff for two years and was one of the editors in his last year. Always interested in athletics, he won his monogram in football and was manager of the track team.

In much of this, Ernest was definitely kidding the kids and was taken, apparently, seriously. But he was also under increasing pressure about his uncertain future. Our parents had harbored definite hopes that this fling at soldiering had taught him a lesson, that now he would suddenly show a keen interest in some "sensible" way of life. But if nothing else, Ernest had begun a legend to live up to—one that would never be so easy that it would be less than a challenge.

Not all of Ernest's wounds were physical. Like hundreds of thousands of other soldiers before and since, he had received some psychic shock. He was plagued by insomnia and couldn't sleep unless he had a light in his room. To his friend Guy Hickok he described how he felt when the mortar shell exploded. "I felt my soul or something coming right out of my body like you'd pull a silk handkerchief out of a pocket by one corner. It flew around and then came back and went in again and I wasn't dead any more."

The older bartender in "A Clean Well-Lighted Place" knew something of that feeling. Nick Adams says in "Now I Lay Me," "If I could have a light I was not afraid to sleep, because I knew my soul would only go out of me if it were dark."

In those first months Ernest's welcome home had all the genuine reverence due a national hero, within the confines of Oak

Park. At home he was enshrined in his third-floor room. The steep climb could not have been easy for him, but it probably helped to strengthen that trick knee. And in his room he had war souvenirs, pictures of Europe, maps, uniforms, guns, bayonets, medals, an unexploded live hand grenade, and a secret bottle to pass around to friends who came to visit. On rare and wondrous occasions I was allowed to follow the clumping footsteps up the back stairs to the third floor. I watched in awe while Ernest and his friends handled the guns, sighted them out the windows, snapped their actions, and asked questions. Besides the Austrian star-shell pistol he had brought back an Austrian Mannlicher carbine with a straight-pull bolt.

"That's a sniper's rifle," he told me. "I killed the sniper who was using it to pick off our troops from up in a tree."

It baffled me, young as I was, that he bothered to tell me these marvelous stories only when he had other friends around. But he gave me a shiny medal with a portrait of King Victor Emmanuel on it, which hung from a red-and-green ribbon. And for a long time I refused to go out of the house without that medal pinned to the front of my shirt. I was the only kid I knew whose brother had been in the war in Italy, and I had the medal that could prove it. In those days I didn't know the only American units in Italy until the war was nearly over were Red Cross units.

The actual combat decorations Ernest won, a silver medal and a bronze one, were kept in a velvet-lined case upstairs. The silver one had been presented to him by the Italian King. It was shown only to friends who had seen the other trophies. Later Ernest gave it to a local girl of great beauty.

Ernest and his girl, Kathryn Longwell, often went on canoe trips on the Des Plaines River. "We'd paddle for miles," she told me many years later, "and other times we would come to my home and read stories he had written, while eating little Italian cakes that he brought from the city."

One Sunday afternoon that spring a large group of Ernest's Italian friends came out to our house, led by Manfredi, a veteran whom he had known in Milan during the war. Cooking fires were lit in two places on Iowa Street right beside the yard, and spaghetti and meat balls were prepared in the open air for the fiesta honoring Tenente Ernesto and Miss Longwell. There was a certain amount of red wine in evidence and Ernest did his best to placate our parents, reminding them that they had both traveled in Europe and that his friends were accustomed to the Old World way of life. Father refused to enter into the spirit of the thing, but Ernest and Kathryn enjoyed it immensely.

When a kid brother, about four years old, becomes properly overawed, he's sure to be a pest. One day I was ordered to go downstairs, away from the wonderful aura of snapping rifles and shining blades. Ernest was talking to Jack Pentecost, one of the fellow members of Section Four in Italy and a childhood friend. They both turned sternly when Ernest said, "Get downstairs, kid, or we'll put you in the spanking machine."

"What's that?" I quavered.

They were both eager to explain about the wonderful European machine in which small boys were strapped down until bloody while the paddles went round and round and nobody got tired of spanking except the little boys. There undoubtedly were more details, but by then I was downstairs and out of certain hearing.

Our family and Ernest's friends soon began observing Ernest's daily life with indifference. It did not ease Ernest's mood of rebellion to find himself being moved around with the air of long-suffering patience some families use with difficult young men. Our father switched from being fascinated with Ernest's war wounds and hospital experiences to urging him to "Go have those tonsils tended to!"

Ernest had been bothered with sore throats frequently during his high school days. These might have been caused, it was thought, by infections lodging in the tonsils he had half-amputated with a stick when he was a child. Sore throats were a regular annoyance. Finally, Father got him to go to his friend of medical school days, Dr. Wesley Hamilton Peck, an eye-ear-nose-and-throat specialist, to have the tonsils properly removed. Immediately after the operation Ernest had a serious throat infection.

The irony, like that of Grandfather Hemingway's cannon-ball wound, grated on Ernest for years. "I nearly died when I had those tonsils out—after surviving the damned war," he said. In the forty years following the operation he was plagued with more sore throats than an average opera star.

That first postwar summer up at Walloon Lake was a marvelous one for me because Ernest was there. The pleasure in this company was completely one-sided. Soon after the cottage was opened, I was doing my dawn-hour exploring before the rest of the family got up. Then I heard strange sounds from under the porch annex. Stealthily I flattened against the ground and found myself face to face with two big rabbits, Belgian hare types, orange and white. They looked enormous to me as we shared frightened, eye-level stares.

How they got there was no mystery. They belonged to the Bacon farm where we bought milk, eggs, and corn. The Bacons let their rabbits forage for natural food around the orchard, uncaged.

I backed away and went down to the beach. Soon I heard the muffled crack of Ernest's .22 rifle. Shortly after that I saw that sure enough he'd got them both, maybe with one shot. I didn't know for certain but it sounded good.

"My brother got two of your rabbits with one shot, I think."

"Where was this?" Mrs. Bacon wanted to know.

"Over at our house, first thing this morning."

That afternoon there was some fuss between Ernest and the Bacons. Then the rabbits were duly paid for. I didn't quite understand at the time, nor even later when I was given a fierce chewing out. His voice was low, but cold with anger.

"You understand me, kid?" He waited while I nodded, staring.

"If you ever again tell anybody anything that you saw, heard, or understood that I did—if you *ever* do—I'll have to reduce you to a nasty pulp, see?" He showed his fists. I nodded again.

Many years passed before he directly reversed himself. About the only thing I really understood of that first summer after the war was that Ernest was in an agitated state, and being around the family did not calm him at all.

Chapter 3

That first summer after the experience of being alone and near death was a time of personal triumph and humiliation, one of violent emotion. Ernest savored the delights of roaming afoot through the woods. He loved the smells of pine needles and new-mown hay, the fresh-caught trout when laid in ferns, and the sound of cowbells carrying far on the calm evening air. He was like an animal that has traveled far and returned to the place where he was raised, finding reassurance that things were as he remembered them and that this was truly the place.

Strict parental restraint was behind him, though Mother and Father had not completely faced that fact. Ernest was a personality, a former lieutenant in the Red Cross. As an ex-newspaper reporter and ex-officer, with the snobbery of combat and wounds, Ernest felt he had lived more deeply than his fellow men. He was moody and bored, and he had not yet decided what to do about it. He made another speech on his war experiences before a civic group in Petoskey. For this he dressed in an Italian uniform and allowed himself to be photographed afterward. But the unlimited enthusiasm of his first days back home was gone. What he liked best was to see old friends, go fishing, and get away from people who had no personal knowledge of experiences such as he had recently gone through.

In between fishing trips that summer, Ernest wrote a lot. He wrote what seemed good to him. When the summer ended, he decided to stay on and write some more. He had never before been able to stay in Michigan during the fall when the hunting was best and he was eager to experience the fine autumn storms, the grouse shooting, and the approach of real winter on the lonely lake. Most of all he looked forward to the seclusion he would have when the rest of the family left for Oak Park.

Ernest worked hard on paper at Windemere during the autumn months. But nothing he wrote that summer or fall hit the market. Each manuscript bounced for one reason or another, which was doubly discouraging because of our parents' disapproval of his chosen field. Fortunately, he had sympathetic friends in Petoskey. Through Edwin "Dutch" Pailthorpe, Ernest met Ralph Connable, the head of Woolworth's stores in Canada. Connable had planned to take young Pailthorpe to Toronto with him and when there were complications Ernest was suggested as an alternate, to tutor Connable's son. Ernest was interested, particularly if Connable would agree to introduce him to someone on the *Toronto Star*, where he knew he would like to work.

So in the winter of 1919, Ernest and "Dutch" both went to Toronto where Mr. Connable introduced Ernest to Gregory Clark, feature editor of the *Weekly Star* magazine. Clark explained what the paper was interested in buying, what it paid, and how to get copy in. It was a free-lance opportunity. With this opening, Ernest wrote newspaper copy again, saw his name in print, and sold enough material to feel he was earning a living. During that winter and spring he sold fifteen articles for a total of less than a hundred and fifty dollars. But the articles kept appearing during the spring, summer, and fall. Writing independently and getting money for his copy gave him confidence. It wasn't great. But it was better than trying to sell to magazines that would not buy what he produced.

By the spring of 1920, however, Ernest was again longing to be in northern Michigan, outwitting the local trout with both nat-

ural bait and flies. He delighted in the many places there where
the eye could move over the country without seeing a sign of
man anywhere. And it was the time of year that he loved best.
So he came again to the rivers and streams and the woods and
wild life of the northern end of the lower peninsula.

On this summer of his coming of age, he finally fought openly
with our parents. As is usual in such contests, it ended in a draw.
Both sides acknowledged misunderstanding. On the surface the
quarrel was smoothed over. But underneath, nothing was ever
the same again, and each side realized it.

Our parents ran their lives and those of their children on the
basis of the Victorian morality in which they had been brought
up. There were rules which could not be broken, and expectations
which absolutely had to be met. The individual and his special
needs and circumstances were secondary. If the order of things
somehow got fractured, then the wisest course might be a fine
and noble pretense which was known as "living it down." You
did this with the law, the Church, and public opinion.

Though Mother was temperamental, she was a basically honest
person who was simply a poor observer. She would get so involved
looking at her side of a problem she could forget there was another
side. The situation at Walloon Lake that summer might have
been very different if Father had not needed to be back in Oak
Park attending patients most of the time. Yet the events and attitudes leading to the break had been building up over the previous years, and had to come out in the open.

But that summer was a beaut, as far as parental estrangement
went. Self-righteousness was the order of the day. And while mis-
understood artists and writers are the norm, Ernest is the only one
I know who, having already shown talent, courage, humor, and
a genuine affection for his family, got formally drummed out of
the home just after his twenty-first birthday. Mother and Father
managed to carry it off with a magnificent show of solidarity.
They not only did it—when it was all over they congratulated
each other on the stand they had taken.

Ernest was staying with friends over at Horton's Bay when the
family arrived at Walloon Lake the first week of June that summer.

Since he was unemployed—free-lance writing could hardly be called self-employment when the returns are so small—he was expected to help get cottage life rolling, as long as he was nearby. That was the least a young man could do when, in our parents' judgment, he refused to show any real ambition. It was not a lot to ask. On the other hand, Ernest's negligence was not as serious as it was described. What rankled was that the family would not consider his writing as work.

At first Father was cautious in reacting to Mother's complaints. On June 11, he wrote: "Dear ones at Windemere: Hope Ernest has been over to help you. . . ." On June 13: "I will write to Ernest this afternoon. Hope he has been over and helped you. . . ." June 16: "I had a letter from Ernest in this morning's mail. He expected to go over and see you soon. He was expecting Jack Pentecost. Says he and Bill have worked very hard all the time since he arrived. Trust my box of salted almonds arrived all right. Also the can openers. All the special curtains returned from Mrs. Fisher are neatly put on your bed—flat and covered. . . ." On June 17: "Had a Borden emergency that will help my milk bill a lot this season. I am sending a lot of *Youth's Companions* for the girls to read. Ernest wrote that he had found my rubber boots and would bring them over to Walloon as soon as convenient. Keep them under the bed, so as to avoid their getting a puncture. If they do not now leak I will be surprised. . . ." And on June 19: ". . . I am glad to hear those other items are there from Gum Ward that you failed to put on your check list. You have never acknowledged the original list that I sent you the day after you left . . . I am pleased to know Ernest has been over to see you. We are still having fine cool weather. Glad you have the same."

On June 28, our father was still sweltering through practice in Oak Park and trying to keep things running smoothly at Windemere from that distance, though it was not easy. "My dear Gracie and Ursula and Sunny," he wrote. "Herewith I acknowledge all your good letters that came today to freshen my memories of the wonderful Walloon Lake. Thanks for the local color, from rabbits to canoeing and the pretty garden behind the boathouse. I have a plan to dispose of all the rabbits. Ask Ernest to try his .22 and

slaughter them and plant at the foot of the nut trees on Longfield. If he does not succeed I will do the job when I get there.
Dungs? If they are a nuisance they should all be used for fertilizer.
What became of the ferocious cat and the many Bacon dogs?
The heat here is fierce, 92 Saturday, 94 Sunday, and right now at
three o'clock it is 96. I have written to Dr. Pottoff, and will hope
to have a favorable report from him in a few days. Do not worry
about anything, as there you can regulate your speed to your own
inclinations. I will commence to pick up all the many things that
you so desire and will with pleasure 'fetch' them to you at the earliest possible opportunity. Canoe varnish to tacks. I long to get
a dip in lovely Walloona. I think I had better write a letter to
Warren and have some of you deliver it, so it will not stay in his
box in Boyne City for a week. If the hay should be cut before I
get there, do not wait for me. I sent a lot of papers last night
and will send more today . . . I had a big bunch of radishes
from Leicester's garden to take to mother's for Sunday dinner
yesterday. They were wonderful. The catalpa trees are now dropping their white blossoms, and the lawn is as white as snow under
the trees . . . Too hot to cook even spaghetti. Drink strong farmers
and eat crackers and gingersnaps. I had a postal from Ted Brumback from Vanderbilt, said he and Ernest were away over on the
Black and would go over to see you all at Walloon when they returned. Uncle Tyley Hancock called here Sunday evening. He was
very well, but awfully disappointed that he had heard nothing from
Ernest, and had received no rod case so far. . . . I think he would
like to be invited to the lake. Do whatever you think wise. . . ."

On July 2, father got Dr. Pottoff to take over his patients and
came to Windemere for two weeks. While he was there, the situation ripened fast. Tired and knowing that he by no means had all
the answers to life's problems, Father was worried. He was baffled
by Ernest's refusal to settle down and frightened to think of where
further independent behavior might lead.

Back in Oak Park after an uneasy vacation, he sent Mother a
letter dated July 18: "I have written Ernest and sent him the
check as we talked over. I advised him to go with Ted down
Travers City way and work at good wages and at least cut down

his living expenses. I also most sincerely hoped now that he had attained the legal age he would be more considerate of others and use less vitriolistic words." July 21: ". . . Today is Ernest's twenty-first birthday anniversary and I hope he will have a good day. He has not written me yet, but I took for granted he had done the spraying as per your Thursday letter, and so sent him the five dollars and the birthday five. I hope he will now write me a good letter. . . ." July 22: ". . . I am greatly distressed about the reports from Warren. If Ernest delivered the note to him that I wrote and handed to Ernest the day I left, there should be no trouble whatsoever. . . . I think Ernest is trying to irritate us in some way, so as to have a witness in Brummy in hearing us say we would be glad if he was to go away and stay. I have written him that I wanted him to get busy and be more self-supporting and respect-ful, and leave the Bay and go to work down Travers City way. I will write to him and enclose herewith for you to read and hand to him. Keep up your courage, my darling. We are all at work and very soon he will settle down and suffer the loss of his friends the way he is fast using them up. He will have to move into new fields to conquer. . . . You read Ernest's letter enclosed! If he has gone, seal it and *stamp* it and mail it to *him!*"

July 25: ". . . In the last mail last night I received your big envelope letter and the letter of Thursday evening, after Ernest's birthday supper. I hope he went back to the Bay with Bill and that you read and have mailed him the letter I wrote to him to stay away from Windemere until he was again invited. You surely gave him and his friends a good time. . . ."

July 26: "My dear Gracie: I have just received your letter written Saturday the 24th and am indeed sorry for you. I hope you have handed Ernest the letter that I enclosed for him, advising him he must move on and get to work and stay away from Windemere until he is again invited to return. It is a great insult that he and Ted Brumback should take it for granted that they can lay down on the family as they have been doing. I supposed of course they would have gone back to the Bay when Bill Smith went back the night after the wonderful 21st supper you wrote about. I am now also distressed to receive a letter from Warren, which proves that

Ernest did not deliver to Warren the note I wrote the day I left and asked Ernest to deliver to Warren that same night. I have just answered the questions that Warren will see now just what I want and we will have no misunderstandings. I so wish that Ernest would show some decent loyalty to you and not keep on the sponge game with his friend Ted. I will write to him again at the Bay, so if he is still at Windemere tell him that you know there is mail for him at the Bay. I will also write Ted at the Bay advising him that it is altogether too much for you to entertain him longer at Windemere, and request that he and Ernest not return to Windemere until they are invited *by you.* . . . It is hard to work here in the heat, but harder to know you are suffering such insults as to cause the breaking up of the family circle from he who has had so much done for him and his friends. . . . I shall continue to pray for Ernest, that he will develop a sense of greater responsibility, for if he does not the Great Creator will cause him to suffer a whole lot more than he ever has so far."

July 28: "My darlings at Windemere: I have had no letter from you today but received a very definite letter of denial from Ernest. He is a very unusual youth that does not realize that his mother and father have done a lot more for him than any of his chums. He is sure to suffer a lot. I will pay no attention to his statements that he has done nothing wrong at Windemere. He says Brummy was there at your particular request and that he had painted the house for you and dug garbage holes and washed dishes and done all the work of a 'hired man.' Let it go. If they will only now stay away from irritating you. He says in a letter to Father that he lost his pocket book while fishing on Spring brook and in it was the cash of a check I sent to him and a check from Father. He will have a second check from Father for the two dollars. He did not tell me a kind thing. All denial of my statements as to the reasons I was sure it was best for he and Brummy to stay away from Windemere until he was again invited by you. He says he does not want to hear from me any more along those lines. I hope it will not be necessary. He does not answer a question about their trip that I spoke of to him. I shall not let his fiery letter bother me and I will wait a while to write to him again. Reading over the copies I am sure I only wrote just what you would want me to do. In his letter to Father he was as sweet as pie. Said he saw all his Connable friends from Toronto in Petoskey last Sunday. Did he tell you whether or not he delivered that letter to Warren the night of the day I left?"

July 30: "I am greatly relieved to know Ernest has at last gone, and trust he will stay away and now you can get what you so much need this summer. The last act of his was his finish, and it will be just so all along the line. Oh, if he alone could do the suffering. I am glad that Ursula is having a few days at Marjorie Bumps. Hope she will not see Ernest. . . . If those big boys had gumption at all they would have volunteered all the paint work and had it done long ago. . . . You better buy up there what you need in the way of supplies. I knew the boys were getting into the supplies with no idea of replacing anything. I am anxious for you to tell me what Ted had to say when you delivered your ultimatum. Ernest's last letter to me after reading the one I sent you to hand him, does not require an answer. It was written in anger and was filled with expressions that were untrue to a gentleman and a son who has had everything done for him. We have done too much. He must get busy and make his own way, and suffering alone will be the means of softening his Iron Heart of selfishness. . . ."

The passage of time was valuable in this hoedown. On August 27, our long-suffering father wrote from Oak Park: ". . . I had a very nice letter from Ernest today, written yesterday in Petoskey. He says he has been fishing with Sam Nickey and had some good times, and had some wonderful fishing. He surely feels as if he had a great injustice done him at Windemere. I do not in any way discuss the matter with him. I am glad he has cooled off and again writes to his father, who will always love him, and will continue to pray for him to be an honest and unselfish and considerate Christian gentleman and loyal to those who love him. He was starting out again to fish to the end of the season, which I think is September first. He was going over on the Sturgeon. So I hope you will go over to the Bay the very first of the week. . . .

"This has been an ideal harvest day. I long for the fields and the open life. I had such a nice note from Warren. He expected soon to go down and do my plowing all right. . . . Make a list of what you will want me to bring up. It will not be before the fifteenth and maybe a little later. I still have three OB's to deliver and finish, before I can come up. My old friend Peter is to be here all day tomorrow to clean rugs and house in general. I have finished up my pickle-making for another year, twenty-seven quarts to the good. Sweet and spiced. They will make some few people happy. I am sure you rejoice in the Full Equal Rights for women and the Passage of the Nineteenth Amendment. Old Tennessee did the trick all right."

Mother was not so ready to be reconciled with her wayward son, however, and on September 2, Father wrote: ". . . I am glad to receive your letter this morning with the copy of the letter you sent to Ernest. That is a masterpiece. I will always prize it as the right conception of the Mother's part of the game of Family life. Keep up your courage, my darling, as I know you will recover from this summer's shocks. It is a long session of the family's existence, and we must be brave. There are relatively few storms in our sea of life as compared to many you and I know, if you only stop and count your blessings."

Another letter came from Ernest later and Father wavered even more in his belief that all had been as represented to him. On September 15 he wrote: "My dear Gracie and Leicester, I was greatly pleased to receive your letter of Monday morning today. . . . We too are having fine weather. . . . The girls are all doing very well in school. . . . I continue to pray for Ernest and believe that God will soften his heart and that we all shall again be united in love. If you falsely accused him, be sure to beg his pardon, even if he had made many mistakes. For false accusations grow more sore all the time and separate many dear friends and relatives. . . ."

And by September 19, Father was feeling somewhat more piqued with his absent wife than with Ernest. ". . . A wonderful sermon. Wish so much you had been with me too. Many ask when you are to return. Mrs. Imhoff wants you to recommend a contralto for her Third Church Quartette. I wrote to Ernest last night and hope you will invite him over to help you pack up. He is stronger than I am and can do all that is necessary. Love him my dear, he is our boy and we must always love and forgive each other. . . . I am certainly unable to get who you suggest namely: 'Some perfectly responsible individual' to look after our girls and our home. So I am to stay here until you come home. I asked a certain person to recommend a 'perfectly responsible individual' and was answered that 'there ain't no such animal.' . . ."

That was how the big rift came and passed. Years later, on being shown the long letter formally drumming Ernest out of the family's summer home, which our mother had written for his birthday, I was surprised. With all the emotion and mutual recriminations, anyone would think some dreadful sins had been committed. Actually Mother did some mighty belaboring of his lack of courtesy and gainful employment, enumerating all the ways he had changed since she remembered him as her dear little boy, listing some trivial actions she deemed worthy of censure, and commanding him to leave Windemere, not to return unless specifically invited. Few affronts to personal dignity could top that of holding a ceremonial dinner on a twenty-first birthday, while getting ready to slip the guest of honor a letter asking him to kindly leave the family premises.

It was this break that enabled Ernest to write as truthfully as he could about what he knew, including our parents and their reactions to stress, in the years following. He could be indifferent to any criticism that he had violated the right of privacy. Without the break, he could not have done it. Those of his readers who have always been at a loss to understand how he could say such things can cease being baffled and begin to understand a little of what went on in those postwar summer days.

At the age of five, I knew there were difficulties between Ernest and our parents, but I didn't have the answers either. I figured they were foolish not to go fishing and just skip the "you said" and "I said" business.

To me the high point of the summer was the day that Ernest ate a raw snipe.

It all started down on the beach one day in front of the cottage. "I'm hungry enough to eat a skunk," Ernest said.

Ted Brumback glanced back through the trees. "Not a skunk in sight. There's a snipe though."

Our sisters giggled. Ernest said, "Okay, a snipe then."

"You wouldn't eat a snipe," Brumback said.

"Sure I would. Raw."

"Five says you couldn't do it."

"Five says I will."

A few minutes later a flight of little shore birds went fluttering off the beach. Over the quiet water a shotgun roared. One bird dropped with a splash. Soon Ernest had cleaned it and put on a fine savage performance of crunching noises, munching sounds, and low gutturals, until the bird was reduced to a few dainty bones and the bet was solemnly noted for future collection. Downy snipe feathers littered the sand below the tall tamaracks. They were testimony that the tale our sisters told was true. Mother was terribly distressed. It was not just that the snack had been so "uncivilized." It seemed a brutal needling of her complaints that Ernest was decreasing the family larder while continuing to be a bum.

In October, after Mother had returned with me to Oak Park, Father was able to visit Windemere again. He wrote that he "saw Ernest picking apples up at Mrs. Charles. He is all well again. Now Bill Smith is laid up with a sprained ankle. They had expected to drive down next week, if Bill gets well. . . ."

But though the feud was over, Ernest remained emotionally as well as legally of age. He would have nothing more to do with family lodgings. That fall he and Bill Smith headed for the Near North Side of Chicago where they both had friends. Ernest looked up Bill Horne, who was making money selling machinery and knew that Ernest wanted to write. They shared a furnished room for months and ate regularly at a restaurant down the block called Kitsos, which was owned by a couple of Greeks of the same name, Bill Horne recalls. "You could get one of their good steaks, plus French fries and coffee, for sixty-five cents and we did, night after night." The counter, the stools, the serving window, and the layout of this little restaurant later came to be known to readers around the world. This restaurant served as the model for the restaurant scene in "The Killers."

Ernest and Bill then moved in with Y. K. Smith and his wife who had a large apartment on Division Street. The Smiths spent their summers at Horton's Bay and Ernest had been a friend of Y. K.'s younger sister Kate in earlier days. The Smiths had many friends in the writing world. Through Y. K. Ernest met Sherwood Anderson.

At the Smith's apartment Ernest also met Hadley Richardson, whom he married the following summer. Hadley was a tall, well-formed, English-looking girl. She had studied piano for years. That winter she had come up from St. Louis to visit Kate.

"The moment she entered the room," Ernest said afterward, "an intense feeling came over me. I knew she was the girl I was going to marry."

That winter Ernest got a job editing the *Cooperative Commonwealth*, a folksy house organ for an organization that sounded good, but was suspect within. He was an associate editor at first and did a lot of feature and human interest articles which the publication needed. After his apprenticeship on the two *Star* papers, the material came easily. It was his first job in Chicago and paid him fifty dollars a week, which was not bad. It gave him time to write on his own, too. He sold more features to the *Toronto Star*. His magazine writing still did not sell, but he was learning more all the time, and he was just past twenty-one.

Best of all, he was financially independent of our critical parents. As during the previous winter, he was living in an establishment operated by somebody else. But this time he was supporting himself and saving a little money as well.

It didn't take more than a couple of months for the sweet settling down to become unsettled again. The *Commonwealth* job got to be more unpleasant as he learned what went on in the organization. Saving went slowly and time went fast and he had big plans he wanted to get on with. In April he wrote to Father, then in Florida blowing his savings in what was to become the real estate bubble, saying that the Italian lire he'd bought at around

3.50 had risen to 5. He could sell at a profit. But he was buying them because he wanted the lire. He wanted to go to Italy next year. He wished he could rate a vacation—but it was back at the treadmill again—and he was going to beat the machine by going to Italy for a while in the fall. He noted the authorities had hanged Cardinella and Cosmano and some other killer that day, but Lopez, who was to hang, was reprieved. He figured Cardinella was a good man to swing and when he passed the County Jail that morning there was a big crowd standing outside waiting.

More than just getting back to Europe, Ernest wanted to land a job that would pay his expenses over and allow him to get around once he landed. He was dickering with the people on the *Toronto Star*. And in that summer of 1921, a great many things worked out well.

Ernest and Hadley decided to get married that summer. And they did not want the fuss and formality that would go with a ceremony back in Hash's home town. Ernest was strong for Horton's Bay and Hadley liked the idea of spending some time in northern Michigan after the wedding.

It took some sharp organization to get the word to all the friends and relatives about the impending event, and to get straight the arrangements for transportation as well as the usual flurry with flowers and fittings. Few members of the wedding party were normally up in Michigan, especially then. It meant days of time away from work for most of them and the confusion of a shifting of headquarters among friends at Horton's Bay.

These friends faced the travel test very well. Among the immediate family at Windemere the confusion was something to see. Closing the cottage for the season had always been a grand hassle with so many harum-scarum kids, a calm but disorganized mother, and a haggard father who showed the strain by hurrying through everything and then fretting about it long afterward. That year the Hemingway dither involved getting each member impeccably groomed for the great event and being ready to head for Oak Park immediately afterward. For Ernest and Hash were spending their honeymoon at Windemere.

It was a really beautiful wedding. Everybody said so. The big elm trees that grew along both sides of the road through Horton's Bay were well dusted by end-of-summer traffic. The wedding party assembled up beyond the store just before four o'clock on that September 3 afternoon. The single white spire of the small Methodist church stood back from the road in a clearing.

The family was seated right at the front. It was exciting with the sweet smells of flowers and perfumes, as the organist from the Episcopal Church in Petoskey began the Wedding March from *Lohengrin*. Outside there was bright sunlight. The west windows let in golden bars of light among the shadows of the pews.

Hash looked like an angel, her bridal radiance covered with considerable flowing white veil, as she came up the aisle. Then came Ernest, the debonair war hero, my personal idol—but with legs moving from side to side as well as forward. His heavy white serge trousers semed to have a serious case of shivers. It was the first time I had ever seen unconcealed shaking, and it baffled me. Then suddenly the kneeling part was over, the organ's vibrant strains filled the church, and everyone milled around laughing and congratulating everyone else and hurrying out to the lawn for picture-taking. I was relieved to see that Ernest was "well" again and that the shaking had stopped.

Over at Dilworth's later there was a huge, delicious cake, though its cutting seemed to take forever. There were more pictures in the yard with everyone smiling, trying not to squint against the sun. Just at dusk Father herded us into his Ford touring car and we drove south. When we reached Oak Park late the next day, he went to his typewriter and got out the announcement for the papers:

Ernest Miller Hemingway, First Lieutenant in the Italian Army during the World War and son of Dr. and Mrs. Clarence E. Hemingway of Oak Park, was married at Horton's Bay, Michigan, on September 3, 1921, to Miss Hadley Richardson of St. Louis, Missouri. The young people preferred a simple country wedding and honeymoon spent at Windemere, Walloon Lake, Michigan, the summer home of the Hemingways, to the usual formal church wedding in St. Louis. The little white church at Horton's Bay was decorated with masses of swamp lilies, bittersweet, and boughs of balsam. After the ceremony a dinner was served at Pinehurst Cottage to the bridal party, consisting of Miss Catherine Foster Smith of Chicago, Miss Ruth Bradfield and Mrs. D. Charles of St. Louis, and Mrs. Roland C. Usher, sister of the bride, and Mrs. George J. Breaker of St. Louis, Mr. William D. Smith, Mr. George J. Breaker, Mr. J. C. Edgar of St. Joseph, Missouri, Mr. William D. Horne, Jr., of Yonkers, New York, Howell Griffiths Jenkins of Chicago, and Arthur Meyer. The last three were in the Italian service with the groom. Mr. George J. Breaker gave the bride away in the absence of Professor Usher. Other guests at the dinner were Mrs. Ralph Connable and son of Toronto, Mr. Edwin Pailthorpe and Mr. Luman Ramsdell of Petoskey, Michigan, Dr. and Mrs. Clarence E. Hemingway, Misses Ursula and Carol Hemingway and Master Leicester Hemingway, of Oak Park. Many telegrams were received from people of high social and state positions in Italy where Lieutenant Hemingway received such signal honors and decorations at the close of the war. The young couple expect to spend the winter in Italy.

Ernest and Hadley moved into a small apartment on the Near North Side of Chicago. Our parents entertained brief hopes that a wife was what he had needed all along to help him conform to the social pattern of the Chicago suburbs. But late that fall the newlyweds closed up their apartment to go to Toronto; they also were making plans for a trip to Europe. Father was helping with the baggage. When he came down to the car where I was waiting, I knew something was wrong. He shoved some boxes into the back of the car and climbed behind the steering wheel where he sat for a moment shaking his head in bewilderment.

"Those young people," he spluttered. "Do you know what they were cooking their eggs in? Well, I won't say it." The car bucked out into the traffic at a greater speed than usual.

Sherwood Anderson had come back to Chicago after months in Europe. He was full of anecdotes and gossip about the literary activity there and gave Ernest several letters of introduction. As a return gesture, Ernest and Hadley went over to Anderson's apartment one evening just before they left, carrying a knapsack of canned goods as a gift for an established writer settling down again.

It made for good feeling all around, and Anderson told about it for years afterward, when they no longer saw each other.

Before they left, Ernest had one more ceremony to go through. This was for an award that had been going through channels for a long time. In late November the Italian Consulate in Chicago got in touch with him. At a ceremony attended by friends and local Italian war veterans, General Diaz formally presented him with the Silver Medal of Military Valor, followed by toasts and much good feeling. Everyone, even our father, was impressed all over again.

But then Father examined Ernest's Marlin .22. After the honeymoon at Windemere, there had been the matter of a bill for milk and other farm produce, with Ernest foreseeing a need for cash in the near future. It had been agreed that our father would pay the milk bill in exchange for the rifle. There were short, bitter exclamations. He turned to me, in a lesson-teaching mood. "Look at this." He held up the barrel of the dismantled rifle. "This is the gun I taught Ernest to take care of properly. He let something get into the bore and then tried to shoot it out. . . . Now it will have to be completely rebored. Medals for military valor, but he ruins a good weapon like this." Our father was lost in sad bewilderment again.

The arrangements with the *Toronto Star* were finally made, and Ernest and Hadley were able to go to Europe as they had hoped, though without a salary for security. Instead, Ernest was to file dispatches by mail, be paid space rates for everything the paper used, and be paid expenses incurred in getting the stories used. This meant financing themselves for the first few weeks, and playing it low and slow until they got to Paris where they would set up headquarters. The arrangement kept the *Star* from risking anything, but it allowed Ernest great freedom to work on his own writing whenever he was not working for eating money on special articles for the *Star*. With the lire and other money he had saved, the plan was workable. Living was cheap in Europe then, if you had dollars to exchange. Both Ernest and Hadley were delighted at the firm commitment and made plans to get to France as soon as possible.

Chapter 4

To be headed for postwar Europe with a beautiful wife, plenty of letters of introduction, writing assignments lined up, and enough money ahead to insure a few months of inexpensive living was the fulfillment of a young writer's dream. Ernest already thought of himself as a writer as well as a newspaper correspondent. A news story from Charlevoix during his honeymoon had described him this way. The word could have come only from Ernest or a close friend. He had written reams of material. And though he had so far sold only to newspapers, things were working out beautifully. With Hadley's love and enthusiasm, he had plenty of reason for self-confidence.

Paris was to be their first headquarters in a year and a half of life in Europe. They traveled light, having stored most of their possessions in Oak Park. Our practical father insisted on putting up a food box for them. And Mother, in her own way more practical, made them a going-away gift of a check. In New York they saw friends and were sent *bon voyage* gifts by other relatives. Then they boarded the old French liner *Leopoldina*.

The mid-December voyage across the North Atlantic was not easy because of high winds and head colds. But it was fun. Hadley was in great demand because of her piano playing. Ernest boxed three rounds with Henry Cuddy, a Salt Lake City middleweight who was also headed for Paris with fights scheduled. Hash was described as the real champion in Ernest's corner, sponging him off between rounds and cheering him on. Ernest was given the decision in one shipboard match. And Cuddy, impressed by his excellent showing, urged Ernest to consider fighting professionally in France. This was the kind of praise that delighted Ernest most.

When the steamer touched at Vigo, Ernest wrote to the family describing the harbor and its great schools of tuna, some jumping six and eight feet out of water chasing sardines. He said they had seen a whale off Cape Finisterre and noted that Vigo harbor had been a great hiding place for German submarines during the war, and that Hash was talking French to three Argentinians who were all in love with her.

They landed in Le Havre and reached Paris three days before Christmas. In the Hotel Jacob they took living quarters and Ernest arranged for a small room on the fourth floor where he could work completely alone. Settled at last, they were both promptly laid low by colds and tonsillitis.

By the first week of January, Ernest wrote that they were looking forward to taking a small apartment on the Rue Cardinal Lemoine. There Hadley could have a piano and work on some Scriabin. She was excited by Paris and loved just being there. In her delightful letters to our family she described in amazement the complete dinners that could be had for seven or eight francs, then about sixty cents, and the breakfasts of marvelous coffee with hot milk and crescent rolls that came to a tenth of that.

At that time Paris was again in vogue as a haven for artists and writers, as it had been in spurts over several centuries. After every war, with inflation hitting everywhere, Paris has seemed particularly attractive to individuals who want to live inexpensively while producing in the fine arts, or dreaming of such production.

The Americans and English then living in Paris soon came to know each other as they would in Soho or Greenwich Village. With their friend Sherwood Anderson, a mature, well-published Midwestern writer, having been in Paris earlier in the year, Ernest and Hadley had been thoroughly briefed on the outstanding characters before they arrived.

They soon met and made friends with Sylvia Beach, who ran the Shakespeare and Company bookstore. Through Anderson's introductions, they got to know Gertrude Stein, Alice Toklas, Ezra Pound, Lewis Galantière, and some other serious workers, as well as dozens of fakes and dilettantes.

During their first three months in Europe, Ernest made one short trip to Switzerland. He brought back enough material to turn out thick envelopes of feature articles. At the end of March, his Toronto office asked him to go to Genoa to cover the European economic conference. This turned into a two-month job, and further solidified his status with the paper, where his by-lined articles began to appear daily. The *Star* upped his status to that of foreign correspondent, and began paying him seventy-five dollars a week plus expenses.

Ernest was feeling very good about his newspaper work. At the conference he had met Mussolini, Lincoln Steffens, Max Beerbohm, Max Eastman, and others. Back in Paris and laid up with another sore throat, he wrote cheerfully that May Day was quiet, although the Comrades had shot a couple of policemen. He told of meeting Lloyd George, Chicherin, and Litvinov, and said he hoped he would be going to Russia for the paper very soon— a trip that he was never to make.

He complained of the rotten weather—rain always depressed Ernest—but described the countryside around Paris, with fields full of big black-and-white magpies walking along the plow furrows, and said he'd seen a crossbill on one walk. He was impressed with the forests, bare of underbrush. With Hash he had hiked forty miles through the forests of Chantilly and Compiègne, seeing deer, wild boar, foxes, and rabbits. They had eaten a meat pie of wild boar with carrots and onions and mushrooms in a fine brown crust and Ernest was looking forward to good bird shooting in the fall. Of the rebuilding of the towns of eastern France, Ernest commented that the new French architecture was ugly.

At that time he was working on his portable Corona, usually propped up in bed and feeling miserable, but writing steadily. By way of remembering the old grind at the *Cooperative Commonwealth* in the Wells Building at 128 North Wells Street, Chicago, the year before, he used that organization's blank second-class mailing wrappers as stationery to write us the news of Europe as he saw it. His Paris apartment was a nice vantage point from which to look back twelve months to the time that he had been hopefully saving lire for a trip to Europe while hating his job of the moment.

Weeks later, Ernest and Hash headed for Montreux to go trout fishing with Ernest's friend, Major Dorman-Smith. They planned to walk over the St. Bernard pass and down into Italy before going back to Paris. He wrote that the country around Montreux was exhilarating. They had climbed Cap au Moine, a tricky, steep height that allowed them to coast down the snow fields by simply sitting down and letting go. The lower valleys were full of narcissus and he said that just below the snow line they had seen two fine martens.

Ernest was enthusiastic over the fly fishing in the Rhone valley, where the water was just clear enough to fool the trout. He had regained the weight he had lost in the recent bouts of infection, but his throat still bothered him. Despite all that the doctors seemed able to do for it, Ernest said he supposed it would bother him for the rest of his life. Hadley, though, was looking as healthy and as brown as an Indian, he said.

That was how things stood when Ernest finally got his credentials from the *Star* enabling him to go to Russia. He also got a large check for back expenses and was feeling ready for new territory, when the whole project was called off by the management with no explanation.

That summer Ernest continued writing the stories that seemed important. He got on paper some of the strongest impressions he had of northern Michigan. He was also learning from Gertrude Stein, with whom he discussed his work regularly. He also learned about the publishing ventures of several people who were determined to start small magazines. He was doing some careful listening. It seemed to him that publication in these magazines might bring recognition quickly, rather than late in life.

In July of that year, Ernest and Hadley went off on a long trip through Germany with Bill Bird of the Consolidated Press and his wife. They were bent on fishing and getting feature material for magazines. They were moving out of the city's heat in the most pleasant way possible, and catching many trout on the way. From Triberg Ernest wrote the family about the wonderful time they were having, with Hash catching three good trout the first time she fished, and he and Bill steadily taking several fish daily. He was still using his old McGintys and noted they seemed to have an international flavor.

The thing that shocked him was the economics of fierce inflation. He pointed out that because the mark kept dropping they actually had more money at that moment than when they'd started out weeks earlier, and that if they stayed long enough they might be able to live scot-free. With that letter he enclosed some German paper money for Father. The sixty-two marks he sent would then buy six steins of beer, ten newspapers, five pounds of eating apples, or a seat at the theater, he said. He was impressed with the artistry of the notes and said that for quite awhile he had saved others to send but had spent them.

From where they were, more hills and forest stretched ahead. They took a boat down the Rhine from Frankfurt to Cologne where a British friend was stationed with his regiment. After that Ernest and Bill planned to get back to the business of earning their livings with their typewriters.

During that summer I wrote Ernest his first fan mail from the family. Like most fan mail, it was a letter asking for something, and offering only gratitude in return. I'd been fascinated with the German money Ernest had sent home, and in my first letter ever addressed to Europe, I said I had talked with Dad about it, and he had said he would pay the postage if I wanted to scrawl a note to my big brother way over there in Germany and France. I asked if he would please get me some unused postage stamps. I had just started a collection, and he was the only person I knew in that part of the world who might get the stamps before they'd gone through the mail.

Ernest replied with a very friendly letter, together with a packet of bright and fascinating shapes, from Fiume, from Italy, France, Belgium, and Luxemburg. This put me nicely ahead in my collecting, taught me more geography, and heightened my admiration for my big brother and his ability to produce.

Later, because we talked about the way German money was "going to the devil" as Dad phrased it, I wrote Ernest again, asking if he could get any more of that wild German money. He afterward sent me an entire album of the beautiful currency that was being rolled off the presses too slowly to keep pace with inflation. I didn't get to thank him for it until he came home from Toronto just before Christmas the following year.

"That money collection was very pretty, wasn't it, kid?"

I gratefully insisted it was a pure wonder.

"Hang onto it," he said. "It's worth very little now, but you never know."

That fall the pressure of work kept Ernest and Hadley apart for several weeks. The *Star* ordered him to Constantinople, where a Turkish attack on the Greek army in Thrace was expected. The situation could have started another large war and the assignment was ideal for a young writer who wanted to know more about violence.

Before leaving, Ernest had wangled an interview with Clemenceau, the wartime French premier who had personally killed many men in duels. Though he had obtained valuable statements and quotes, the *Star* would not use the piece. Ernest was so angry he welcomed a chance to get away from feature interviews, even though it meant being away from Hadley.

Before he left for Turkey, Ernest got Frank Mason, who ran the INS bureau in Paris, to let him file additional material for INS under the name of John Hadley. Mason agreed to pay expenses on it. This gave Ernest more money, for he was able to file twice as much material on the same crisis.

He had the freedom to decide where he wanted to go and to maneuver his way there. The armistice talks in Turkey were not very interesting to cover. But fighting and the evacuation of cities were. Other correspondents were on the scene and also military observers who knew a great deal but, of course, who could write nothing of what they knew for publication.

Ernest made friends quickly with the people who had the most information and were free to talk as long as they were not directly quoted. He skipped the interminable wrangles about high politics, conceding that both sides were being manipulated toward the end of controlling the oil of the Middle East. But he wrote some wonderful feature material on the inhabitants, the places where they lived, and what was happening to their lives during this fight over oil.

Following the armies west through Thrace, Ernest got to know how mucking awful war could be among agrarian people in a modern age. Moving through troop-occupied territory, he finally reached the areas of civilian suffering. What he saw and the horror he felt gave him material for scenes which later shocked many a reader. But his observations gave him additional conviction that to write truly was the most important thing to do in a lifetime. He had known missionary zeal and fervor at work within our family. He was convinced that, for him, a better way to do something about human conditions was to show these things as clearly as he could so that men elsewhere would be incensed enough to take action. It was the beginning of a credo for him. In later years he developed it to the classic status of a moral responsibility.

Whether outraged over some international event or over a personal conflict, he used to sum up his sense of immediate involvement with "If you're any damned good at all, *everything* is your own damned fault." This statement was always clearly enunciated and with a tremendous outward calm.

When Ernest got back to Paris in October, he and Hadley made up for time lost while he had been away. It was a wonderful season to be in the City of Light. To our parents, Hadley wrote joyously, "I didn't know anyone *could* be so glad to get anyone back!" With great pride she said she thought he had done a brilliant writing job on this assignment and asked if our parents had seen the grand introductory paragraph to the first of the series. But, she said, he had "paid for his glory in bad discomfort—his throat came on

again and he had fever to such an extent that he took quinine as
a part of his diet. And the bites—he was covered with them—bad
ones, and there are a lot of small ones still not faded out. Had to
have his hair cut very short to get the animals out! Besides all that
he had loads of work to do and very little money to do it with
and found few people to hobnob with. No encouragement from
anybody and fishing nil! In addition, my letters were never received
on account of postal stupidity and . . . we both felt pretty bad.
But now it's all over and we're together again and I've done tons
of things to improve the apartment and he's crazy about it. He
brought me a chain of great heavy wong beads and one of amber,
big beads with black coral and silver that belonged to some royal
Russian who is now a waiter in Constantinople. . . ."

But Ernest was soon given another assignment. The new job
involved digging news out of a very difficult subject—the Lausanne
peace conference. As one who had actually seen the problems of
Greece and Turkey that were under discussion, Ernest had an
unusual understanding for writing background material.

Through Hank Wales of the *Chicago Tribune*, Ernest landed
another spot as legman for Universal News while at the conference. This was invaluable because Switzerland was an expensive
country in which to work. The *Star* paid whatever expense accounts it okayed but always well after their submission. The "foreign" press was being used by each delegation to the conference
as a public relations outlet. No reporters were trusted for off-the-
record interviews, which made digging difficult. The results were
disappointing. Though everyone sensed what was going on, no
one could say it and back statements with documentary proof.

Bill Ryall of the *Manchester Guardian* taught Ernest a great
deal about political maneuvers. Ryall was a former infantry officer
who knew how the British Foreign Office worked. He understood
the human motives, including the cold, calculated drive for power
behind many a bland gesture. Later, writing as William Bolitho,
his first two given names, Ryall showed the world the depth of his
understanding in his book, *Twelve Against the Gods*. He thought
for himself and needled others into doing the same thing. Ernest
reasoned with him, drank with him, and became his great admirer.

Just before Christmas, Hadley gathered up Ernest's papers, his short stories, and part of a novel he had been working on for a long while. Packing the manuscripts into one suitcase, she took a smaller bag of personal things and left the apartment, headed for a holiday with her husband in Switzerland. She got there, but the baggage did not. The bag with the manuscripts apparently was stolen in the railway station in Paris.

Ernest did everything within his power to recover that suitcase. He had no luck. The thief, probably unable to read English and most likely disappointed that the loot was hard to sell, may have destroyed the contents as a worthless haul. Ernest finally had to accept the loss. Later he said it was the hardest thing he had had to do in his life, up to that point.

After the holidays, Ernest wrote a series of character sketches of the various personalities at the Lausanne conference. He depicted the Turks, the Russians and their secret police, the Italians and their Fascist show-offs, and particularly Mussolini. Then he and Hadley went down to Rapallo to talk with Ezra Pound.

Ezra introduced Ernest to Robert McAlmon, another American. McAlmon had a small printing press and had just published the first of Pound's *Cantos*. McAlmon had been briefed on Ernest and was interested in his work. It was an incredibly sad moment when Ernest had to explain that almost all of his work had been lost. There remained only a few poems and scattered pieces. But he and McAlmon talked well. They liked each other and figured something good would yet come of their meeting. Later that year it did.

In spite of the setback, there was good skiing at Cortina d'Ampezzo in the Italian Alps. Ernest and Hadley enjoyed several weeks of happy living before they headed back to Paris. When they got there, Ernest learned that Grandmother Hemingway had died. Genuinely distressed, he wrote Grandfather that it was impossible for him to believe it—because she was not the kind of person that could die. When he'd finished the letter, he went out and got quietly squiffed.

In March, the *Star* set him planning a series of stories on the Ruhr and what the French occupation was like. Ernest wrote to the family to make everyone aware of his plans, schedules, and future production. The new series, he said, was planned as twelve articles for the daily *Star* and should appear in the middle of April. He told Father how much he appreciated his letters and apologized for not writing more himself. He told of being thirty-eight hours on the train and being "pooped." He had traveled nearly 10,000 miles by railroad that year, going to Italy three times, back and forth, and from Switzerland to Paris six times, and to Constantinople. He had had for the moment a bellyful of traveling.

After the Ruhr series, Ernest plunged into work on his own fiction, reconstructing from fragments some of the work lost at the time the suitcase disappeared. An arrangement for McAlmon to publish *Three Stories and Ten Poems*, his first book, was under way. And Bill Bird had him pulling together sketches and stories for a volume to be called *In Our Time*. That summer Ernest corrected proofs while working on new material.

In June he wrote to thank Father for the sporting magazines he sent regularly. Ernest said he and Hadley both read them in bed and that they made him want to get out on the Sturgeon or the Black or some other good northern river to fish.

He said he and Ezra Pound had watched Battling Siki, a wonderful Negro Ernest believed would be a world champion fighter if he would only stop training in the cafés. He said he was looking forward to seeing more fights—if only the rain would end. It was making Paris "entirely disagreeable" for him.

He told Father he had lived with a bunch of bullfighters while he was in Spain and predicted that the experience would make some very fine stories. He had wanted to go in as a picador, but union rules would not allow it at that time. Nevertheless, he said that if he and Father were ever some place where there was a bull he would show him some of the stuff.

Ernest was very pleased that the family had liked his Franco-German articles. After he had written nine of them, the *Star* had cabled him for still more, so he wrote eleven in all and was convinced that they were handled well, making events real to the readers.

Late in July 1923, McAlmon, at Dijon in eastern France, had

printed and bound the first copies of *Three Stories and Ten Poems*.
It was a small edition of only three hundred copies. But it was a
book and it was for sale to the public. Now, almost forty years
later, each surviving copy of this edition is valued at several hundred
dollars or more. The Library of Congress keeps its copies in the
Rare Book Collection.

When the book came out, Hadley was some six months pregnant. In order to insure skilled medical care and either U. S. or
Canadian citizenship for their coming child, they decided the
shrewd thing to do was head for Toronto at the end of August.
There Ernest believed he could talk the *Star* management into a
job on the daily paper.

By mid-September Ernest and Hadley were comfortably relo-
cated in the Hotel Selby in Toronto. From there they spread the
good news. Hadley explained to our parents that she and Ernest
had decided to let the two families know only after making a safe
passage, so that they would not worry. It had seemed the best way
to keep them from feeling anxious, since there was nothing anyone
back home could do to help.

In Toronto they were welcomed by Ernest's old friends, who
were eager to do everything for them. They had found an apartment a half-hour's car ride from the *Star* office, yet right at the
edge of the country. Hadley was busily furnishing it, hemming
linen, and finishing baby clothes.

The new apartment was at the Cedawah Mansions, 1599 Bath-
hurst Street. To that address Father sent their stored wedding
presents, all packages carefully marked "Settler's Household
Goods" to avoid customs duties.

Father wrote in response to the news in great excitement. "I
have just returned from my week's rest up north and found the
joyous news awaiting me here. I was so delighted and thrilled. I
congratulate you both as parents and rest assured I will do all I
can to help you in every way. I was so pleased with your letter
written aboard ship and anxiously waited for an address to write
to you before I went North. . . . I am especially anxious to hear
from Ernest. Did you receive the long envelope for your birthday
on time? I have thought about you a lot, dear boy, and don't for-

get your old Dad loves you and so does your mother. She would greatly appreciate hearing from you. . . ."

Hadley produced a fine, healthy son on October 10, 1923. They named him John Hadley Nicanor Hemingway. At the time Ernest was on his way back from Montreal where he had covered the visit of Lloyd George. While both families rejoiced in the birth of John Hadley and in Ernest's settling into "a good job" on this side of the ocean, Ernest himself was miserable.

The paper's assistant managing editor was out to break the spirit of every prima donna in the newspaper business and he considered Ernest a definite prima donna. Ernest's friends Cranston and Clark had long before been transferred to the *Weekly Star,* where there was less unpleasantness than on the daily. Ernest looked forward to a switch himself. If it didn't work out, he planned to climb off the merry-go-round before it got him down.

On November 7, he wrote the family thanking them for the check, which he said had come at a very difficult time. He had been up around Cobalt and Sudbury near Hudson Bay on stories and had interviewed Count Aponyi, Sir William Lister, and Dr. Banting, as well as Lloyd George. He had also written two interesting articles on bullfighting for the *Weekly.*

The actual birth of his son had done little, as yet, to modify the apprehension of becoming a father he had voiced months earlier to Gertrude Stein in his often-quoted comment, "I am too young." To our parents he wrote that the baby, with his squalling, was a nuisance and that he supposed there would be plenty of yelling for the next couple of years.

Father had relayed the congratulations of several of Ernest's high school teachers. To Mr. Platt, Ernest said he sent his best but as for McDaniel he said he saw no reason to feel kindly toward someone simply because that person was no longer in a position to do him harm.

The weather was rotten again and depressing and so was the country. He remembered that the summer before he'd been out on the Marne shooting crows and had shot a pike in the river with his .22 automatic pistol. In the fine open country of Thrace he had shot more than twenty quail in one day with a 12-gauge

double. He said he longed to get back to Spain. Galicia had the
best trout fishing in Europe. And Spain was the best country—
though he thought almost any place would be more pleasant than
where he was. It had been a mistake to return to Canada, and he
wanted to pay for his mistakes and move beyond them as quickly
as he could.

Just before Christmas Ernest broke the news to us at home that
he had decided it would be unwise for Hadley to bring the new
grandson to Oak Park. They were determined that nothing should
interfere with her nursing the baby because they were sailing for
Europe January 19 and it would be risky if they had to switch to
bottle-feeding while traveling.

Instead, Ernest came down to Oak Park alone for two fast days,
hurrying back to Toronto in time to spend Christmas with Hadley.
After a blow-up in the office, he had chopped all ties with the
Toronto Star, and with Hadley and young John he caught the
boat from Montreal to France. Hadley agreed with Ernest that
the most logical thing for them was to get back to where living
was inexpensive, friends more expansive, and his second book, *In
Our Time* (Paris, 1924, a limited edition of 170 copies), was due
for publication in a matter of weeks. By now, Ernest was betting
completely on himself and on his ability to survive by creative
writing. He felt that if he did what he wanted to do as well as he
could, the results would justify the belt-tightening means.

Going to Paris immediately they found an inexpensive apartment at 113 Rue Notre Dame des Champs where Hadley said "a
carpenter makes the sawdust fly down below and Ernest keeps
the keys of his Corona flying on the floor just above." He had to
get out a lot of work in a hurry, for the savings from those four
hectic months in Toronto would have to stretch until there were
new returns on his writing.

By April they had established their routine. Hadley wrote
Mother thanking her for some family pjctures which they had
shown to John Hadley's godparents, Gertrude Stein and Alice
Toklas, who were "wild over the whole family." Describing family
life, she said the baby slept all day in his bed right by the big
French window all dressed for outdoors. He came in to meals with

pink cheeks and laughter. For his six-month birthday they'd had Gertrude Stein and Alice Toklas over. The baby had received rubber animals from them and a beautiful silver cup for his orange juice. Then the adults had gone to the dining room and had oysters before dinner and white wine for toasts. Hadley had begun to regret the location of their new apartment, however, because it was in the line of march of many friends and some boring acquaintances as well. There was not enough peace for Ernest to work. He wrote in the mornings while she cooked for the baby, fed, and bathed him. In the afternoons a housekeeper came to take care of Bumby, as John Hadley was called.

Ernest and Hadley had joined a tennis club and Ernest was boxing twice a week with George O'Neil at their apartment. To reassure Mother and Father on Bumby's welfare, Hadley reminded them that Gertrude Stein had been an obstetrical surgeon—a Johns Hopkins graduate—and that she came over every few days.

She said that Ernest was making a *great* name for himself among literary people and that Ford Madox Ford, editor of the *Transatlantic Review*, who taught Joseph Conrad to write English, had told him, when Ernest was complaining that it took a man years to get his name known, "Nonsense! *You* will have a *great* name in no time at all!"

That summer Ford Madox Ford made a highly successful lecture tour in the United States. While covering the Middle West, he phoned out to our house. He wanted to talk with Mother about her remarkable son and was, of course, invited for tea the very next day.

Mr. Ford was not only a big man in the literary world, he was a very big man in person. He seemed to tower over Mother, who was a very tall woman herself, and he looked to weigh about three hundred pounds.

"This is my other son, Leicester," Mother said. We solemnly shook hands, and then I was sent out to bring the tea into the living room, a pleasantly cool place with dark oak-paneled walls. There were a good many cookies with the tea. They discussed England, which Mother loved, France, of which she had seen little, and Ernest. The cookies disappeared. So did the tea. I re-

filled the pot and in the course of the next hour it was refilled
again.

Consuming more than twelve cups of tea, Mother and Mr. Ford
really covered Ernest's early life. She got out the *Tabulas* to which
he'd contributed during high school, showed his baby books, and
told anecdotes which even I hadn't heard before. When our courtly
guest departed, he was one of the best-briefed ever to have visited
our house.

Ernest went to Spain that summer with Donald Ogden Stewart,
John Dos Passos, and Bob McAlmon. They all did some serious
drinking and had a lot of fun during the Pamplona fiesta. One
bullfighting incident made headlines back in the States. The
Chicago Tribune told it this way:

> Madrid, July 28 [1924]—MacDonald Ogden Stewart and Ernest
> Hemingway, two American writers, were gored by a bull in the
> bull ring at Pamplona, where they went to attend a fiesta. Mr.
> Stewart had two ribs broken and Mr. Hemingway was bruised.
> Both their lives were saved.
>
> Mr. Stewart, Mr. Hemingway, John Dos Passos, and Robert
> McAlmon, all American writers resident of Paris, went to
> Pamplona, Spain, on account of an old fashioned celebration. It
> is the custom there to barricade the side streets and drive the
> bulls for the day's fighting from the station to the arena, the
> larger part of the populace flying before them. Afterwards an-
> other bull with bandaged horns is sent to the arena where the
> toreadors play leap frog and tag with the animal.
>
> Part of the initiation of young manhood in Pamplona con-
> sists of being thrown by a bandaged bull. Mr. Stewart and Mr.
> Hemingway participated in the first day successfully and on the
> second day Mr. Stewart was thrown. It occurred when he said
> he could leap on the bull's back and blow smoke in the bull's eyes
> and then beat him down. The chief toreador presented Mr.
> Stewart with a scarlet cloak, which he could not refuse, and dur-
> ing the handshaking the bull rushed for Mr. Stewart, lifted him
> on his horns and tossed him over and then threw him into the
> air and tried to horn him. Mr. Hemingway rushed to rescue Mr.
> Stewart and was also gored, but was saved from death on account
> of the horn bandages.

Other Chicago papers and the *Toronto Star* soon got into the act and the story was enlarged. Father liked the heady feeling of "being besieged by reporter friends all day." Supplying the *Tribune* staff's Paul Augsburg with a picture of Ernest taken in Milan during December, 1918, he noted, "This to you is the only photo furnished anyone, so if by chance any further news comes through the cables, please let me know and you have the 'Scoop.'" No sudden Hollywood star ever had a better family following at this point in his career.

Besides working on his own material that year, Ernest was periodically devoting time to Ford Madox Ford's *Transatlantic Review*. He worked as an unpaid associate editor, reading and rewriting manuscripts and, in turn, doing favors through the magazine for people who had helped him, like Gertrude Stein. Ernest and Bill Bird and Ivan Beede did much of the leg work around the magazine's headquarters. Ernest helped convince the others that Gertrude's *The Making of Americans* would be a fine piece to run as a serial. Ernest personally transcribed the first fifty pages of her only copy of the manuscript and then edited and proofed it so that it could reach a discerning public after lying around for years in Gertrude's apartment. The magazine also served as a launching pad for several of Ernest's stories.

Things were going very well for Ernest, with his home life as well as with his writing. Bumby was beginning to talk and Ernest was learning that a child could be more fun than fret. With wife and son he took off for Schruns in the Vorarlberg when good skiing weather set in. For months they were deep in the snow up there, working and enjoying the sports, before returning to Paris in mid-March.

Ernest wrote the family that when they camped in the mountains, up above 2,000 meters, there had been lots of ptarmigan and foxes, too. The deer and chamois were lower down.

He said Bumby weighed twenty-nine pounds, played in a sand pile with shovel and pail, and was always jolly. His own writing was going very well. *In Our Time* was out of print and bringing high prices, he said, while his stories were being translated into Russian and German. He and Hash were "black as Senegal niggers" from the sun and he enclosed a picture of the group on skis by a hut where they had stayed.

Hadley added other details, thanking the family for the Christmas box which had been delayed more than two months in customs, but had arrived without damage to the fruit cake—Mother's one culinary triumph besides meat loaf. She wrote that Bumby had a wonderful nurse who had taken care of him while she and Ernest spent days at a stretch in mountain huts to be near good snow. The joyful climax of the trip had been at Madlinnhaus, one of the big huts of the Alpine Club where a friend had brought up two telegrams from Don Stewart and Harold Loeb (formerly of the *Broom* magazine) saying that Boni and Liveright had taken Ernest's book of short stories, *In Our Time*. Hadley mentioned that Ernest's fishing story "Big Two-Hearted River" was appearing in the opening number of *This Quarter*, an American and English magazine, and that the story of Manuel the bullfighter in "The Undefeated" was to be in *Der Querschnitt*, the March or April number.

She added that they were all three terrifically happy, the baby was so handsome it hurt, and could talk in three languages. Ernest was again corresponding with Bill Smith and they were hoping to see him and Jenks (Howell Jenkins) in Europe that summer.

Hadley's public relations work with our parents paid off to the extent that Father wrote and asked to see more of Ernest's work. Ernest's reply of March 20, 1925, was a calmly logical statement of his literary aims. He very much wanted Father's understanding and approval, but he had gained enough maturity to keep his emotions under control.

He said he was glad Father had liked the Doctor story ("The Doctor and the Doctor's Wife") and that he had used the real names of Dick Boulton and Billy Tabeshaw because he doubted they would have access to a copy of the *Transatlantic Review*. He said he had written a number of stories about the Michigan country and that the country was always true, but that what happened in the stories was fiction.

Ernest also promised to try to get a copy of *This Quarter* for Father when it came out because he was sure he would like "Big

Two-Hearted River." He said the river was really the Fox above Seney.

Then he threw a straight ball. He said the reason he had not sent more copies of his work home was because Mother and Dad, having prejudged his work with a puritanical viewpoint, had returned the copies of *In Our Time*. That had looked to him as if they did not want to see anything more.

He said what he was trying to do in all of his stories was to get the feeling of actual life across—not just to depict it or to criticize it. He hoped that when anyone read his work he would actually experience the thing. He believed this could not be unless he put in the bad and the ugly as well as the beautiful. If he put in only the beautiful, the reader could not believe it because it would not be real. Only by showing both sides—putting in three dimensions and, if possible, four, could he achieve what he wanted. When Father saw some of his work that he didn't like, Ernest asked him to remember that he was sincere and was working toward a definite goal. Though some particular work might seem ugly or hateful, our parents should realize that the next work might be something they would like very much.

Then he thanked Dad for sending the sporting magazines and reviews and said that though he lent them out regularly to other marooned sportsmen, he always got them back for his magazine file. He said he hoped to get in some good fishing in Spain though for a while it had looked impossible. With a two-hundred-dollar advance against royalties from Boni and Liveright he was counting on it. He hoped the book would sell. His others were all out of print. Someone had stolen his copy of *In Our Time* and when he had gone to the publishers he had found that every copy had been sold. He congratulated Mother on her painting, asked to be sent reproductions, and signed the letter with love.

Those spring and summer days of 1925 were a time of intense production. Ernest had a tremendous lot of work in process, and the two things needed were time and money with which to live through the period so the work could get done.

One evening when funds were low, Ernest had a hunch. Telling Hadley that he would be back shortly and to hold dinner until he arrived, he put on his coat and went down to a gambling spot nearby where things were less rigged than elsewhere. "I had a kind of feeling. I don't know how to explain it," he said to me afterward. Putting a few francs into play, he soon ran them up until he had the equivalent of fifty dollars. "I cashed in then and came back upstairs to dinner, feeling very good. We had enough to live on for another month and get more work done—all in less than half an hour's time with the right hunch."

Ernest had worked hard enough for the money he had earned on the *Toronto Star*. With independent writing, he earned much less and was forced to learn the art of stretching every sou so he could get his work done. In later years the knowledge of how it was to be low in funds made him an easy touch. He was so openly generous with gifts to friends, he sometimes reached the point of regaining that old feeling of being broke.

Ernest's first books, published in France, made only a few hundred dollars. But that spring, Scott Fitzgerald came to Paris as a successful young American writer. He had heard about Ernest, read some of his work, and wanted to talk with him. The two proceeded to think the world of each other, while occasionally testing each other's capacity for strong drink. Scott came as an unofficial representative of his publisher, Scribner's, though Ernest had already signed a contract with Boni and Liveright which contained an option for his next work.

By the summer of 1925, Ernest was deep into *The Sun Also Rises*, and was excited by the way the book was shaping up. This was the first serious novel of his career. He later told of writing the first draft in six weeks, though the revision required about five months. Its title was from Ecclesiastes and its motto Gertrude Stein's famous remark, "You are all a lost generation." The book captured the imagination of thousands of perceptive readers and made them feel they had a new understanding of the postwar youth of their day.

On September 25, 1925, Ernest wrote to Father that he and Hadley were going to move sometime between then and December and to send future mail in care of his bank which would always forward it. The bigger news was that he had just finished his novel of some 80,000 words. He said he was feeling very tired and was going away on a trip though he was not sure where. He thought he and Dos Passos might go down to the Riff. Dos was at Antibes on the Riviera then. Hadley and Bumby were both well, and Bumby had come back from the country big and brown and blonder than ever, but talking only Breton.

He said that *In Our Time* would be out October 1 in the States and that he hoped some of the people in Oak Park would buy it. He noted that a reviewer in a Minneapolis paper had mentioned that he had a brother who was a banker and super business promoter and that, unless I had come on very fast, our Uncle George must be getting credit for being his brother.

Ernest said he hoped Dad would get a chance to go shooting that fall. He himself had been invited to shoot and hunt in England, but had not had either the guns or the riding clothes for it, though he hoped sometime to shoot grouse in August in Scotland.

On November 20, Ernest wrote again to thank Dad for his letters from Florida and Look-Out Mountain, Tennessee. He said he hoped he and Hadley might see Florida before it was completely chopped up into town lots, though at the rate that was happening he didn't know if they could. He had been working very hard on some new material that was going well. Dos Passos was back and his company was very enjoyable.

Clippings and reviews of Ernest's book had been coming in from all over. He had received more than fifty in one recent mail and was enclosing three from the most influential New York papers for our parents to read. He said he hoped they would arrange for the *Oak Leaves* or the *Oak Parker* to see them so that the local reviewers would hear that, in New York at least, he was not considered a bum. There had been a long article on him, and information about Hadley and Bumby, with a picture, in the November issue of *Arts and Decoration* and he thought it might interest the family. He hoped his book would sell well in Chicago and Oak Park because he wanted the people he knew to see what he was doing, no matter what their opinion was. He said he thought Dad would like the fishing story "Big Two-Hearted River" and that both he and Mother might like "Cat in the Rain."

At that time, Ernest was working swiftly and surely on *The Torrents of Spring*, in a move that might bring Boni and Liveright to reject this new manuscript on which they had an option. If that happened, Ernest would be free to choose another publisher, which he wanted very much to do. He wanted to be free to go to Scribner's, where Max Perkins was an editor, and where Scott Fitzgerald had been given such a good deal. It would take a manuscript like *The Torrents of Spring*, which spoofed the style of Sherwood Anderson and some other people, to get the firm of Boni and Liveright to turn down its option.

Writing from Schruns in the Alps on December 14, he gave the family a preview of things to come. After congratulating Mother on her success with her paintings, he thanked her for sending the *New Republic* review and the review of Anderson's book from the *Atlantic Monthly*. Archibald MacLeish, reviewer of Anderson's *Dark Laughter*, was very intelligent, Ernest said. They had the same opinions about Anderson's book, except that Ernest considered it an even more pretentious fake, with only a few patches of real writing in it.

Ernest said he would be delighted to get the book Mother was sending and that he would be in the Alps until March. By the end of March, they would be visiting friends on the Riviera, and from there they would go to Spain. They were planning to return to the United States in September.

Ernest had a new camera and promised to send more pictures of Bumby, who was at that moment out sledding with his nurse. There had been a heavy snow when they arrived two days earlier. He was working very hard, though he had been feeling run down when they left Paris. He had another book off to the publisher, and had been working so much he had not had time for exercise. So he had developed a bad cough and had lost weight. But he felt certain that the mountains would fix that. It was pretty country. He and Hadley knew everyone in the village of green-and-white plastered houses. He played in the weekly poker game and belonged to the ski club. They were the only foreigners and that was the best way to learn the language.

Pauline Pfeiffer, a friend of Hadley's, was coming for Christmas

Ernest Miller Hemingway, age three months, and our proud mother in the Oak Park style of 1899.

An early candid portrait, 1900: Ernest, one year, and Marcelline, two and a half, with our parents.

Walloon Lake, Mich.

"*Windemere*"

The post cards sent by the family in 1900 showed Ernest and
Marcelline in the water.

Ursula Hemingway and brother Ernest in cowboy and soldier suits
pose with a friend.

Ernest, at six years, was proud of his sailor suit.

In March 1912, Ernest was a serious student.

A year later, he was ready to be graduated from grade school.

In Oriental costume, Marcelline, Ernest, cousin Marguerite Hemingway, and Ursula, behind the fan.

Ernest, the happy hunter, with a friend and porcupine trophy; Ernest's first gun stands beside him.

These brook trout were caught
by Ernest in Horton's Creek.

At high school graduation in
1917 Marcelline and Ernest pose
on the front lawn at 600 North
Kenilworth Avenue, Oak Park.

The young sports enthusiast before heading for Kansas City and
his first professional work.

Ernest was serious when this senior class picture was taken.

Ernest's gun club in 1917: members included Señor Ernest De La Mancha y O'Brien Hemingway; Sir Raymond Charles Ohlsen; John Lewis Pentecost, Jr., the Fifth; C. Bayley Savage, Jr.; and Fred Wilcoxen.

The six Hemingway children: Ursula and Madelaine standing, Carol on Marcelline's lap, Leicester held by Ernest.

and Dos Passos was in Morocco on an assignment for *Harper's* magazine and would not be back until February. Then they planned to go to Munich together. They would fly over the Alps, land on a high mountain plateau—in the Selvretta—and ski down from there. It was a new stunt people were trying that year, and they would be among the first to do it. With five of them going, the cost would be only about twenty-five marks each.

In closing, Ernest commented that the *New Republic* review of his own work had been just a lot of blah blah.

It was a big winter at Schruns and Ernest had done a lot of traveling. By May 23, he wrote from Madrid telling Dad he was happy to hear about his splendid Smoky Mountain trip. Ernest and Hadley were still planning to come to America in the fall and would probably spend the winter in Piggott, Arkansas. Though that was the plan, Ernest pointed out that nothing had been settled definitely.

Ernest reported making a fast trip to New York while Father was in Florida but he had stayed only a week on business. He had wanted to visit the family but had booked passage on the *President Roosevelt* and figured it would only complicate matters if they tried to get together, while everyone would feel worse if they did not. So he had not mentioned the trip at all.

Ernest's plan to make a shift to Scribner's had worked and now he had an excellent contract with them. They would be bringing out his satire, *The Torrents of Spring*, that month. *The Sun Also Rises* would be out in the fall. At that moment, Ernest was writing stories to be published in *Scribner's* magazine later on.

He said Hadley had taken Bumby and the baby's nurse to Antibes when he had come to Madrid. She had expected to join him there but Bumby had developed whooping cough, so Ernest expected to go back to Antibes until Bumby was well. Then they would all return to Spain until August.

Ernest and Hadley planned to come to Chicago when they got back to the States and hoped to stay three or four days with the family—if our parents wanted them to stay. Hadley wanted to see her people in St. Louis, but Ernest did not want to get caught in the entertaining there so he thought he would stay on in Oak

Park and just go on down for a single day of facing relatives before they all went on to Piggott. He said he hoped that in Piggott he would be far enough away so that no one would want to bother and he could just work. He had another novel to work on and though some writers might feel sociable all the time, he knew he was about as pleasant to be around as a bear with sore paws. Pauline Pfeiffer, who had been in Austria with them and was going to Spain that summer, lived in Piggott, Arkansas, when she was in America and was getting them a house there. Ernest said he had heard Father was upset about his wanting to spend the winter at the cottage of Windemere and had decided not to bother him on that score.

As casually as his usual comment on the weather, Ernest mentioned that he had been to Mass that morning and was due at a bullfight that afternoon and that he wished Father could come along. Since both Ernest and Hadley had been brought up as Protestants, the comment about Mass was not taken casually by our parents. But then, it was a letter that said a great deal.

That spring *The Torrents of Spring* was published and in the fall *The Sun Also Rises* came out in an American edition four times as large as the earlier book. *The Sun Also Rises* became a best-seller, impressed the critics of two continents, and was a success in England as well.

But at home, Ernest was trying to toss snowballs through a brick wall in attempting to get our parents to understand what he had written and the value of writing it was concerned. Before he could go into that problem further, Ernest received news of our Grandfather Hemingway's death. He hastened to reply on October 22, the day *The Sun Also Rises* was being published in New York, telling Dad he was dreadfully sorry to hear of the death. It had brought great sadness not to see him again before he died, but Ernest was glad that he had at least died happily and peacefully.

He then announced that his own plans had been entirely upset. The only thing that was certain was that they would not get to America that fall.

What Ernest did not tell our parents was that he and Hadley had separated. He was not about to break that news before it became absolutely necessary. As it was, our parents, in their disappointment at not seeing their grandson when they had hoped, wrote with even greater concern about the child's health and well-being. To reassure them, Ernest wrote on December 1, 1926, that he felt terrible not to be getting back in the fall and to miss the hunting with Father, but that things had not worked out. He advised them to stop worrying about Bumby's health. The child was not living in a studio, but in a sixth-floor apartment, well-heated, comfortable, with all modern comforts and a lovely view as well. He had recovered completely from the whooping cough and was tremendously healthy and strong. He spoke French, German, and some English and was saying some very intelligent things. Ernest pointed out that it was he who worked in the studio where nobody had the address so that he would not be interrupted.

He said that the reviews of his novel had been splendid, and that, according to an ad in the *New York World* late in November, the book was in its second printing. The *Boston Transcript* had given it two columns and the *New York Times*, *World*, and *Tribune* had all had good reviews. It was soon to be published in England. *In Our Time* had been published there already and had received a good press. He offered to save some of the reviews Scribner's was sending him and forward them to Father, if he would like to see them.

He said he thought he had another story in the December *Scribner's* magazine, and that there would be one in the next number, too. He had read the proof on both stories but was not sure when they were appearing.

Ernest promised the family a fine new picture of Bumby for Christmas. Man Ray had made it. He also said Bumby had declared he was going to Spain with his papa next year and sleep with the bulls. Recently, Bumby had pretended to have drunk some cleaning fluid. When Hadley told him that if he had drunk it it would kill him and then he would go to heaven with the baby Jesus, Bumby quickly said in French that that was true but that if the baby Jesus should drink the cleaning fluid, it would kill him too. Ernest said he had taught Bumby all his prayers in English but that he didn't take them very seriously as yet. When Ernest

had taken him to church, Bumby had considered it a fine place
because it was full of lions.

It was at the time the Man Ray photographs were taken, a few
weeks earlier, that Ernest got dangerously clipped on the forehead
by a falling glass skylight. The Montparnasse party, in the apartment of a friend, was already running late when Ernest pulled on
the skylight chain, and the whole thing gave. It could have ended
his career had it fallen at a slightly different angle. As it was, a
two-inch piece of flesh was sliced loose and had to be stitched up.
The scar remained. And he was photographed both with a bandage
over it and without.

Ernest continued to work well despite the emotional misery he
was going through that winter. Some of the stories he was sweating
out, phrase by phrase, will stand as examples of emotional honesty
transferred from one mind to another, as long as men continue to
read.

Our parents, when they finally read *The Sun Also Rises*, were
as bewildered and shocked as convent girls visiting a bawdy house.
Their reading of it at all was as unlikely as such a visit, except that
their son was the author. They did not know what to make of the
scenes and characters in the book. Their emotions were thoroughly
shaken and life at home, I remember, was like trying to walk on
empty eggshells without cracking any. It was referred to as "that
book," in horrified tones.

On February 5, Ernest wrote to our parents from Switzerland.
He thanked them for sending the catalogue of the Marshall Field
exhibit with the reproduction of Mother's painting of the Black-
smith Shop. He said he would have liked to see the original.

Then he launched into the subject he had avoided for some
time. He said he had not answered Mother's letter about the *Sun*
book because he had been angry. It was foolish, he had decided,
to write angry letters, and worse than foolish to write such letters
to one's own mother. He said it was natural for Mother not to like
the book and that he was sorry she had read it if it caused her pain
or disgust.

On the other hand, he assured them he was in no way ashamed
of it, except in that he might have failed to portray accurately the

people about whom he had written, or might have failed to make them alive for the reader. He was sure the book was unpleasant, though not *all* unpleasant, and surely no more unpleasant than the true inner lives of some of the best families in Oak Park. He asked Mother to remember that in such a book the worst of lives was shown, while in life there was a lovely side for the public and also the kind of thing he himself had observed behind closed doors. He asked Mother, as an artist, to realize that a writer should not have to defend his choice of subject, but only his treatment of that subject. He said that the people about whom he had written were indeed burned out, hollow and smashed, and that that was how he had tried to show them. He was ashamed only if he had failed to show truly the people he had tried to present. In future books, and he believed he would write others, the subjects might be different—but they would all be, he hoped, human beings.

Warming up to the subject, Ernest added that if the good ladies of some book study club under the direction of a local reviewer, who was *not* an intelligent reviewer and her praise would have made Ernest feel silly, had all agreed Ernest was prostituting his talent for low ends, then the good ladies said very foolish things.

Ernest then broke the news about his family life. He and Hadley had been living apart since the previous September, though they were still best of friends. She and Bumby were both happy and well. Ernest had ordered all profits from *The Sun Also Rises* paid to Hadley, and the book was doing well. It had gone into five printings for a total of 15,000 copies as of January, he said, and had been published in England under the title of *Fiesta*. He could not resist pointing out that Hadley would soon be back in the States, so the family would finally see Bumby on the profits of *The Sun Also Rises*.

Getting back on the subject of his writing, Ernest said that while he and our parents had a fundamental disagreement about what constituted good writing, they would be sadly deceived if they let the world's nit pickers tell them he was pandering to sensationalism. He told them he was getting letters from *Vanity Fair, Cosmopolitan,* and other magazines asking to see his work. But he was

not going to be publishing anything for a few months, except for
some stories already sold to Scribner's, because it was a crucial time
in his life and it was most important to him to write in tranquillity.
He wanted to write as well as he could without thinking of markets
or money. And he did not want to fall into the money-making
trap that handled American writers the way the cornhusking machine handled Uncle Will's thumb.

Ernest said he was sorry if he had caused our parents to worry,
and urged them not to because, though his life might smash up
in many ways, he would always do all he could for the people he
loved. And though they might never like any of his work, it was
probable that in the future they might find something they liked
very much. In any case, he asked them to realize that he was sincere. He felt that Dad had been very loyal while Mother had not
been loyal at all. But he assured her he knew it was because she
felt she had to correct him in a path that to her seemed disastrous.
He hoped they could drop all that. If our parents believed everything they heard, he supposed they would often believe that he had
disgraced them. But he was sure that, with a little shot of loyalty
for an anaesthetic, they would survive his disreputability and find,
in the end, that he had not disgraced them at all.

That spring of 1927 there was no talk of our older brother
bandied around the dinner table. Mother and Dad made a brave,
determined effort to limit the conversation to the school work my
sister Carol and I were doing, our sister Sunny's progress in nursing, our older sisters' marriages and their small granddaughters in
Minneapolis and Detroit. The very fact that Ernest had become a
taboo subject and that he was such a well-known object of interest
indicated that something hidden and perhaps sinister was going on.
When I asked Carol what she knew about the situation, I was
told, "Don't be nosy," the standard remark made to younger
brothers of all ages in all countries. The gloomy atmosphere
bothered her, too, and soon it was her turn to ask, "Do *you* know
what's going on?" I shook my head.

The only thing I knew was something that baffled me. It explained absolutely nothing at the time. From the murmur and fade
of voices behind the closed doors of the front bedroom one night,

I had overheard Mother say, as I went up the stairs, "It's the shame and the suffering . . ."

Then Father had said, "No. It's the disgrace. I'd rather see him in his grave."

The coming vacation that summer was something I longed for. It was an enormous relief to get away from Oak Park. Mother and Dad both seemed a little more cheerful when we left the Chicago area. Up in the quiet of Walloon Lake, the grand calamity was finally brought into the open.

One morning, while Dad and I were digging worms for bait, he said, "You know, of course, that your brother has brought great shame on our family by divorcing Hadley, don't you?"

"No, I didn't," I answered truthfully, but with interest. "When did that happen?"

"This last spring. And it's all over now. What I wanted to tell you was that Bumby will be coming to visit us. We'll see him in Oak Park when you go back for school again."

"Gee, wonderful!" I remember saying. "Do you think he really talks French the way Stein says he can?"

"I don't know . . . I don't know." And then, maybe because I had not seemed properly shocked by the big news, Father added, ". . . Oh, the shame of it—Ernest and Hadley divorced! There hasn't been a divorce in the family for generations—for seventy years."

I wanted to ask who had been divorced seventy years earlier, but Dad had nearly choked on the words. And since it was a quiet morning and the lake was so peaceful, I saw no reason to feel outraged. I was happy at the prospect of seeing my own nephew, a fabulous child of three who was reputed to speak three languages already.

That fall, Bumby and Hadley came to see us in Oak Park, and Bumby was as wonderful as his advance billing. He was full of questions, always in French. Clasping my brother's cello lovingly, he called it a violón. I thought he was the nicest, brightest nephew anyone could ever have.

Many years passed before I saw the story that was run by the *Chicago Tribune* on Ernest's divorce from Hadley. The correspondent, filing on March 11, 1927, revealed his own feelings in the opening sentence: "Ernest M. Hemingway, a figure in the Montparnasse literary set and the author of *The Sun Also Rises*, reputed to be a best-seller in America, today was divorced by his wife on grounds of incompatibility. . . ." The story went on, but the attitude was already familiar. Ernest's literary detractors had already set to work.

In more than seven pages of longhand (that he called the longest letter he'd written since he learned to use pen and ink) Ernest tried with painstaking care to explain to Dad the divorce and his marriage that summer to Pauline Pfeiffer. It is a great credit to his diplomacy and his sincerity that he was able to smooth things over to the point where he and the family were again exchanging news, though in fairly terse dispatches.

By October 20, 1927, he wrote thanking Father for his fine letter with the pictures and said they had been having fine October weather and that he was working hard on his new book. He had some 30,000 words done. He said he had met Bumby and Hadley at Havre the week earlier. Bumby was living with Ernest and Pauline while Hadley fixed up her new apartment. Ernest said it was wonderful having him back and then apologized for not writing longer letters, explaining that his work on the book kept him feeling sucked pretty well dry. He hoped to finish it by Christmas.

The book he was working on then was *Men Without Women*, which Scribner's brought out the following fall. Hugh Walpole, discussing "The Killers," one of the short stories in it, said, "We have no short story writer alive in England as good as the author of 'The Killers,' but then neither has America."

Chapter 5

The "Key West period" for Ernest begins in the public mind with a picture of a bronzed giant fighting huge fish, then heading inshore for the roughest, toughest bar to celebrate the catch, possibly pausing somewhere to beat out a letter to *Esquire*, using words growled from one corner of the mouth. It was not like that ever. And the contrast between such a picture and the actual beginning is striking.

Ernest and Pauline came back from Europe early in 1928, when they knew Pauline was pregnant. The winter weather in Arkansas was bad for sore throats. To give Pauline a chance to be as healthy as possible, with lots of sun and rest, they headed for Florida, determined to go to the southern tip if possible.

Driving a yellow Model A Ford convertible coupé, they made their way down over the bridges and ferry crossings and finally reached Key West. This southernmost town in the United States was so far removed from the rest of Florida that the great real estate boom and bust had never reached it. It was a quiet, subtropical town whose last big excitement had been thirty years earlier when the Spanish-American War had made the port a haven for coaling steamers, and a dispatch point for news and naval forces.

That spring, Ernest and Pauline rested, fished, and saw the wild everglades land and neglected keys for the first time. Ernest was writing well. They were enjoying the feeling of being away from everyone who knew them or cared what they did. And then their mail caught up with them. They had not told the family their plans. Letters had crossed the Atlantic, were readdressed and sent back to the States, and finally reached Ernest in Key West. That was how he learned that Dad and Mother were in St. Petersburg. On April 10, he wired them there that he had just found out they were in Florida from a letter forwarded from Paris. He invited them to come down for a few days' fishing, explaining that he had a car and some tackle.

The telegram was so openly friendly that our parents immediately caught a train down. They met Pauline, who was such a wonderful person that everyone liked her once they talked with her. Our parents were no exception. They took pictures of each other and agreed that everyone in the family was pretty fine after all.

On April 23, Ernest wrote to Father back in Oak Park, saying it had been grand seeing him and Mother and Uncle Bill and that Pauline had enjoyed it tremendously. He said he was working hard and hoped to stay in Key West until the book was finished. He had had some fine fishing, had landed a sixty-three-pound tarpon and a five-foot barracuda. He had caught a small barracuda on the fly rod. He said he and Pauline had been living on snappers and grunts. He was going out after tarpon that night, and the night before he had gone out about sundown and had taken a ten-pound jack that had fought well.

Ernest was working smoothly on A *Farewell to Arms* at that time. Because of Pauline's pregnancy they went to visit her family in Piggott, Arkansas. From there, Ernest wrote to Father on June 1 that he was anxious to get the trip over and get back to work on his book. He said he had 238 pages done, nearly 200 written at Key West.

He said that while they were in the Keys, he had caught five tarpon altogether—the largest weighing seventy-one pounds, the smallest, forty pounds. He had also caught a big kingfish, some sixty barracuda, three amberjacks, many jack crevalles, snappers, groupers, whip rays, and sharks, including hammerheads, man-eaters, and nurse sharks.

He said he had been out to the Marquesas Islands, twenty-five miles out beyond the keys, and that there he had found the best tarpon fishing and had also shot some plover, cranes, and curlew. He urged Dad to come down for a trip to the Marquesas Keys. Waldo Pierce, the painter, had landed a six-foot-five-inch tarpon weighing 150 pounds. It had taken him one hour and twenty minutes to bring him in after hooking him in the channel inside an atoll. Ernest said he had taken a tarpon of more than sixty pounds on bass tackle, without a brake or a drag on the reel. It had taken a full hour, for the fish had jumped twelve times. They had also harpooned many sharks and whip rays.

Ernest wanted to know when Dad planned to go north. He hoped that they might come to Oak Park for a few days during the next two weeks, and then go on up to Walloon. The baby was due June 27, and he wondered if there was a good hospital at Petoskey, and if Pauline could have the baby there as comfortably as at Kansas City. He asked who had the Loomis cottage at Walloon Lake, and if they could get a cook and a nurse up there. If Pauline had the baby at Kansas City, he did not know how soon they could travel and he found that he was getting very homesick for the north.

In asking about the availability of servants and a comparison of hospitals, Ernest hurt Dad's feelings seriously. Our father's answer was prompt but stiffly worded. On June 4, he wrote:

My dear Ernest,
  Yours of June 1st from Piggott, Ark. received this A.M. . . . As to the Weyburn-Loomis Cottage on Walloon, it is now owned by your sister Marcelline and her husband, Sterling S. Sanford. They bought it just two years ago. Also to answer your first question: We would be very pleased to see you at any time. We do not know just when we can get up to Windemere now, but probably not until after July Fourth. You would best consider having your new baby in Kansas City or St. Louis as the Petoskey Hospitals are really only best for local emergencies. Nurses and maids

are very scarce up there. Both Mrs. Dilworth and Uncle George
have difficulty to get help for their own families. Wesley and
Katherine had twins this early spring. All doing well. Also, it is
a very backward cool spring in Michigan. If you want to have me
attend your wife at the Oak Park Hospital, I am glad to offer you
my services.

Just last night Marcelline returned to Detroit, leaving her little
Carol with us till she will go to Walloon with our Carol and
Lucile Dick and baby boy and husband, Waldon Edwards, who
are to occupy their cottage while Marcelline is in Europe. She
wants Hadley's address very badly. Marc sails this week June 8th
at midnight on the S.S. Olympic from New York, and you please
send the enclosed to her at once upon the urgent request of your
Mother. I congratulate you upon your great fishing success. Wish
I had been with you. Some time we will. Hope to be with you
and Leicester this summer. Write to me often and God bless you
and yours.   Lovingly, your father.

Beneath his signature Dad penned "C. E. Hemingway, M.D."
Ernest decided Pauline would be happier in Kansas City. They
got there safely and Pauline gave birth to a fine son at the end of
the month. On July 4, Ernest wrote to our parents to thank them
for their letters. He said they had named the boy Patrick and that
he was very big and strong. He was too big, Ernest reported, and
had almost killed his mother. A Caesarean was finally done and
Ernest had been very worried about Pauline. He said she had
suffered terribly but that her fever was finally down.

The temperature had been over 90 in the shade in Kansas City,
ever since the baby's birth. He noted that his earlier plans for
coming to Walloon had seemed to conflict with the plans of the
family and he did not see how he could come now. He had seen
the chance to come to Oak Park before the baby was born, but
Dad had seemed against it. They could not now move around with
such a young baby in the summer and so would have to stay awhile
wherever they went.

The letter was not mailed until July 15. By then he added a
postscript saying that Pauline would write as soon as she could to

thank them for the lovely presents to Patrick who was gaining well. He weighed nine pounds, ten ounces then.

Ernest thanked Dad for sending the clippings and added that the one from the local village critic was charming. He had never before read such a collection of drool and had been tempted to send her a wire, but decided it would be better not to notice her. He said he had been working hard all the time, and with the strain of Pauline's danger and the heat he had 456 pages done— there was only one-third more to go. He said he would take Pauline and Patrick back to Piggott and from there he would find a place where he knew no one and finish the book. Much as he would love to go to Walloon, he observed that he would be about as pleasant a companion as a bear with carbuncles until the book was finished.

That fall Ernest and Pauline stayed in Piggott until quail-hunting time, and then headed down for Key West with Patrick, savoring the good sights and feelings they had experienced the spring before in the keys. A *Farewell to Arms* was in the rewrite stage. Ernest knew what a wonderful story he had created. He was simply doing his best to make it even better and sweating the production through.

In Oak Park it was a time of harassments for our father. He had been thoroughly clipped in the unforeseen bust of the Florida real estate boom. He had lost his savings that he had invested in land which suddenly had no resale value. The year before he had successfully passed the Florida State medical examinations and he had looked forward to retiring there in a moderate practice. Then this prospect disappeared. Collections on current bills owed him were far behind.

That fall Dad suspected that he had diabetes, and when he didn't like living with the suspicion any longer, he underwent some laboratory tests. Sure enough, he had "a touch of the sugar," as I heard him tell a colleague over the phone that final week. But like most physicians, he was slow to put himself in the care of another doctor. No one knows why but he put off any treatment. In the course of several days of cold, rainy, late fall weather, he underwent a serious loss of morale.

During that first week of December, Carol was busy with home-
work. I was home in bed with a bad cold for three days. Mother
was preoccupied with the work of the Nineteenth Century Club
and the preparations for Christmas only three weeks away. Our
other sisters were busy with their own lives. On the morning of
December 6, Dad took some personal papers and mementos down
to the furnace and burned them. Then he went upstairs again,
closed his bedroom door, got out my grandfather's Smith and
Wesson revolver, and shot himself just behind the ear.

Within minutes the house was in an uproar, with policemen,
relatives, and strangers moving about and talking to each other as
though we residents had no right to be there. Carol was reached
by telephone at school. As soon as she got home, she did the most
sensible thing anyone could do. She suggested that a telegram be
sent to Ernest, in care of his publisher in New York. This message,
reaching Ernest while he was on a train between New York and
Arkansas, allowed him to make a swift change of direction and
reach Chicago a few hours later.

When Ernest arrived, he took charge of the situation and soon
had the necessary funeral and other arrangements made. Mother
was incapacitated by shock, and was able to make decisions only
after a day of sedation. Ernest moved into the big, second-story
bedroom at the east end of the house, and was to be found there,
in between minor crises, during the next several days.

One of the things that had been on Father's mind was a sum
of money for which he had signed a note with a relative. The sum
itself was not large, but with collections slow, and his own refusal
ever to use a collection agency, his situation must have seemed far
more desperate than it actually was. For he had a conscience of
heroic size, and the note was coming due. The relative who had
issued the note had spoken unsympathetically about the facts of
life and how business was business. In desperation, Father wrote
Ernest the circumstances and asked his help. Then he waited, the
tension building up beneath an exterior that was designed to soothe
others in time of need. Ernest immediately answered, enclosing a
check to cover the note. When Ernest reached the house he found
his letter had arrived. It lay unopened, with others, on top of

Father's white painted bedside table. It had reached the house that very morning, and could only have been carried upstairs and placed there by the man to whom it was addressed, and who must have been dazed and bewildered, possibly by lack of insulin, beyond any close touch with reality.

Father's impending funeral provided a situation most of us would have liked to skip. He had been a deacon of the Church, knew intimate details of the lives of many of the parishioners, and in the narrow-minded hypocritical view of many local residents, had disgraced himself pretty thoroughly by committing suicide. Emotional illness was very little understood even thirty years ago. Ernest took me aside and pointed out some of the realities, and his own interpretation, as soon as he had a chance.

"At the funeral, I want no crying. You understand, kid? There will be some others who will weep, and let them. But not in our family. We're here to honor him for the kind of life he lived, and the people he taught and helped. And, if you will, really pray as hard as you can, to help get his soul out of purgatory. There are plenty of heathens around here who should be ashamed of themselves. They think it's all over, and what they don't seem able to understand is that things go right on from here. I'm going to give Marcelline a piece of my mind, first chance I get. Now . . . what about Grandfather's gun, the revolver that was used? Will you get it for me? You and Mother will have to go to the police, or the Cook County sheriff. But request that it be returned to the family, as a historical keepsake. It will take time, but you're going to be here. I won't be able to follow this through, from down South. But that's the only gun I want. You can have all the others. And as his sons, we divide these things by agreement. All right with you? Then that's settled. When you get the gun, have Mother ship it to me. Now remember what I said about the funeral." I nodded, and was dismissed.

Two months after the funeral Mother and I did finally get the paper work straightened out, and down at City Hall in Chicago, in the County Sheriff's office, were given back both the revolver and its cylinder that had been seized and impounded as evidence. The gun was then shipped to Ernest as he had requested.

Before Ernest left to go back to Pauline and Patrick, he lent me
two of Zane Grey's early books on salt-water fishing and told me
about the wonders of the Florida Keys. He said that if things got
too rough in Oak Park, I could always come down there and go to
school and get to learn about a completely different section of the
country. The idea appealed to me but I was, of course, unable
to accept the proposal.

The thing Ernest needed most right then was a good secretary.
Sunny was then working as a dentist's assistant.

"Look, keed, I'll give you whatever wages you're getting now.
But I need you to do a clean typing job on a long manuscript.
Are you willing?" Sunny reached Key West soon afterward. That
winter she helped take care of Patrick and did the copying so
Pauline could get some rest. She had the honor of being the first
person to read A Farewell to Arms as she unrolled finished pages
from the typewriter.

The Key West in which Ernest and Pauline were doing their
pioneering had not had any resident writers or artists since John
James Audubon stopped by half a century earlier. When Audubon
was there, the quiet, gray town had been a booming seaport, full
of affluent wreckers and salvage merchants, their families and re-
tainers. But in the late 1920s, it was an almost-forgotten place.

Some early Florida fishing books written at the turn of the
century were what interested Ernest in Key West in the beginning.
He and Pauline had returned to it because it was a wonderfully
quiet place to work in, an inexpensive place to live in, and an easy
place to relax and raise children. It had all the fishing and
swimming and fine weather anyone could use, with no real distractions.

When they first came to Key West, Ernest rented an apartment
in a building directly across from the present post office. In the
next four years he and Pauline lived in at least three other houses.
One was a house in Conchtown, near the Garrison bight. The
other two were near South Beach, but more than a mile from each
other. They were trying various parts of the island before finally
settling on one spot.

The spot was finally located when Ernest bought the old Spanish house at 907 Whitehead Street, just across from the Key West lighthouse where the commandant of the Coast Guard lived. This house had possibilities, Pauline said. And she proceeded to clean it, rewire it, and build an extension to the rear. What later became the pool house, with showers and dressing rooms and a laundry downstairs, also had an upstairs workroom for Ernest. This was separated from the main house, but could be reached by the catwalk off the second-story balcony.

In 1929, Ernest found plenty to do besides fishing, completing a book, and raising a small child. One of his delights in Key West was the weekly fights. In those days before television, boxing matches had to be created, not just watched. There was an arena near the upper end of Whitehead Street that had been used for cockfights in the old days when the cigar-making business was good. The bleachers, made of bare pine boards, completely encircled the main area and were still intact. A raised platform had been added. The Saturday night fights were held there.

Generally more honor than money was involved, for the entrance fee was modest. Only side bets were allowed. And in a town like Key West, everybody knew everybody. Sometimes everybody knew who was changing whose mind and for what figure. As was natural with nonprofessionals, there were some who caught on faster than others. Some fighters began throwing fights on which the betting had become worth while. A need for vigilantes was felt. Ernest, by his very nature, was one of these.

Real dirty work was afoot one night. Not many spectators saw it. A blow was struck and suddenly the boy who was the heavy favorite began to sink to his knees. As he sagged, Ernest leaped. Eyewitnesses of integrity said Ernest grabbed the boy who'd struck the foul by one ear. Ernest bent low and said something. Almost immediately the nonfavorite leaped toward the center of the ring yelling, "He was fouled. I fouled him."

Then a great cheer rose from the bleachers. As happens now and then, right had triumphed over wrong. Or so swore the local gamblers as they pocketed the bets they had very nearly lost.

Ernest soon settled into the relatively quiet life of Key West. But like any shrewd animal in a new place, he had to explore the surrounding area. The great bay of Florida stretched northward, the uninhabited keys stretched to the west, and out beyond them lay the Dry Tortugas, the tip end of the barrier reef that curves down for more than two hundred miles west of Miami.

In Bra Saunders' boat with its big, slow-chuffing Palmer engine, and two fishing chairs made by mounting captain's chairs in the cockpit, the first trips began. Fishing for tarpon was excellent in the spring, as Ernest had discovered the year earlier. Through the Calda channel that winds north and east of the main northwest channel into Florida Bay, Ernest and Pauline, Charles Thompson and his wife, Lorraine, and Bra Saunders went out trolling in the evening, season after season.

Patrick and later Gregory, who was born in 1931, were usually left with Ada, the nurse who had charge of them during most of their waking hours when they were young. Pauline would pack the frosted bottles of Gilbey's gin, plenty of key limes, sugar, and a thermos of ice water. Then they would load into the Ford roadster and be off to the docks.

Pauline, my second favorite sister-in-law, had a marvelous sense of humor, a petite figure, and was an amazingly good sport. Charles Thompson was an all-around friend as well as sportsman. He ran the hardware store of the Thompson enterprises on the island. These took in the pineapple factory, turtle cannery, ice-house, and the fishery, including the fishing boats. A large, well-built man with a broad forehead and the calm manner of a business executive, he was the most amiable, down-to-earth member of the group. Lorraine Thompson was an outspoken Georgia girl with a ready wit. Bra Saunders was a true conch. Of English background, his family had originally settled on Green Turtle Cay in the Bahamas. Bra had the pale, watery eyes that come from staring into the sun-glare for years on end. He was thin and wiry and would take any chance offered. No one ever doubted the occasional guarded reference he made to his colorful past.

Ernest dominated the group. He was slender in those days, but his blue-striped Basque fishing shirts were always stretched at the seams over his immense, barrel-chested frame. He never bothered to put his belt through the loops of his khaki pants. Instead, he flipped it around his middle, below the loops. As one horrified local lady declared, "He always looked like he'd just pulled his pants on and planned to pull them off again any second."

This was the regular gang—though there were often other friends—who went fishing. They took fish right in midchannel and also on the flats extending all the way to Boca Grande. Sometimes they went in Charles Thompson's round-bottom open launch, a sweet little shoal-draft hull with plenty of room that Charles kept just beyond the turtle pens. Bra's boat became the exploratory vessel for longer trips. While going over charts, Ernest told me that he always tried to picture the places in his mind's eye. Then he had to explore them in order to satisfy his curiosity.

Out in the Marquesas that first spring, after a certain amount of gin and lime, Waldo Pierce proposed to wrestle all over again the tarpon he'd taken. His fish was slipped back into the water. Fortunately for Waldo, it was groggy. Amid great splashing, shouting, and general jest Waldo and the tarpon wrestled for some wonderful "which-one's-the-fish" type pictures.

Being almost halfway to Tortugas, the Marquesas were unspoiled then. All kinds of flotsam and jetsam drifted ashore. Flocks of frigate birds, ibises, and pelicans nested in the islands, around the northern edge of the atoll particularly. The fish inside the lagoon were so thick that barracuda lay in schools, idly sunning themselves in the clear water. Anchored out there at night you could hear splashing and diving sounds regularly through the dark hours. And if something disturbed the birds, you'd be jolted awake by the ruckus only an aroused rookery makes.

But the real exploring was to the westward. Out at Tortugas, eighty years before it became a national monument, the Union had built a great fort named after Jefferson, for blockade use. Dr. Samuel Mudd was imprisoned there for setting the leg of John Wilkes Booth the night Lincoln was assassinated. No caretaker guarded the empty fort at Garden Key against souvenir hunters in those days. The crews of Cuban fishing smacks had removed what metal they could, to sell for scrap and ballast. Those keys farthest out had the kind of isolation that made any man feel humility, especially if he were gazing around the horizon for help. When Ernest was asked about the author of *Of Time and the*

River, he observed, "If Wolfe were to spend a little time on Tortugas, he'd write better."

John Herrmann, a talented but undisciplined writer from Grand Rapids Ernest had known in Europe, loved the desolation, the fishing, and the feeling of wind and water. He had a keen eye, a good voice, and a fine sense of humor. And he had an immense liking for people. Once when cruising westward, Ernest was armed with a bottle of Bacardi, John with a bottle of Fundador. They felt they were in great form. Starting by trading swigs, they began singing, "We're in the outhouse now." This parody on grand opera, with hilarious variations on all the arias from all the things they could remember, literally rocked the boat with laughter.

There came a day at Fort Jefferson when the engine of Bra's fishing boat refused to run. Something had cracked and repair parts were available only in Key West. In those days it was wise to have an outboard along so that you could get help should you need it. The lighthouse keeper was on another key. A tender visited the lighthouse every month, but anyone at Tortugas had to look after himself. The islands are called dry because there is no fresh water. Men have perished there from thirst.

The outboard of this particular Hemingway expedition was a big Johnson. "You gents take the little boat and start early before the wind gets up," Ernest told Bra Saunders and John Herrmann. "Then make a quick trip and be back tomorrow evening. But get back safely, because we're depending on you."

Like all two-cycle engines of the time, that one had its difficult days. But on this trip, it ran well. More than thirty miles of open water separate Tortugas and the nearest of the Marquesas Keys. But the engine ran smoothly in the spray and the big swells. Once they reached the lee of Cosgrove shoals, Bra opened her another notch. The rest of the trip was made in record time.

In Key West the fun began. To celebrate, John and Bra had a few quick ones. Then they got the replacement parts and had a few more. After that, the only sensible thing seemed to be to make a day of it. Hadn't they just made a record run of some sixty miles at sea in an open boat? Hangovers, of course, required eye openers. New days of celebration followed the first. John and Bra finally returned to Tortugas, feeling intrepid yet unwilling to boast of their exploit. The weather had been good the whole time, so they could not use that for an excuse. And after waiting three days for their return, Ernest was angry indeed. "You unprintable, unrepeatable, questionable so-and-so's," he shouted in words to that effect. "What if somebody'd gotten sick or hurt? Bra's easy to lead, but somebody had to lead him. . . . John, what did you do all that time?"

"We just got to celebrating. You know . . ."

Ernest knew. John figured, with some logic, that the same thing might have happened had Ernest been in his place, so he supposed there might be a scene, then understanding and forgiveness. But Ernest could be severe. And he was. From then on, he and John had no further communication. When Ernest banished someone, he prided himself on enforcement of the decision. Should he decide to forgive, the recipient might spend the rest of his life in gratitude at being freed from Ernest's version of Coventry, so strong was his moral position. In years of observation, I have never seen any one of the "forgiven" recover completely the status previously enjoyed. This was a psychological device Ernest learned from having had it used on him.

That experience made Ernest feel a certain disenchantment for the Tortugas. But the fishing there is still wonderful, and the bird-life is unequaled. The east wind still blows for weeks at a time, and now the danger of being stranded is far less because of two-way radios and many visitors.

After A Farewell to Arms was published, just before the great stock crash of 1929, Ernest decided it was time to break new ground and explore more territory. Sport fishing off the Cuban coast was about to begin.

Havana is one of the loveliest, wickedest, most mysterious and enchanting cities in the world. It lies just ninety miles south of Sand Key light on the Florida reef. It is the largest city in the world with a grandstand seat beside the Gulf Stream. Here a magnificent assortment of free-roving fishes files past. Food for the fish may vary from scarce to abundant, but the stream has been warm and heavy with nutrient salts for centuries.

Ernest first heard about the great fishing on the other side of the stream from Josey Russell. Joe had made the run between Cuba and the keys regularly for a number of years, carrying profitable cargo that gurgled. He had guts beyond any mere conception of the word. Harry Morgan of *To Have and Have Not* was modeled after Josey.

Ernest would stop in at Josey's bar off Duval Street for a few beers and some talk. "Ernest," Josey began one afternoon in the dark, cool end away from the door, "those big fish are the most exciting things to catch there is." He described the marlin fishermen he had often seen many miles from land in their open boats. Josey said they handlined for market fish, risking their time and tackle against long odds to make a living. But they made out because the big fish were really there.

So in the beginning, Ernest chartered the *Anita*, Josey's thirty-four-foot fishing boat. They crossed the stream together and fished out of Havana, using Cojimar and then Mariel and Bahía Honda as bases for stretches of hard fishing. They bought bait from the local boatmen and fished the stream to the east or the west depending on the reports of local catches, depths, and concentrations.

The *Anita* was a low-slung, sponger-type launch. Her cabin had less than full headroom. But it made less wind resistance. With a reliable, medium-speed Kermath of a hundred horsepower, the *Anita* never did more than eight knots an hour, with her stern pulling low. But she trolled nicely, had sun protection on deck, and plenty of room aft to fight a big fish from either chair. After one particular summer of marlin fishing the hull of the *Anita* had eight separate swordfish bills sticking in her hull. She was expertly fished and was a wonderful boat.

In those days, Havana provided great hospitality. Though close to the United States, that city's American residents were fond of entertaining other Americans.

Among Ernest's first friends there were Grant and Jane Mason.

Their friendship survived great changes in all their lives. Grant was then local manager of Pan American Airways, during Pan Am's beginning years. A large, strikingly handsome man, he had inherited a fortune, but was determined to make something of his life.

His bride, Jane, was a society belle from the Kendall and Lee families. Her grave beauty had a madonnalike quality accentuated by a middle part in her smoothed-back blond hair. She had large eyes and fine features. Even "Silent Cal" Coolidge was moved to comment when he first saw her. He said she was the "likeliest young lady ever to enter the White House."

The Masons entertained with an openheartedness that was astonishing. Having lived at the height of the social and diplomatic tide in Washington, Jane had friends everywhere. And a passion for fishing. With our sister, Carol, Jane spent all one summer holding the rods between strikes while Ernest trolled off the north Cuban coast. She fitted admirably into the fishing fever. Her sense of humor and good sportsmanship were profound.

Jane liked to drink and managed it well—an accomplishment Ernest openly admired. For sheer excitement, they used to enjoy "cross-country runs" in her small, imported sports car. These runs were somewhat removed from cross-country driving in the usual sense.

Before lunch, they would have plenty of daiquiris and then take off. The object was to see how long whoever was passenger could ride without saying "slow down" or "watch out." The driver was free to cut away from the road and actually head out cross-country. Ditches, fences, hedges, and thorn patches were legitimate hazards. So were cattle, egrets, royal palms, and fallen logs. Ox carts, parked cars, or corners of houses counted one point each. But they couldn't be smacked—only grazed.

Jane and Ernest would each take a turn driving. The game lasted until one called a halt. It was a primitive game of "chicken" played in some of the most rugged terrain imaginable.

"Ernest was always a gentleman about letting me win," Jane recalled. "But I lost as many times as I won because when he drove he'd take off his glasses, in case of solid impact. He was

awfully nearsighted, so half the time he didn't know enough to
be scared, and I was terrified."

Tremendous drinking parties were held aboard Grant Mason's
forty-six-foot Matthews cruiser, the *Pelican II*, and at the Mason
residence in Jaimanitas, as well as the Floridita Bar. Yet none of
these compared with the natural parties that developed during the
comparsas, the great festival dances at Mardi Gras time in Havana.
Then the whole city went wild.

Then there was the time Ernest and Grant got an entire suburb
of Havana cockeyed—on the finest vintage brandy in the world.
That party lasted two solid days and into a third.

Ernest was in Cuba with Josey Russell and Charles Thompson
on the *Anita*. It had been a great season. They had caught marlin
with a total weight of nearly a thousand pounds on several fine
days, while fishing down the coast. No foreigner could fish com-
mercially in Cuban waters, but sport fishermen were allowed to
sell their marlin for gas money. On this particular trip, they had
been fishing for several weeks without Ernest's encountering
Grant. Finally the weather turned bad. Putting in at Jaimanitas,
west of Havana, Ernest and Josey and Charles decided to pay a
call on good old Grant. Jaimanitas had a miserable harbor. That
night they wanted companionship more than a drink. The first
thing they learned was that Jane was away up north. The gloomy
weather made Ernest moody. Grant was effusive, but it didn't
do any good. There was Grant, a summer bachelor for the moment, practically avoiding an old fishing pal. That was Ernest's
attitude.

Hoping to mellow him out of it, Grant announced, "Ernest, for
you I have a surprise. A new way to drink called carburetion."

Ernest studied Grant suspiciously and remained slouched in his
chair while Grant went on, "It's based on the principle of carburetion in good engines. What you need most is a good mixture."

"Such as?"

"Say a fine brandy."

"You have some?" Ernest was interested.

Grant had that week purchased five dozen cases at a salvage
auction from a French schooner wrecked down the coast. He

dug out a couple of dilapidated bottles whose water-soaked labels bore the legend "Castillon Cognac."

"Take a large mouthful," Grant said, "but don't swallow it now. Swish it around in your mouth half a minute or so. Hold it. Now exhale through your nose—completely deflate your lungs. That's right. Then swallow the cognac to get it out of the way. Open your mouth. Quickly! Inhale as deeply as you can."

A slow smile of appreciation appeared on Ernest's face.

"See?" Grant was triumphant. "It enters your lungs in a fine mist that way. Goes into your blood stream faster, like a carburetor that gives the best mixture for burning in an engine."

Glasses were quickly produced. Soon the room was filled with exhaling sounds like those of dying porpoises, followed by deep sighs of contentment after the intake. Charles and Josey soon decided they'd had enough and were hoping to make it back to the boat for sleep. By then Ernest's enthusiasm for the new technique of drinking, and Grant's delight at teaching, were practically without bounds.

"Why should the honest fishermen of this barrie sit playing dominoes over who slugs the next stranger when they could be enjoying this boon to humanity?" Ernest asked indignantly. Like a pair of jolly Santas, weighted down with cases of fine cognac, Ernest and Grant headed down the streets of Jaimanitas, knocking on rickety wooden doors.

"Many a fisherman was weaned on cognac that night," Grant recalls. Each recipient learned the art of "carbinación."

Between them, Ernest and Grant distributed three dozen cases. How generous they had been they didn't learn until later. Grant had bought the cognac at salvage for about five dollars a case. But that brandy was from the last of two shipments made by the heir of the Castillon cellars in France. It was rare then. The market value was forty dollars a bottle. Now there are less than a dozen bottles known to exist. They are valued at more than two hundred dollars apiece.

Yet the Mason-Hemingway nor'wester party was far from a total loss. Those tough residents took no gourmet's delight in the rare cognac, perhaps. But they were grateful enough not to hold

anyone accountable for their monumental hangovers. And in the
rioting that flared up in Cuba years later, many houses in Jaimanitas
were looted and set afire. What happened to Grant Mason's house?
It wasn't touched. Instead, local residents pointed it out as "the
house of our friend, Señor Mason. He was the gringo who invented carbinación."

Not even the sport fishing could keep Ernest in Cuba every
season. Between bouts with the first hundred marlin, he lived in
Key West, visited Kansas City again for the birth of his third
son, Gregory Hancock Hemingway, and hunted quail in Arkansas
near Pauline's relatives in Piggott. In the fall he liked the L Bar T
Ranch in Wyoming for big game.

Out West in the fall of 1930, while he was elk hunting, Ernest's
open Ford was forced off the road by an oncoming vehicle. As the
car turned over, his right arm was pinned back by the top of
the windshield and fractured badly, the bone sticking out of the
muscle. There was an agonizing ride of more than forty miles of
rough road to reach the hospital. Ernest kept his right hand
clamped tightly between his knees and with his left hand pulled
back on the fractured arm to keep the jagged bone ends from
chewing up more meat. Nevertheless, quite a bit of muscle had
to be cut away. Setting the arm properly was very difficult because
the muscles kept pulling the bone ends past each other. The
bones were finally notched and spliced with tendon, after about
ten tries.

Soon word got around that Ernest was in the Billings, Montana,
hospital and a serious, well-read young reporter rushed over. He
was so impressed with the authenticity of *The Sun Also Rises* that
he was positive its author must have suffered the loss of part,
if not all, of his genitalia. He figured this was his opportunity
to get the real story, a chance he could not pass up, no matter
how indelicate the subject. As the reporter told me the story,
years afterward, Ernest let him stammer around in embarrassment.
Finally he blurted out the question point-blank. Almost convulsed
with laughter, Ernest flipped back the bedsheet, revealing every-

thing he was born with. The flustered reporter walked off with a rare literary anecdote and a thoroughly exploded rumor.

Ernest returned to Piggott in the fall of 1931, after the birth of Gregory. By then the first motion-picture version of A *Farewell to Arms* had been completed. The studio insisted that the picture's première be held in Piggott, which was then known as Ernest's home. The studio undoubtedly hoped for favorable publicity. But in this it ran into a solid wall of frustration. Ernest took a dislike to the advance arrangements when he learned of them and calmly declined to attend the first showing.

The week of the film's première, I arrived in Piggott for some quail hunting. Ernest's invitation was not the kind you ignored. It had been accompanied by a check that more than covered the train fare, and six boxes of shells. And it turned out to be a memorable week.

The first night there I asked how the picture had turned out.

"Tell you what, Baron. You go. Take Ginny with you."

I went with Pauline's sister Virginia. Later when he asked how certain sequences had been treated, we told him about it. I asked why he didn't go see it.

"Nope. Bad luck to see the picture now."

Next morning we had a large breakfast before sunup, and got the dogs into the back of the car. Bumby had a sore throat and was running a temperature so he couldn't come. We headed for a farm owned by a friend a few miles away. The road was plain mud. When the sun began thawing the frozen muck, we skidded and splashed along.

"It'll be plenty bad by this afternoon when we head back," Ernest said. "But by then we may have the kind of shooting that will make us feel good."

I asked about the dogs, two pointers that rode in the trunk with the top partly up so they got plenty of air.

"The brown-and-white one is a mature bitch," he said. "That black-and-white is a young dog. He has a fine nose, but keeps wanting to chase rabbits. Got to teach him better."

When we reached the far end of a large field, we pulled the car out of the ruts, and let the dogs loose. After they relieved themselves, they headed down the field, the young dog racing out far and wide.

There in the early December chill, moving ever closer to the line of bare trees ahead, the older dog suddenly froze, holding her point. We had about thirty yards to come up, and Ernest motioned me out as we advanced through the stubble toward the dog.

We were almost even with her then when a big quail and then another whirred out of the sparse grass and made for a brush pile near the trees. Ernest fired and got one. He fired again and then I fired. The second bird flew on, curved, and went down on the far side of the brush.

"Tough luck, kid. But we got half of them. Now see what a good animal can do." He waved his hand upward and the dog took a great jump ahead and then commenced crisscrossing over where the first bird had fallen. She was back in a minute, all wet with moving fast through the grass and stubble. She held the bird gently across her mouth.

"Good dog." Ernest took the bird, twisted off its head, threw it close on the ground, and watched the dog chomp the head as he pocketed the bird. Then we reloaded. He talked on as we moved toward the far line of trees.

"I think you shot behind that second one. Try a little more lead, and always figure where you would go if you were the bird. Most of the time they'll break for the nearest cover. That's not necessarily the cover away from you. So think like the bird does, and you'll get more game. Also the hunting becomes more exciting. There, she's on another point." We continued across the field to the next single.

By lunch time when we stopped to get out the sandwiches, we'd skirted several swamps, climbed a number of fences, jumped some very large ditches, and taken fourteen birds. The sandwiches were a hunter's dream. I asked where you could get meat that size.

"Elk steaks from last time we hunted out West."

"But doesn't somebody cut the meat up?"

"Comes only in the large economy size." He winked and took

another mouthful. The bread was homemade, and the sandwiches were from close-grained meat a half-inch thick and at least a foot wide.

That afternoon we had some poor luck with the young dog and also met a party of hunters—three men. Two were local types. One of them carried a sack over his shoulder. It had game in it. The third was a city man with a clean jacket, autoloading shotgun, and no game bird bulges in his pockets. The meeting came soon after the young dog had made a spectacular run just after we'd flushed a single bird and downed it near the other group. Then ahead of the dog, a cottontail had burst out of a small brush pile and bounced along in a wide curve, clean away. The dog came back then, tongue out and really hoping for some praise. It had been a good chase. He was simply following the rabbit when he should have been concentrating on birds. When he came over, Ernest bent down, took him by the loose skin on his back, and gave him a vigorous shaking.

"No. No. No rabbits . . . no, you understand?" Then he let the dog go, stood up, and carefully reloaded.

The other group witnessed this scene. Their own dogs were on the far side. They apparently had permission to hunt over the same land we had. We didn't know each other, but nodded. The taller of the local men called over then. "Used to have a dog chased rabbits like that. Know how I cured him?"

"He's just this year's litter. We're teaching him," Ernest said.

"My dawg kept after rabbits till one day you know what?"

"All right, what?"

"Gave him a load of number eights, about sixty yards. Cured him."

The city man started to laugh but stopped. Ernest just looked at them. We didn't speak again. Suddenly we were moving off. I looked back. They were still staring.

The rest of the afternoon we hunted down singles that had scattered from a big covey the young dog found, and then the covey had flushed right out from under him, after he had come to a point alone, with the older dog some distance off to the right.

From the scattered birds, we took another seven. Ernest had

four and I had three. It involved a lot of walking, but the young
dog was much closer in his work. By coming in on the far side,
the mature bitch several times showed him just where he could look,
like a faithful canine bank messenger at the scene of a holdup.

It wasn't until we were weary and full of contentment after the
day's action that Ernest brought up the other matter.

"It's never easy to reason why they do it, Baron," he said with
a nod toward where we'd seen the other hunters. "You'd think
they'd learn better, but nobody has any right to control an animal
if they'd shoot him for punishment. The chase of game birds is
an instinctive action and I'm damned pleased you've got it, Baron.
The more you use it, the better it gets, like some other things.
But those sons of bitches would do that to their own . . ."

He let it trail and we walked back toward the car, legs tired,
thorn scratches stinging, and the birds heavy in our jackets. On
the far side of the big field we could see the dogs were already
there ahead of us.

The next day started out even better. The air was colder and
the ground stayed frozen until ten o'clock in the morning. By
then we were hunting over farms near the big river and we had
another dog with us. He was a lovely red setter that had been
raised by Ernest's brother-in-law, Carl Pfeiffer.

Over toward the Mississippi there were stretches of flooded
bottom land that had made the high ground invaluable to the
young birds that had hatched the previous spring. These youngsters
didn't have all the survival sense of adults. But they had the same
needs. And in their eagerness to crowd the ditch crowns and levees
and high briar patches, they were fair game.

"You take one ditch, I'll take another, Baron. We'll meet at
intersections. But watch the dog. He'll teach you when I'm not
there." Ernest grinned and moved off. I knew the dog wasn't the
only one under observation.

Every once in awhile I'd hear his 12-gauge double make a "blam"
in the still air. Most of the time he only fired once. I was shooting
my 20-gauge single, and the second day the birds either flew more
steadily, or I was leading them just right. The sound of my own
gun seemed a shameful racket on such a lovely day. But the birds

whirred enticingly, and every one fell with a satisfying grace, the small downy feathers floating off in the breeze.

"Let the dog make all the decisions. He's hunted more than you have," Ernest said when we met at a lateral earthwork farther along. I had pointed out that this dog never looked back and sometimes went right beyond a bird I'd downed and marked through the brush.

"I've hunted with him six weeks," he said, "but he respects you, too, because you bring down the birds he points when you walk up and make them break cover. Just keep shooting well and when you recover the game, give him the heads." He bent down and gathered up the skin on the young dog's head. The dog looked up soulfully.

"When you can drop something cleanly that is trying to get away, or catch it when it is fighting to tear loose, you get that old, primitive sensation. You feel it too, don't you, kid?"

"Yes, but not always. Sometimes I want them to get away free."

"Not when you're hungry. But maybe I'm more eager for the catch than the eating. It's better to feel it than to analyze it, I can tell you that."

We talked a lot that afternoon. Ernest told me about the time Dad had taken him hunting down at our Uncle Frank's farm in Carbondale, Illinois. The shooting had been wonderful and our father had been excited about Ernest's ability. "But I had some bad luck too," he laughed. He told me about the young kid named Red who had trounced him after he'd shot pigeons around the barn and was taking some to a neighbor. He said he'd nearly shot another hunter with a rifle he had been allowed to carry while they went coon hunting at night.

The year before Dad died, he had taken me hunting down at Uncle Frank's place too. But we had had trouble with licenses. I asked Ernest why I didn't need a license there in Arkansas. "You're a member of the family. Down here if you're on your own land or shoot on land owned by friends, no one ever questions your actions. They'd think I was crazy if I tried to buy a license. Other states aren't like that, but this one is."

And we talked about that crane-shooting episode up in Michigan. I mentioned what Dad had told me about how badly he'd felt at not being up there to help Ernest when that trouble developed.

"Let's make it another lesson, Baron. Try always to stay out of any court of law, no matter what the reason might be. They can take you and twist you around so you end up mucking yourself. That's how lawyers use the law."

The third day we tried a tougher terrain. Though it had many thorn hedges, it was reported to be full of birds. Sure enough, the birds were there. The sight and sound of a big covey drumming out in a grand whirring of excitement was all the dogs could stand. Their flanks quivered and mine may have too as we fired, reloaded, marked birds for recovery and chase, and then moved up as quickly as we could so as to keep the dogs in sight as they went crashing around in the briars ahead. We had to know where they were at the moment they discovered new game and froze in position. In one briar patch the birds were so thick we smelled them, too.

"You get that, Baron?" Ernest was inhaling, a far-off look in his eyes.

"Ummmmm. Like birds dusting, but kind of more damp?"

"That's it. You've been close before." He lifted his head, eyes closed. "They're over there." He motioned over toward the right. There the three dogs had converged on a patch of briars tinged with brown where the frost had hit them. The leaves beneath the thorns made it impossible to see more than a foot into the tangle.

As the dogs moved inward, a great explosion suddenly made us snap-shoot, reload, and shoot again as the big quail continued to whirr out of that one incredible patch of briars.

Then there was silence. The dogs began feeling their way through the undergrowth, scuffling for wounded birds and mouthing others to retrieve. I went in gingerly, tripped, and fell forward heavily while trying to reach one almost straight ahead of me. I got the bird, and broke off some thorns in my legs reaching it. Ernest watched, noting the dogs, me, and remembering where birds were downed on both sides. We didn't want to lose any, after having readied them for the crumbs-and-egg dip and the steaming pan. When I came out, bird in hand, sweating, and happy beyond reason at reaching in for a hard one and claiming it through all hazards, Ernest was having a quick one from his flat silver flask.

"You saw that one go down and they missed it completely? Good hunting, Baron. . . . It gives me a lift right here," he patted his groin. "Feeling them take off and then reaching out and pulling them down again does something." He turned away. I saw the flask tip up. Then he let out his breath like a man who has just slaked his thirst with something better than just liquid. He silently offered me one. I shook my head and he put the flask away. We were brothers there on the high ground, whatever situations life and the world might produce elsewhere.

On that visit we had had a lot of time to talk out family problems back in Oak Park since our father's death. He had asked, "Are you making out all right up there? You can come to Key West if you want to, but it would be simpler if you stayed up there with Mother until you finished high school. Then you'll be free to come and you'll learn twice as much, moving on your own."

Shortly after our father's death, when A *Farewell to Arms* had made some real money, he had set up a trust fund with Pauline. He put in thirty thousand, Pauline put in twenty so that our mother would have an adequate income during her lifetime. Then the trust was to be divided with Carol and me getting ten each, our older sisters, Ursula and Sunny, five apiece, and Pauline getting her twenty back.

Our mother had plenty of musical and artistic talent, but she was a far from astute manager of houses, properties, and economic problems. Her income, even after Ernest had set up this trust fund, had been cut somewhat by the big Depression, and Ernest worried about how she was doing.

At the station, just before I caught the train back up to Oak Park, Ernest turned to me. "Sure you have enough to get back on?"

"Absolutely. You financed the entire trip."

"Better have something for emergencies." Then he fished out a cheerful wad of bills from his shirt pocket, and peeled off a large one. This ability to enjoy generosity gave him profound pleasure because of his well-remembered days of low finances when he first started writing.

I'd had a fine vacation, had learned a lot, and had gained even greater respect for Ernest's bird shooting. His corrected vision with glasses was not an ideal 20-20, but he had an amazing sense of where the gun ought to be aimed and how fast to swing in order to take the difficult birds in lowland quail shooting.

In the first four years that Ernest was living in Key West, he and Pauline had visited the Pfeiffer home in Arkansas every year, had been in Kansas City for the birth of each of their two sons, and had managed time to hunt big game out West. They had been in the Florida Keys during the best winter weather and repeatedly had the best spring and summer fishing there, too.

Max Perkins, Ernest's editor at Scribner's, was a good companion and visitor on the fishing trips. But Max was more mature than Ernest, and Ernest was never very content with life unless he had a spiritual kid brother nearby. He needed someone he could show off to as well as teach. He needed uncritical admiration. If the kid brother could show a little worshipful awe, that was a distinct aid in the relationship. I made a good kid brother when I was around, but I couldn't be around regularly.

Jane Mason became another kid brother as the summer expeditions to Cuba for marlin fishing developed. When Jane and Grant adopted two boys, Ernest became the godfather of Anthony, the oldest. And as though to set an example in godfatherly ways, he remained faithful to his charge throughout his life.

In 1932 Ernest began the development of another friendship that was to have a profound influence on his production, as well as to provide him with another spiritual younger brother. This was a relationship he developed with Arnold Gingrich. Contrary to the belief that these two were old wartime buddies, Arnold and Ernest did not even meet until the following year. They had corresponded for many months before that, when Arnold was editing and doing most of the writing for *Apparel Arts*, a beautiful and visually exciting magazine published in Chicago.

Arnold was near Ernest's age, had spent his boyhood in Michigan where his father was a woodcarver of great skill. And Arnold loved trout fishing with a passion equal to Ernest's own.

By the fall of 1932, when the correspondence of these two writers had reached a warm and intimate stage—they were discussing the ideas that went into great titles, and the origins of some of Ernest's titles—Arnold offered to send Ernest a complete set of the files of *Apparel Arts,* if he could get Ernest to inscribe his first-edition copy of *Death in the Afternoon,* which he described as the greatest four-word poem ever written. This was an intriguing offer, for in the several years that Ernest had been writing books, this was the first time anyone had actually offered some kind of exchange of values, instead of allowing the writer to make a straight gift. In December of that year Ernest wrote Arnold saying he would be glad to inscribe the book if it were sent to Key West any time in the next three months, when he would be certain of getting it. He added that he'd be very glad to have the copies of Arnold's magazine, and looked forward to seeing them. Not long after, a package so heavy the mailman was sweating as he lifted it was delivered to the boy who called for Ernest's mail. When carried up to the house it proved to be filled with *Apparel Arts,* at three pounds an issue.

"If we had the dough, I'd gladly go broke buying the leather jackets they show in the illustrations," he told Pauline.

Arnold's gift began a friendship that lasted over the years. Due to his generosity, I am able to fill some important gaps in information about Ernest's life. In the early thirties Ernest was about to reach a popular, nonliterary audience for the first time through a new magazine, "with plenty of *cojones,*" about to be launched under Arnold's editorship. On a midwinter trip to New York, where Arnold had also gone on business, the two met for the first time, and over drinks discussed fishing and writing, until Ernest had to hurry back to his hotel and pack to catch his train.

Later that spring, Ernest said that in the time lapse since their meeting he had written three stories and fifty-some pages on a novel. He said he'd been going very well because of the good weather, and because he was suffering no diseases or accidents. He had finished a long story the day before and was laying off that day to write Mr. Gingrich himself.

A parody of Walter Winchell that Arnold had sent him brought Ernest to Winchell's defense. He said that Pegler, who had written the parody, might be the better writer but was not one one-hundredth the newspaperman, for Winchell was the greatest newspaperman that ever lived. Ernest felt that Pegler wrote a very funny line about sports, but that that was the kind of column that was easy to do. And Winchell had to function six days a week. So if he chose to put in sentimental stuff about his family on his off days, that was okay, because look what he produced the rest of the time.

Answering Arnold's comments about Ezra Pound, Ernest said he believed he had read almost every line Ezra had ever written and that he still felt his best was in the *Cantos*, but it was a matter of opinion. Admitting there were some stale jokes and quite a lot of crap in the *Cantos*, Ernest said there was also some Christwonderful poetry that no one had bettered yet.

Referring to the matter of Arnold's projected quarterly, Ernest said he had two policies about selling stuff. If the publication was a noncommercial one and published in the interest of letters, he would give the stuff away or accept a nominal fee. But he had often found out, in asking for the return of such a manuscript, that the pure-hearted lover of letters would have sold the manuscript for anywhere from ten to a hundred times what he had paid Ernest for the story or article. And Ernest would then have to tear up the pamphlet and use it for a manuscript when it came to publishing a book of stories. He said his second policy was to make all commercial magazines pay the absolute top price they had ever paid anybody. This made them love and appreciate a man's stuff and then they realized what a fine writer you were.

In his letter, Arnold had made a definite offer of no changes in copy, and of an advance payment of two hundred and fifty dollars for any single article Ernest might care to write. Ernest replied that he had several times within the past twelve months needed two hundred and fifty in cash badly. Yet he knew he could always have received many times that for writing a piece such as Arnold had suggested. As for stories, Ernest said the only ones he had not published would get the new magazine into trouble with the authorities. Besides, he wanted to keep a certain amount of post-humous work around to pay for the funeral expenses, since he did not carry insurance of any kind except liability. So where did that bring them? To the fact that two hundred and fifty dollars was nice pocket money but nothing serious to negotiate about, Ernest said.

He told Arnold he planned to go across to Cuba in a small boat on April 12 to fish that coast for two months, in case he went to Spain to make a motion picture. If the movie arrangements did not work out, he would fish four months and then go to Spain. And if he suddenly needed two hundred and fifty dollars, he would knock off and write a piece and would wire Arnold if that were agreeable. He planned to go from Spain to Tanganyika and then to Abyssinia to hunt. He would be back the following January, he thought.

Arnold explained more about the magazine to Ernest. He said it was to be a quarterly because he was used to managing quar-terlies without much of a staff, and that he hoped to make it a consumer magazine that would be to the American male what Vogue was to the female. He envisioned some wonderful adver-tisers and pointed out that if Ernest would give him his personal measurements he would try and get some samples of outdoor clothing being used for illustrations that would both fit and look well on Ernest.

In connection with Ernest's coming African trip, Arnold urged him to count on writing four magazine pieces during the coming year and promised equal payment for each, to be paid in advance if Ernest wished. He suggested the articles be done in the form of letters, which were easy to write and would cut into Ernest's creative time in a minimum way. Then he asked some leading questions about the old writing days and was amazed at Ernest's eager rise to the literary bait.

Answering early in April 1933, Ernest first complimented Arnold on the quality of his letter writing and then launched into the facts so Arnold would be ready in case of any prospective benefits from the magazine's advertisers. He said his collar size was seventeen and a half, he wore a forty-four in jackets, but liked a forty-six even better. His shoes were a wide size eleven. The trousers he wore were a thirty-four by thirty-four. He said he doubted they would send many of those dimensions to photograph but that if Arnold ever did have items like that, to send them parcel post collect and he would promise to wear them out.

The next year, when I saw him nattily dressed in a buckskin jacket while cleaning a pair of big sailfish down on Thompson's dock, there was little doubt as to his attitude.

"Hey, Stein, what're you planning to do, become a male model?"

"Listen, Baron," he said, "none of that, or you'll find yourself down there swimming among the fish guts."

Chapter 6

A curious thing happened the spring that Ernest and Pauline were organizing the first Hemingway safari. One day in mid-April, a man rang the doorbell of our house in Oak Park. I had just arrived home from school and had learned Mother was having a sick headache and was resting upstairs. As I went to the door, I heard the visitor pacing back and forth on the porch, as though he was dreading something or feeling nervous.

The caller was a tall man with a mustache. "Is Mrs. Hemingway in?"

"Yes, but she's not feeling well. Can I help you?"

"Well, I wanted to have a talk with her," he said.

"Is it anything I can help you with? She won't be coming downstairs this afternoon for anything less than a visit by the fire department." This was a standard dodge for salesmen.

"Ha. I like that." He laughed nervously. "Who are you?"

"I'm her son."

"Oh, you're Leicester, then. Well, it's only a social call. I'll be back another day. I saw your brother down in Piggott recently."

"Oh? When was that?"

"Just last month."

"I think he's been in Key West since Christmas."

". . . Maybe, maybe it was earlier, then."

My curiosity was rising fast. "Did you get to go shooting?"

"No, it was way past the season."

His story just didn't add up. But then he told me his name was Hemingway too and that he was from the East. He shook my hand nervously and said he'd come back another time. That was the only time he showed up at our house. But later that week there was a story in the paper about Ernest Hemingway having returned to Chicago and having autographed books at an Evanston bookstore for an eager gathering. Mother said it couldn't have been Ernest. He was either in Key West or Havana, and he would never have come to the Chicago area without seeing the family or letting us know he was there. And she was right.

The stranger was a phony. In spite of his mustache, he did not look much like Ernest. Later we learned this character had traveled all over the country claiming to be Ernest, autographing books, running up bills, and generally raising the devil with Ernest's reputation. Ernest never caught up with him. But in the years following, he was to regret that he hadn't, for his continued impersonations caused a flood of bills to reach Ernest.

That spring of 1933 there were many plans under way and time was running out faster than Ernest would have liked. He had to make a choice.

"What about the movie? Do you think you'll make it this summer?" Pauline wanted to know.

"From what Milestone wrote, we would have had to wait before deciding. Now there isn't time," Ernest said. "We can try again next year. It's too late in the season now. Better to have the African trip well organized than to try to do both things only half as well as they should be done."

Jane Mason had visited Ernest and Pauline in Key West, bringing Major Dick Cooper with her. Ernest and Dick had gone bird shooting on some of the uninhabited keys to the westward where there was an unusual variety of bird life. They got along well together and, before he left, Major Cooper gave Ernest practical information on equipping himself properly for an expedition to the African highlands.

The list included heavy, high-powered rifles, antisnakebite serum, chemicals for purifying drinking water, clothing for the cold nights at high altitudes once the rains had stopped, and certain foods and supplies that could not be had in Africa. Most important on the list was the ammunition, both solid-jacket and soft-nosed bullets of different weights and velocities that would make possible the hunting of elephants, rhinos, buffalo, and all of the lesser, thinner-skinned game from lions to wart hogs.

Major Cooper had owned a coffee shamba in Tanganyika, and had hunted extensively throughout British East Africa. He had been decorated for bravery in the late war, had moved in sporting circles, and knew a good deal of what there was to know about hunting in the best areas still left on the continent. He recommended that Ernest get as his guide Philip Percival, a former game ranger who was then a professional hunter. Mr. P., as he soon came to be called, was as reticent and full of understatement as he was capable and knowledgeable. Through Mr. P. came information that guns, especially big-game rifles, were to be had at a moderate rental.

"I'll own my own guns. I don't want to rent them," Ernest said. He was damned if he was going to become fond of any firearm that might save his life, and then have to turn it back to the owner. Since they would first be going to Cuba to fish until August, and then to Europe from Havana, on a Spanish boat, Ernest decided to put off all gun selection until he reached Paris. He could go to the good armorers there and be outfitted for the expedition ahead.

Ernest also invited his friend Charles Thompson from Key West to be his guest for the months to come. Charles was enthusiastic. He had proved himself as a fisherman and bird shot. He wasn't a literary man, but he was a good sport, brave, and one who would enjoy the excitement without getting on Ernest's nerves. Charles' wife Lorraine had teaching commitments, but it was arranged that she would come over in the spring and meet them all in Palestine. With Charles and Pauline, the expedition was bound to be exciting and a success. The children were to be left with relatives, the nurse remaining in charge of details. For the first time since their marriage, Ernest and Pauline knew they were going on an adventurous trip with minimum worries and the chance for maximum enjoyment. They wanted to see Spain again and planned to stay until the conclusion of the feria of Pilar in October.

Both Pauline and Charles Thompson had plenty of things to look after, so they stayed in Key West while, early in April, Ernest went over to Havana in Joe Russell's boat. When he got there, he found the big fish were not running yet. He used the time to work on his novel and to write some short stories, disciplining himself to getting up at five o'clock in the morning and working until at least ten o'clock and frequently until noon. When the fish finally began to show along the edge of the Stream, he was ready for them, having just put in several weeks of satisfying work at the desk in his fourth-floor room at the Hotel Ambos Mundos on Obispo Street.

That spring, Ernest and Arnold Gingrich were in regular correspondence, exchanging a great deal of information and getting to like each other more and more as their trust developed. Ernest had not liked the proposed title of *Esquire*, feeling it might be too snooty in a depression time, but he liked the intentions of the magazine. By the end of May, he was ready to write the first Cuban letter for the new magazine and was going satisfactorily on his own work, as well as fishing on the days when the breeze came up. The schedule was almost ideal for marlin fishing, which was best when the water was ruffled, and often the day's wind didn't set in until after eleven in the morning, when the day's writing was done.

By the end of May, Ernest had taken twenty-nine marlin and had run into more fish and luck in one three-day period than he'd known anyone else ever to experience, taking seven one day on one rod. When he told me about that day the following summer, he was still ecstatic.

"Think of it, Baron," he said, "seven huge ones, all of them blues and running to a good size—between one hundred twenty and two hundred fifty pounds. I fought each one absolutely alone, with Carlos helping around the cockpit, of course. Caught a hell of a chill, from sweating and being cooled by the wind. My throat gave me hell for three days. But I still think it may have been a world's record."

Ernest was then keeping a daily log of his catches, carefully noting fishing conditions, kind of tackle used, and how it performed, with remarks—some quite comical—on the guests, the happenings, and the feelings aroused. He was in much better shape than when he had started, noting that he had lost twenty-six pounds after a steady month of patrolling the southern edge of the Stream and fighting all the fish that stayed hooked.

By the end of July, with the Cuban piece written and pictures arranged for, and the trip to Europe and Africa shaping up swiftly, Ernest was in high gear. He was excited at the prospect of traveling and of covering some old ground with a fresh point of view gained from five years of writing, hunting, fishing, and family raising entirely in the United States and Cuba.

The trip to Spain was a breeze, on the *Reina de la Pacifica*. Before Ernest left, Arnold Gingrich had paid him for the first of two letters to be used in the new magazine, and Ernest had shrewdly deposited the money in his London account. When he and Pauline reached Madrid, he bought pesetas at a very favorable rate with his English currency. Pleased with his foresight, he wrote Arnold that he would split the profit with him. Inflation was hitting the American dollar as a result of President Roosevelt's having taken the country off the gold standard, and was an upsetting factor in the completion of the safari plans. Ernest was angry about it. In a letter to me that fall he said that their money had been seriously devalued, but that he figured there would still be enough to make the trip. The whole thing was simply going to cost far more than he had expected.

By November, when Ernest and Pauline reached Paris, there were a number of small and cheerful surprises. At Sylvia Beach's bookshop Ernest had a chance to see the first copies of *Winner Take Nothing*, which had just been shipped over by Scribner's. He liked the jacket, which he had not seen before since he'd had to correct proofs by cable and had been out of touch with book-production matters.

He also had a chance to see the first issue of *Esquire*. He was very favorably impressed with the two boxing articles in the issue and wrote Arnold how he felt about the whole presentation. He said he was convinced that at least one-third of the magazine needed to be "snotty." As subjects, shooting and fishing were still two of the least snotty, he was pleased to note, though he figured they were bound to get that way because of advertising.

The final two weeks in France were hectic. Ernest was busy collecting the things needed for the months ahead and writing Arnold a third piece for the magazine. There were an unusual number of letters that had to be written and sent to relatives, banks, children, friends, and editors. After a final round of parties and some compulsory entertaining of old pals who had heard he was in town, the expedition headed for the south of France and a breather on the boat that would take them to East Africa. Before going down through the Red Sea, their French boat stopped at Port Said and Ernest ate something there that had the effect of an intestinal time bomb.

South of Cairo, the trip itself was a revelation. Ernest had taken a number of travel and reference books with him, but many areas remained to be filled in. In discussing his feelings when he finally reached the highlands of British East Africa, Ernest later said that nothing he had read really gave him an accurate idea of the way the whole country was. The plains were immense, he said, and the wonderful animal life was as full of vitality as it must have been thousands of years ago.

The thing Ernest and Pauline and Charles Thompson felt most when they arrived was the altitude. They had been on the sea for seventeen days, and the change had been abrupt. Ernest's energies were lagging and he declared he had no pep to write. It took some overlong nights of sleep to catch up. At night they used two blankets. They felt cool even in the morning sun with the wind moving over the Kapiti plains. In their first week Ernest had taken good heads of Thomson's and Grant's gazelles, as well as kongoni and impala. Charles was shooting well too. Pauline, nicknamed "Poor Old Mama," did a great deal of watching and formed the cheering section.

Ernest did not know it yet, but he was by then seriously ill with amoebic dysentery, which he had picked up at Port Said. The lack of energy was a strong sign. In the next few weeks he came down with the unmistakable evidence to a remarkable degree. However, late in December he was heading after kudu, and then wanted to follow up with lion, buffalo, and rhino.

In Kenya he met Alfred Vanderbilt and Winston Guest, two young and wealthy American sportsmen who were to make their names in racing and polo in the coming years. Alfred was more the ideal kid brother than Winston. He was easier to impress, had more to learn, and needed a papa in many ways. Winston was more accomplished and had already taken two tuskers, one with 117 pounds of ivory, the other with 97, before heading back into the better game areas.

Ernest found he was holding his weight, even with the dysentery and the routine of getting up at five in the morning and moving fast on his feet the whole day. He reported weighing over two hundred pounds again, but said he was so dead tired he could hardly write a letter, much less a chunk of reading matter. In six weeks Ernest expected to finish the safari. Afterward he wanted to go down to the East African coast and fish. They planned to head for Pemba, Zanzibar, and the coast near Mombasa to try for the huge sailfish that Zane Grey had reported as running to tremendous lengths in that area. Grey hadn't fished there himself, but Ernest was determined to. He was already ordering tackle from Hardy Brothers in London so that it would reach the coast by the time he needed it. The African trip was going to be more expensive than ever, but it would be a better trip because of the information he had gained in talking with the local people.

In the next three weeks, Ernest got his lion, rhino, and buffalo. He also got jolted, thoroughly and completely, by the dysentery. "Suddenly Ernest was passing nearly a quart of blood daily," Pauline told me months later. But though the bleeding and loss of energy were severe, the fever lasted only a short time because of prompt treatment. Philip Percival knew the seriousness of the malady and the safari was broken so that Ernest could get several days of bed rest.

Then, dosed so heavily with quinine and emetine that he swore he couldn't make his head go properly, he began thinking out some of his best stories, and wrote a batch of mail to catch up with the correspondence that had finally reached the Nairobi address.

The shooting on the Serengetti plain had been tremendous. Ernest was very fond of his .30-06 Springfield rifle. He had used it a good deal out West on elk and antelope. Now, shooting with heavier loads, he had successfully killed his two buffalo and all his lions with the same rifle. He had come to have tremendous faith in its accuracy and shocking power, even on the most dangerous sort of African game. Charles also had a Springfield, and with it he, too, made some remarkable kills. Both hunters were accounting for most of the game that was allowed on their licenses, and they were excited by the knowledge that they had some wonderful trophy heads to hang on the walls of their Key West homes in the years to come.

The degree of skill they each developed was continually demonstrated by the kills they made with the Springfields. Paris had been disappointing as a city in which to buy ideal weapons for African game. They had stuck with their lighter-weight American equipment, adding a .256 Mannlicher rifle with very little recoil as a fine gun for Pauline to shoot. In Nairobi Philip Percival had strongly suggested they rent heavy double-barreled rifles of over .50 caliber, as emergency protection against charging game. These were obtained at the gun shop across from the New Stanley Hotel. But Charles fired his rented gun only twice, to get the feel. Ernest never fired his heavy gun in all the time they hunted.

Ernest's most exciting moments, he told me later, were after he had wounded a Cape buffalo and then went into dense cover after him. The buff charged, and Ernest dropped him when he was almost close enough to touch.

Pauline was most moved by the lions. They had several times come upon prides trailing a herd of wildebeest that may have numbered more than a million animals. Pauline said one time they came up slowly and, when the lions saw them, all but one got up and moved away. The lone lion stayed there, looking curiously at them. "He seemed to want to be friendly," she said.

Ernest had also managed to take some excellent pictures, using his favorite old four-by-five Graflex camera. It was a cumbersome piece of equipment, but he was used to judging the exposures with it, and stuck to Verichrome film because he knew its speed well.

When the first treatment for his dysentery slowed the course of the disease, Ernest declared himself fit to go hunting on foot again. None of the members of the safari could talk him out of continuing the hunt. He was determined to get the great kudu he had dreamed of stalking and killing alone. And he did, despite periodic recurrences of the painful and dangerous dysentery attacks. When he finally had his fill and the party headed for Malindi, Ernest's weight had dropped again, and for the second time he was forced to pay strict attention to the medicine that had been prescribed.

By the time the shooting was finished in the highlands, Ernest and Pauline had persuaded Philip Percival to take a break from the dangerous game circuit where he was the expert, and to join them for a few weeks of big-game fishing on the coast. There Charles and Ernest could be teachers instead of students. The entire party looked forward to it. Alfred Vanderbilt came along too.

"It was an absolutely wonderful time," Pauline said later. "Mr. P. was every inch the visiting sportsman, and the boat Ernest chartered was one of the most comical craft afloat. Its engine would die every time we'd approach the fish. It seemed to know, somehow. And it wasn't the Hindu engineer, either."

For once Ernest had been thoroughly misled in contracting for equipment. There had not been much choice. He either had to take the only boat available, or skip the entire idea. And skipping it was a thing he could not do. The advance information he had received had sounded fair enough. And his previous dealings with everyone in the area had turned out well. The boat had been described as a husky, 34-foot cabin cruiser with a cruising speed of eight knots. It turned out that she made a bare four, when she ran, which was always in short spurts. She never ran for half an hour straight in all the time they had her chartered, and her bottom was foul.

But they had fair accommodations ashore. And in the time afloat, Ernest and Charles helped Alfred and Mr. P. catch big sailfish, jacks, snapper, dolphin, and kingfish. The dolphin were the easiest, because they were constantly cutting into the schools of bait just off the coast. When the engine broke down, as it did with such weird regularity, the dolphin would strike anything jigging brightly through the deep blue water just a short distance from them.

Catching the liner *Gripsholm* on its way back to Europe from a tour to India, the Hemingway party had an easy time. When the boat stopped at Haifa, they picked up Lorraine Thompson, who had come to meet them. The ship was fast and cool and had a swimming pool. In Paris again, Ernest developed his films, both still and motion picture, and sent away illustrations to *Esquire* with very specific instructions as to how certain pictures were to be run. He wanted to be sure that no hasty reader would get the impression that he had first photographed game and then killed it.

By this time Ernest was thoroughly enjoying writing the kind of sportsman's letters the new magazine needed. He loved the audience participation in the Letters to the Editor column. Since the magazine was going to change from a quarterly to a monthly publication, Ernest offered to do ten more pieces at the same rate. He suggested that his friends Alfred Vanderbilt and Evan Shipman, who knew a great deal about racing, be asked to produce commentaries on thoroughbred racing and trotting. Writing candidly to Arnold, he said he hoped the new magazine was making money, because he personally was broke and it was a pain to be writing such good stuff and getting chicken feed for it. In these letters he was giving how-to information that had cost him many thousands of dollars to learn. Besides that, he was planning to get the kind of boat he really wanted, a boat that would cost seven thousand dollars. Twice he had been close to having enough, but each time the money had dribbled away. Now he knew how to raise half of that. And with that he left the matter up in the air.

By the time the expedition returned to Key West early in April the good news was there as well. Arnold had sent a check for three thousand dollars as an advance for the next ten letters. With that and what he was able to raise elsewhere, Ernest put through his order with the Wheeler Company in New York to complete and deliver the fishing cruiser about which he had been dreaming for so long. He had discussed specifications with members of the Wheeler organization the year before and knew just what he wanted in the way of modifications. He was promised delivery in six weeks, for several similar hulls were being built as conventional yachts and the changes Ernest wanted could be made at the yard itself. The boat would be shipped by railroad to Miami and there launched for delivery.

Chapter 7

Back in Key West, with the house running smoothly again, mainly through Pauline's management, Ernest immediately got down to serious writing. He was in what he called a "belle epoch." His subconscious, held in check for so long while he savored each moment of suspense and action and the natural beauty of Africa, flowed abundantly again. He wrote steadily, expanding the notes he had made on the trip, to make chapters for *The Green Hills of Africa*. He also had in process the long novel that would be called *To Have and Have Not*. For it, he was studying Key West and its inhabitants much as he had already studied some of the Cuban people, as a friendly but accurate observer.

The new boat occupied his conscious thoughts, once the working day was over. He rechecked measurements according to plans and continued making small changes until the final work was completed. She was to be a standard 38-foot hull, planked with white cedar and framed with steam-bent white oak, with frames closely spaced. In the very bow there was a cockpit, useful for storing anchors and with its forward hatch providing access to, as well as ventilation for, the forward cabin, which was a double stateroom. Aft of that was a head, two bunks, and a dinette that became a double bunk, with galley and icebox just under the forward end of the deck cabin.

At the after end of the cockpit, Ernest had the stern cut down a foot to reduce the distance between the level of the sea and the height to which a fish had to be lifted to slip it aboard. Over the transom he had installed a gigantic wooden roller, more than six feet wide, to assist any big fish entering the cockpit.

The new boat would be driven by two gasoline engines, a 75-horsepower Chrysler with a reduction gear that turned a powerful, slow-speed propeller, and a 40-horsepower Lycoming with a straight drive, for trolling. The big engine alone could take the boat out and back from a day's run. With the Chrysler, there was the speed to chase a school of fish, or save a life in case of need. Fuel tanks holding three hundred gallons were provided, as well as tanks for a hundred gallons of fresh water when cruising. She was to be named the *Pilar* after the Spanish shrine.

Like most new boats, the *Pilar* was late for delivery. By the time she was ready and had reached Miami, I had managed to arrive in Key West in a small boat I had built in Alabama during the previous winter. With Al Dudek of Petoskey, Michigan, who had spent the winter in Florida, I had sailed her across the Gulf of Mexico in a passage of twenty-three days.

The day Al and I reached Key West was a time of triumph.

"By God, I'm glad to see you, Baron," Ernest said, grinning clear to his ears. The trip was to have taken ten days and for more than a week we had been presumed lost at sea. Our mishaps had been comical and the fact that we had survived on a diet of wormy water and half a potato a day won genuine admiration from Ernest. We were a little wobbly from the experience.

"Did you really build her yourself?" Ernest asked.

"Every blasted plank," I glowed. "A Rabl design from *Modern Mechanix*."

"A little beamy," Ernest observed. Then he began checking her over, right down to the individual fastenings. This was a minor preview of the critical study he would be giving his own boat later that same week. "She looks awfully good for anything built by a Hemingway," he said finally.

Al and I planned to stay aboard our boat until Ernest got his down from Miami. "You gents come up to the house as often as you have any needs we can help you with," he told us. "Charles and Lorraine will have you over to dinner and we'll do the same in a few days. I've got to be in Miami to take delivery of the new boat, but when we get her back here, we'll fish every day, I promise you. I'll try and get permission for you to move your boat into the submarine base where it will be safe."

Later that week, Al and I were in the welcoming committee that saluted, whooped, and blew horns as the *Pilar* entered the harbor, resplendent in her new varnish and gleaming black paint. It was the first boat Ernest had had since the *Sunny* on Walloon Lake. And a boat of one's own is as different from a boat under charter as a wife is from a secretary.

Fortunately, I kept a log that year for my own boat, as well as a notebook filled with the sights, sounds, impressions, and conversations that developed day after day as Ernest felt his way along with his new boat. The Key West of the early thirties was unlike that of any other time. The great American Depression had not hit it all at once. It just wafted in and smothered many of the households to the level of bare existence. Finally even the Federal government took note of the plight of the inhabitants and moved in with the FERA, an organization that made jobs and spread money around in amounts that, however small, helped.

In town many people were living on grits and grunts, a classic poor man's diet in the keys. Hominy grits were less than ten cents a pound and grunts, members of the snapper family, were small eating fish you could catch in any channel or from any pier, with a little patience. Grunts earn their name from the sound they make as if in protest against being taken from the water. Commercial fishermen were mainly handliners after grouper, snapper, and yellowtail. But the grouper were being bought by the only fish house for two cents a pound. Shark fishermen had gone broke and mackerel fishermen could fish only the winter months when the mackerel schooled, using nets they could scarcely afford. Bootlegging was considered an honorable activity, but even there you needed a good boat and gear to make a run. So most of the inhabitants of Key West were quietly engaged in the simple business of living. Those with the best survival attitudes became Ernest's lifelong friends.

When the *Pilar* pulled into the dock, a representative of the Wheeler Company was also aboard with Bra Saunders and the new Captain Hemingway. Ernest introduced the man from Wheeler and explained he had come along to check engine performance and operation. He showed Pauline and the Thompsons and Al and me over the boat and explained everything while we marveled. "Ah, citizens, it was a lovely trip," he told us. "Bra's eyes aren't what they used to be, but he could absolutely feel those markers coming up. He knew every light before we could see it, all the way down Hawk Channel. Just wait until tomorrow when we make the first fishing trip in her. You'll see how she handles."

Ernest was soon involved in final checking with the Wheeler representative, who did not want to lose a day before catching the train up the keys to the mainland and New York. Oil changing and refueling were also necessary before making even a day's run out into the Stream.

During this time of activity and before the first drinks of the evening were hoisted in toast to "the new skiff," as Ernest called her, Bra got to talking. "Now you boys know somethin' about boats. . . . This one rides so high, lighter than any craft around here, or the Bahama boats or the Cubans either. She whines like her big engine is burnin' up, but it's not. It's that reduction gear." He poked an index finger in one ear reflectively, and turned it as though adjusting for tone.

The next day we both heard and saw what the *Pilar* could do. Heading out the ship channel with the morning breeze dappling the light blue water to the east, Ernest peered over the chart as he hadn't done for years. With his own boat under him and out on its first try at big fish, the situation for him had suddenly changed from almost a spectator sport, with others doing all the drudgery, to an intense effort, with all hands responsible for the safety and peak performance of the new vessel.

Pauline had come too, and down below there were hampers of sandwiches, fruit, cold drinks, plenty of beer, ice, and even paper towels and napkins with which to keep everything looking new and unused.

It was a hectic day. We trolled the eastern dry rocks, and then down to Sand Key and the western dry rocks, and back again. We caught barracuda, grouper, and an amberjack. But the big billfish were not to be found, and the expected excitement of the big chase and combat did not develop. Ernest was in no way disappointed. He had gained additional confidence in the feel of the boat, and he was very proud of how she handled.

"Ho, you mariners, look at this," he called from up forward. Then he swung the *Pilar* into a hard turn to starboard and then to port. Moving at homecoming speed, about ten knots, we were thrown sharply over, first one way and then another. Everyone nodded in appreciation, glad that no one of us had lost his balance and gone overboard.

Then Ernest opened both engines up and the *Pilar* seemed to plane. She was throwing a great wake, and she was a big boat by any standards, in those days.

"How fast we moving, Stein?" I asked.

"Better than fifteen, kid. Check the exhaust water, will you?"

I went aft, watched the steady flow from both exhausts, and signaled with my hand. He grinned, then eased the throttles down a little. We were still making plenty of knots and at that rate would be in port in half the time we had used to come out.

"Want to take the wheel?" Ernest asked me.

"Sure. What's the course?"

"Just keep her on the old red brick Post Office, until you get close."

All the way in, Ernest was moving over the boat, checking for vibration, feeling temperatures, raising and lowering engine hatches, moving forward and aft along the deck coamings so as to get the feel and sound of the boat running from every point on board. Several times in the following weeks he did the same things when we were out at sea. When one or the other of us would ask what he was looking for, or hoped to find, he would say, "I want to know what she's like all over." He was learning in the very best way, through sensitive personal observation, just what the boat could do and how she reacted to different conditions of sea and wind, in moderate weather. Later, his knowledge proved invaluable in handling the *Pilar* in foul weather. For no boat is so large or powerful that she can force her way anywhere. She must make her way, in the best manner possible, against superior forces when the sea and wind get tough.

Our fishing expeditions became a way of life many people dream of. Pauline came for a while, but then began staying ashore, realizing that Ernest was so involved with being captain of the boat and locating the fish that he was having damned little time to fish himself. That was less than ideal. Previously, it had always been the fishing that had given him the greatest personal satisfaction. Yet Ernest was taking such obvious delight in acting as host and champion fishing guide that his morning work continued to go well in the room over the little house in the back yard. His self-discipline was excellent and, late one morning just after we started out, he explained to me his own private system of rewards.

"Writing is damned hard work, Baron. If I get up early, and really produce, it gives me a feeling of reward to know you gents are down at the dock waiting to go fishing and I will have the rest of the day out on the water with you. If I don't do so well, I know I won't enjoy the rest of the day as much either. The anticipation helps me do the best I can."

After we had cast off, with bait, lunches, beer, ice, and the day's guests on board, Ernest would discuss the possibilities. He wanted to go everywhere he had ever gone in any other boat, and some new places as well. But the day's weather was what usually influenced his decision most.

"The breeze is up early, gentlemen," he'd say. "How about going down to American Shoals and then running before it along the edge of the Stream?"

Whatever the suggestion, we were likely to be unanimous in our agreement. Some days we were able to lure Joe Russell out of the bar he tended regularly. Mr. Josey would put on his genuine fishing pants, oilskins flecked with dried blood which had seen many fights with big fish. Then we'd try for all the sails and marlin that could be raised on the north side of the Stream. Other days Charles

Thompson would come out, leaving the store in the hands of an assistant. Charles had learned more about fishing around the Keys in his early years than many of the local conches would know in a lifetime.

Once, when we were trolling in from the deep toward the reef below Sand Key, Charles was watching when something took one of the lures that was trolling well below the surface. "Dammit," Ernest said, "why didn't somebody take that line in so we wouldn't snag the bottom? Now we've got to bust off and rig another lure."

"Let's put her astern, Ernest," Charles advised. "I think it's a grouper."

"Grouper my eye. We're into the bottom. Didn't you hear that steady run?"

"Just try going dead astern, will you?"

Ernest took the suggestion. As we recovered line, we all made guesses, both ways, before another couple of short rushes helped revise opinions as to what kind of bottom we'd snagged.

"You're right, Bo. Bottom never moves," Ernest admitted.

Finally when the line was straight up and down, we peered over. There, in about six fathoms of water, we could see a great tail waving some three feet out of a hole in the reef. The big grouper had his head and gills jammed into an aperture that held him securely. Despite Charles' most skillful handling of the rod tip, the line finally parted on the coral before the fish could be coaxed out of there. He was some fish, all right.

"How'd you know it was a grouper, Carl?"

"It just sounded different, after the strike." He frowned modestly and we knew we'd had another lesson in how to fish the Great Florida Reef.

One morning Ernest finished his work earlier than usual. Al and I were ready with the necessary supplies. We had long since had an early morning swim at the submarine base and had walked across town for the day-old sweet rolls and coffee on which we lived, aside from the sensational lunches Pauline always saw were provided as ship's provisions.

"No breeze at all," Ernest observed. "You gents like to look over the reef out there?"

We were all for it, as usual. And Ernest was too. He savored the
lure of the unknown. And while the location of the reefs that ran
along the keys only seven or eight miles out was well known,
nobody knew all about them, not even the chart makers. They
didn't, for instance, list all the wrecks, nor even the obvious ones
that were very old.

"There's a wreck out near Cosgrove shoal that nobody seems to
know anything about. It's plenty grown over, and could be a lot
more to it than just some old piles of ballast stones and humps
of sea bottom. It's inside the main reef. Want to see it?"

We were eager.

"You gents are awfully lucky in plenty of ways," he observed.
"You're getting a look at real water before it's all fished out, and you
have the advantages of going out on a daily charter. In even the
conch boats, it would be thirty-five dollars a day." He had pointed
this out frequently, but we didn't mind. It was all true and we
were plenty thankful. In those days there were no charter boats for
exclusive sport fishing in all the keys. Instead, commercial fishermen could be induced, by the juicy fee, to forget their own hopes
of making three to five dollars a day handlining bottom fish. But
few of them had the tackle, chairs, and manners of a marine
headwaiter and chambermaid that were deemed necessary to handle a party of sports from up North. The few that dealt with this
trade did not regard it as a living. They fished elsewhere, and for
real volume, when the fish were in.

As we eased out of the ship channel to cut across the edge of
the kingfish flats above Little Sand Key, and then on the long
southeastward slant to Cosgrove, every feature of the bottom was
visible. We took turns standing in the bow so we could see directly
down in the water through the unruffled surface. It was a revelation. Patches of rocks and weed we had been moving over regularly
were at last clear to us. They were not even on the chart. An occasional turtle, even schools of fish getting ready for spawning season,
were in sight for considerable periods before they made off at the
approach of the boat's sound and shadow.

It was a long, exciting run out to the reef beyond Boca Grande.
We saw things many fishermen have never seen because the sea

out there is so seldom calm. When it is, you may not have the advantage of a height from which to observe, as we did from the bow and atop the *Pilar's* cabin.

Out along the reef, we circled and then began working back over the area, with Ernest directing the boat the way a good dog would cover a field, in wide, searching sweeps. "Dammit, there's nothing harder to locate than a spot underwater you've only seen clearly once before. You gents spot any likely places? Look for straight lines. Those are the outlines of cannon beneath the coral. We saw a dozen out here a few years ago. Out of a dozen, one might be bronze. And bronze guns, even small ones, are worth real dough."

We continued searching.

"Muck it," Ernest finally announced. "I'm going to cut the power. Wherever we drift, throw the hook there. We'll swim around and see what we can see."

It was a neat solution. No man alive could predict what we would come upon, moving as we were. When the engine died, the silence was profound—for a moment.

"Hey, I see something," Al said.

"Where?"

"Over. Over further. That's it." His arm gesture allowed Ernest to swing the wheel. The boat's momentum did the rest.

"Get the hook overside," Ernest commanded. We leaped forward to obey. "This looks like the sea area, all right. See those?" We nodded. Down through the surface shimmers were several oblong shapes, wider at one end than the other. Some were piled like jackstraws, and others lay around singly. It was a sight, as we glided in, fetched up, and swung, to make any skin diver's mouth water. Yet overside, there was very little we could do. We tried making fast a line on one of the gun muzzles. It wouldn't budge, with even the little windlass pulling over, a spoke hole at a time. Nothing else would come loose that we could see. But Ernest spotted a handsome sea fan, one of those lacy, spongelike growths that can only bend against the current and hope to subsist from the passing riches.

"Let's see you get that fan, Baron." He indicated his choice.

I dived from beside him, breast-stroking down to save time.

When I was almost down to the fan, about thirty feet below, a large set of teeth in a narrow head seemed to flow around one dark area in the coral. I gave it one glance, plucked at the sea fan, and began paddling wildly up. I broke water, flung the fan, and made for the boarding ladder at *Pilar's* stern.

"I want a grains pole."

"We left it ashore," Ernest said.

"Then I want to hold the rifle. There was a moray down there looked meaner than Mr. McDaniel." McDaniel had been the principal when both Ernest and I were in high school.

"We'll get him another time, Baron. You did all right."

The trip home is often expected to be the dullest part of the day. But for me, that time was in many ways the most interesting. There was always the whining roar of the engines. Because we were making knots, it was no time to neglect the safety of the vessel. Ernest always managed to stay within easy reach of the control panel. He usually stuck with whoever had been given the job of helmsman to note how well he performed and to advise or order a change of course if for any reason that seemed like a good idea. Ernest and I had some wonderful long talks during these return trips. That particular afternoon we got to talking about high school days and the writing we had both done for the *Trapeze*.

"What was really the first story you ever sold for dough?" I asked.

"That's a funny one." He grinned. "You know, nobody ever asked me that before. It isn't listed, because it happened before I'd put out a book. When I was working up in Toronto, another gent and I were sticking around late one night and we got talking. We made a bet on whether either of us could write a story in one hour that a current magazine would buy. Then we sat down and wrote our pieces. Both stories sold . . . but that was a market I wanted to skip."

After a moment, he gave me a gentle punch on the shoulder. "Of course that story didn't win any awards." He laughed, referring to an award I'd won in a national short story contest while I was in high school. "Are you serious about wanting to be a writer, Baron?"

"Well, yes, I am," I said and felt suddenly self-conscious, because Ernest was studying me so intently.

"You've got a hell of a load ahead," he said finally. "Everything you do they'll say you're riding on my reputation. You know that, don't you?"

I nodded. "It came up, even in that contest thing. But the entries were all numbered. There weren't any names involved."

"I know, I know. It'll be even tougher, but you can't care too much what people say. You're a good observer. In this fishing, you've learned easily, but you've got a hell of a lot of learning to do—especially if you're going to skip college. You'll need to read a lot. You've read *Huck Finn*, haven't you? And Kipling and the long ones of Stephen Crane? You should study Tolstoy and Dostoevski now, Joyce and the short stories of Henry James, de Maupassant, and Flaubert—especially *Madame Bovary*. When you've finished those try Stendhal, and Thomas Mann's *Buddenbrooks*. . . . We've got a lot of these up at the house. Borrow anything you like—but bring them back. I'm not giving my books away, even to a kid brother, understand?"

I understood.

"You ought to try for a newspaper job. That's the best way to learn to write fluently. But this is a rough year for getting a job on any paper. For the time being you might as well keep on sailing. You're learning a lot, but this stuff comes easily because I think you've got real love for it."

"Anything that makes me tremble inside is for me."

"Outside too, Baron. Remember that first big fish? Try to remember everything about everything. When something gives you the emotional shakes, try to figure out exactly what it was that shook you and remember every detail of it so you can tell what it was. If anybody else is around, find out if they were shaken too and how much and why. The more sides you can see to anything, the more you know. Right now you're too worried about what other people think of you—because you're young, maybe. With luck you'll learn other people are mainly interested in the impression they are making. Anyway, forget about yourself and try to get inside other people more and to see things from their point of view.

"If you really want to write, Bo, then go ahead and write. The more you write, the more you learn about writing. It's the only way to learn that there is. I'm not going to help you if I can avoid it. I've helped a lot of guys, and will again. But mainly it weakens them.

"Now, advice is different. Advice doesn't do anybody's work for him. With good advice you can save some time and effort. The hell of it is, you need judgment to know which is good advice. By the time you've got that, you can give your own advice."

The next week, Archibald MacLeish came down. "Let's have plenty of politeness on board, gents," Ernest said when he briefed us. "Archie is a Pulitzer Prize-winning poet and a *Fortune* editor as well."

We fished midday and during the afternoon regularly and in the evening when weather conditions were good. We took a number of sailfish. Al got a big one of over eighty pounds, after a rugged fight. When the fish was led alongside, we saw it had a bill so short only a single handhold was needed for lifting the fish aboard. Ernest looked it over carefully, checking to see if it might be a variation of species. "That's not it," he finally announced. "One side of the tip is more rounded than the other. It must have broken off years ago. No wonder he was a fighter. He was used to getting out to smack a new breakfast every day with a sore nose."

The next day the weather turned soft again. When Ernest had his morning's work completed, he and Archie drove down to the dock anyway. The food hamper was bulging. Everything else was on board and we were ready to cast off. "Can't say what it'll be like out there. Looks like squalls making up. The glass is low, so the best thing we can do is go out and see." Ernest tapped the barometer repeatedly, and the needle made a slight correction.

Out in the ship channel, a long, low, oily swell moved in from the east. The air was muggy as we moved out, the clouds to the south seeming to change around and become more dense. But in the area where we were, the sun beat down as it often does on a windless day close to the Tropic of Cancer.

Inside, the water was still roiled from yesterday's breeze, with poor visibility. But on the outer side of the great reef we sighted the first fish of the day—a big hammerhead shark. When I say big, I mean fifteen to sixteen feet. We passed the baits in front of his nose and we circled, thinking that he might have been daydreaming during the first pass. It was no good and only when we headed right for him did he sink out of sight.

"Not what you'd expect," Ernest noted, "but then this is not a usual day."

Later we saw a big fish of some kind cutting in through the baits close to the reef, where the dark patches became a mean yellow-brown near the surface. This fish also refused to strike, though our baits were easy to follow and larger and more enticing than the sprats that rose and flashed away at almost every surge of the sea around the coral.

Another big shark, larger than the first, was sighted swimming slowly on the surface to the south. We went out, and ritually passed him the baits. Ernest was clearly annoyed at the way any predator of the sea could ignore the fare we offered.

"Go below and bring me the Woodsman," he said.

I quickly handed him the Colt .22 autoloading pistol with which he was a fine shot. He strapped on the belt, loaded a magazine, and, slipping it in, pulled back the receiver and let it snap a fresh round into the chamber.

"Come around again, Al. We'll come up with him and run parallel while I find out if he's immune to lead poisoning."

While the shark was still ahead of us and we could see it clearly, Ernest commenced firing. He was right on it, just a hair over, and into the great body went every pistol shot. There was no counting aloud, but he must have hit the big shark seven or eight times, above and down along the spine, before the wide-ranging tail quickened and the dorsal fin entered the sea again. There was no sign of blood. That great hammerhead, seeming four feet across, just wigwagged on down and the rest of the heavy, long body followed.

Moving outside the reef, we trolled for miles without result. A squall finally made up further out and we watched it move off without ever bringing us either rain or shade.

"What about a swim?" Archie had the public pulse.

"Hmm. All right. I'll cut the engine. But wait until we stop drifting, and we can take turns on watch with the rifle, in case any sharks want to join the fun."

Within a minute we had the boarding ladder rigged. Ernest was first off the stern. Al and I took turns on watch, the other diving in. It was such a warm day, the water felt like a cool gift as it closed over our bodies. Once in, the thing was to relax, yet head back to the boarding ladder so we could climb up and out at the first sign of trouble. Because trouble, should it come, would arrive suddenly. Archie was an excellent diver. But he didn't waste any time getting back on board.

"What are the chances of a fish . . ."

"Nobody knows," Ernest said. "That's what makes it interesting. A mako, or any other shark that is traveling, seldom moves on the surface. Those fish we saw earlier were stuffed. One with an appetite stays down where he can watch large areas of surface at a time. When he sees something that looks interesting, like splashing around a boat, he comes up fast right out of the deep. Like those we've watched trying to take our sailfish when we've got them half whipped. First there's a little dot, down in the deep blue. Then wham! He's life-size. And if he didn't get you on the first charge, he's coming around again to try for you on the surface. That's where the rifle comes in. The noise, the bullet splat, maybe the shock of contact will surprise him. But nobody can predict how good a judge of distance he is, how active you are, or how long it's been since the shark had his last good meal. That's why I insisted on the rifle. There'd be hell to pay if I brought home no fish, and no crew and no guests either."

After this little illumination we continued diving but even more warily. Soon Ernest announced, "Last dive for everyone. We're cooled off enough to troll down the River Styx now."

The squalls that made up still stayed farther out in the Stream. It was so muggy that sweat trickled off every one of us as we braced ourselves to the roll of the long swells, watched the baits, and waited.

Finally a tern came winging in from the west, spotted our baits, and dived for one. He had a royal time, trying for each one of them, and going "creee, creeee" as he hovered above first one and then the other, between attacks.

"Bloody sea bird trying to bollix our baits." Ernest's temper was feeling the heat.

"He can't hurt them, can he?"

"Not if I line him up right. Bring me the pistol, Baron."

This was sheer exhibition shooting. Ernest let each one of us have a try. The tern was flighty and an incredibly difficult target in motion, with the pistol. Then he took his turn. On the third shot, the bird folded and hit the water with a plop. It floated there as we moved away, so unexpected was the successful shot.

"Somebody get the bird. We need something to bring home from a day like this . . ."

I wasn't holding anything or in charge of anything. So I dived overboard, well clear of the baits. In four or five strokes, I had the bird's body in one hand and began treading water. The *Pilar* was cutting a wide circle and Ernest was shouting something. Then the boat swung around more and I realized they were turning to pick me up, but the hull was turning so slowly they would cut outside the circumference of the circle that would have reached me. As they came around the rest of the way, they realized this.

I started swimming over, the bird in one hand. Its body was warm, but very small comfort as it continued dribbling blood there in the Stream.

"Stay there. There!" They pointed, shouted, and the rifle was much in evidence. "We'll get you the next time." The big black hull got rapidly smaller as they went into the turn again, having waited until they were sure she'd come fully around to alongside me.

Finally they were beside me, the boarding ladder out. I was helped into the cockpit and I handed the bird to the captain. He tossed it to one side. "Thought for a minute we might have tried too hard for that bird." He bashed me on the back and handed me a beer. "When I make a suggestion, you don't always have to take it as an order. Understand?"

I understood. It had been more of an order than a suggestion but he had seen the danger too late.

A couple of days later, when Archie had to go back up North, I found he'd left his swim cap on the boat. "A good sign," Ernest said. "Shows he wants to come back."

"He seemed to have a good time," I said.

"Listen, Archie is one of the most intelligent people I've ever known. He was a champion swimmer on the Princeton team. What Archie has is a wonderful imagination. He just sometimes has difficulty turning it off. He's a hell of a clear thinker. That's what Archie is."

One of the most exciting events that season was the afternoon of May 23, when Ernest boated the biggest Atlantic sailfish ever taken on rod and reel. The fish was not an official record because a guest had hooked it and fought it for the first fourteen minutes. But it was a wonderful fight.

A sporting priest who was interested in Ernest's writing ability had come down to visit. He had a great fund of stories and Ernest and Pauline were delighted with him. He was immediately invited out for the morrow's fishing.

The day was one of those lazy openers, with a long, slow swell working and no wind. It was 2:30 P.M. when Ernest came down, after a long morning's work and a light lunch at the house. He explained that we were going out so as to give the priest whatever sport was possible.

"This is my kid brother, the Baron, Father McGrath," he said. "He gaffs pretty well for his age." I beamed and shook hands.

We worked to the east and picked up 'cuda and grouper over the reef, but the Stream remained quiet until a few cat's-paws began darkening the water between the long, smooth swells. By 3:30 we had been through the additional sandwiches and half a case of beer, with new bottles icing all the time. Ernest liked to be well-equipped for hot days and could become lyrical on occasion.

"Sun and sea air, as they dry your body, make for almost effortless beer consumption. The body needs liquid of a nourishing kind. The palate craves coolness. The optic nerve delights in the sensation of chill that comes from its nearness to the palate as you swallow. Then the skin suddenly blossoms with thousands of happy beads of perspiration as you quaff."

The priest agreed. Talk continued on other edifying subjects. As we worked to the westward, the breeze finally came in. It was like turning a switch. Fish began leaping in the distance, birds were working over bait that surfaced, and suddenly the priest got a fine strike. Ernest was the only one who had seen the billfish come in.

"Aiiiii!" Father McGrath couldn't stay calm any more than we could, as the sailfish leaped clear in a long arc, and then went porpoising out another hundred and fifty yards.

"Pump him back, Father." Ernest said. "I counted. He took seven jumps. You saw him."

"Better than that. I felt him," the good Father managed to say between efforts with the rod.

"Reel as fast as you can, Father. We're going over toward him and you need to recover line so if he does that . . ."

The fish jumped again and made a couple of bobbles, skittering as he landed. But he was moving to our right. There was considerable belly in the line.

"Give the reel everything you've got," Ernest was insistent. "His air sac is distended with this jumping. I doubt he can sound, but he's likely to be taken on the surface like . . ."

Again the fish jumped. Now he was coming toward us. One, two, three jumps clear, then he was in again.

"That was four more," Ernest said. "I don't like it. Something scared him. Keep reeling . . ." He stopped speaking. The line had gone slack. There was a swirl in the water near his last sighting. Father McGrath continued reeling and the line came much more easily. Finally the double line and the leader showed. It had been cut clean off.

"Shark took him, Father. But it was a grand fight. You almost had him in our laps, the way you turned him there."

Father McGrath was breathing hard, perspiring well, and flexing his left hand repeatedly, seeming not to realize it. We got him an extra-cold beer and everybody patted him on the back after he'd taken the first couple of swallows.

"I wish I'd regained that line faster. How big was he?"

"Certainly over sixty, probably seventy-five pounds. You were great. What's with your hand . . . the left?" Ernest was the soul of consideration.

"Arthritis."

"Holy . . . Excuse me, Father. Look, tell us the next time, will you? Now let's get the other bait out. When you get the next strike, remember—let it spool out while you count to ten, slowly, before you sock it to him. How's the beer?"

In less than a minute, another bait was tapped by a large brown shape. We all saw this one.

"Maybe a marlin," Ernest said. "Slack it to him. Count slowly and then after you reach ten, set your drag and sock it to him."

The Father was excited but he knew the value of doing what he was told and followed instructions well. When he finally threw down the drag, Ernest was right there coaching. "Sock him once more, Father. Keep the tip high as he jumps."

Far off—it seemed three hundred yards but may have been half that distance—a really big sailfish bolted out of the water and then went flip-flip-flipping along sideways on the momentum of his falling body.

"What a fish! What a beauty! Fight him, Father." Ernest was in there chanting advice every second. The priest was perspiring with the abandon of a sinner approaching the suburbs of Hell. Part of it was the excitement in Ernest's voice. Part was the feeling of being fairly hooked to a fish much longer than himself and in considerably better shape to conduct a test of strength and stamina.

Then the sailfish jumped again. In all he jumped twenty-eight times, with some success if you counted his ability to throw off the remoras hanging on his underside. But he had no chance to fling the sharp hook out of his mouth.

"With all that jumping, he's filled his air bladder," Ernest said. "Now you'll have another good fight right on top. He can't sound on you."

We watched a rapidly tiring member of the clergy. The strain, the pouring perspiration, and the bad hand were too much for a man unused to violent exertion.

"Ernest, you must help me. I can't handle this fish any longer."

"Look—he's yours. He's a sailfish, not a marlin as I first thought. He may be record size. If I take over, the fish will be disqualified for any kind of record."

"But I can't go on," Father McGrath said. He made sideways motions with the rod and tried to get out of the chair.

Al and I felt for both of them right then. The priest was simply incapable of continuing what must have been the most thrilling sports event of his lifetime. Ernest had been frustrated beyond belief because he was not holding the rod at the moment of such a magnificent strike. Now he was about to take over. But he knew the values had changed.

"All right," he said grimly. "We have to get this fish in, if only to get our tackle back."

Once he had taken over he was again caught up in the excitement.

"What a lovely!" He began to pump and work the fish around.

Al and I had been staying out of the way. Now the priest needed help. We had to steer, get ready for new maneuvers, and keep a lookout for the fish and the line and any sharks that might appear on either side of the boat at the same time. Al and I spelled each other, one taking the controls while the other was lookout on the cabin top, then switching places again. Ernest was determined to take that fish if it were humanly possible. Father McGrath alternately rested on the shaded seats over the gas tanks and then bounded out to Ernest's side whenever the fish changed direction.

Ernest pumped the fish fiercely. He worked the big sail in close twice. "We're getting somewhere. Look at him come," he called out, reeling as fast as he could to recover the now slack line.

It was true. The fish was swimming toward the boat of his own accord. It seemed great luck until the thing every big-game fisherman dreads suddenly happened. Ernest recovered the last of the bellying line as the fish paused about twenty feet from our starboard side. Then it suddenly darted under the hull.

"He's changing sides!" I yelled.

Ernest acknowledged the fact with an unprintable but descriptive comment as he saw the line go under. Then he loosened the drag so more line could play out. "Now where is he?"

"The other side—about the same position." None of us knew then what sweat this was going to cause.

"Here, Al!" Ernest called. "Hang onto me. I'm going to pass the line under the boat and try to keep the propeller from cutting us off. Tell me if the fish moves. Put her in neutral, Baron."

Neutral on the *Pilar's* main engine was a theoretical point, because the wheel was always turning, either slow or fast, if the engine was running. The clutch had not had time to wear in. It wasn't important, except at a time like this.

Ernest bent down low over the stern. Holding the rod in one hand he made a long, curving sweep underwater and brought the tip up on the port side. Then he began recovering slack. The line was still whole. It had passed safely below the propeller. The big sailfish was still on, though very nervous. When he felt the pressure of the hook again, he spurted off on another long run.

"What absolute luck," Ernest said, wiping the sweat from his forehead. Then he was pumping again, steadily pumping, to get the fish headed around on a converging course with us. As he approached the fish, Ernest was warier while gentling him in. This time the fish's dark sail lay folded down in the dorsal slot. The living stripes along his sides flashed in the weaving distortion of the rising-falling surface water. He seemed to roll his big eye and hang there, just a little way beyond reach of the gaff.

"Put her in neutral again," Ernest called. Then he turned. "Use the gloved hand, Al, and ease him a little closer. Be ready to let go if he lunges . . ."

He was interrupted by a heavy splosh. The big sailfish bolted under the hull again. Luckily, Ernest had taken the drag off the reel or the line would have popped right then. As it was, the line was tight and forward of the propeller.

"Going to try it again," Ernest said. He got down on the afterdeck, pushed the rod tip straight down so the reel was in the water, and made the slow arc that brought the rod up on the port side. There the fish was pacing us in our forward motion. As Ernest took up slack even more gently, the fish made another sprint. But he was still hooked. The line had again cleared the hazards of passing under the hull. We all breathed deeply.

"Nice maneuvering," the Father said, beaming in admiration.

"He's not in yet," Ernest cautioned. For another twenty minutes there was more sweat, though he was working him in in the gentlest way. We were all wondering to what extent the line might have been nicked in passing under that last time.

Finally another chance came to get the fish and boat close together. The fish was winded, but still in fine condition. He seemed curious about the big, green underbody with the whining, churning spinner that had attached itself to him when he had mouthed a passing mullet.

This time when Al eased in on the leader, the fish came just enough closer. Snaking out with his gaffing arm, he fought for control of the writhing, shuddering body and brought the big head in against the planking. We all eagerly grabbed along his bill and skinned our palms as we hoisted. In the cockpit, with the gaff removed, the big fish spattered himself furiously about until he was banged squarely on the forehead with the wooden persuader.

I was still studying the big fish in wordless wonder when Ernest's eager voice said, "Maybe we'll get another." He had already put on a new bait so as to have a fine trolling from each side as we hooked up to move toward Sand Key and Key West.

The sailfish was the biggest Ernest had ever seen, and he had far more experience than the rest of us. It measured over nine feet. Nine feet, one and three-quarter inches, as I remember. We didn't have any scales on board to weigh it so we all became authorities. Each one of us believed it would tip the scales at over a hundred pounds.

"How long was I with the fish?" the priest wanted to know.

"We didn't time you exactly, Father," Ernest said, "but I think about fourteen minutes. The whole landing of it was something just under an hour."

It was dark when we finally reached the submarine base. Charles Thompson met us and we loaded the big sailfish onto the rear bumper of Charles' green roadster. It actually stuck out on both sides enough to make us concerned about damaging it as we went through the Navy Yard gate. I promised I would stick with the fish until it was safely in the freezing room at the icehouse. The others headed for the big house on Whitehead Street to celebrate. The celebration was well under way before I arrived. When I told them the weight, they turned joyous.

"A hundred and nineteen pounds! Way over the record, Father! You should have stuck with him the whole way."

"If I had, we'd have lost him sure. I couldn't have lasted another minute, much less have done that rod work under the boat."

"Sure you could have." Ernest could afford to be modest. He had done some phenomenal maneuvering that day. "The fish might have behaved better if he'd seen it was you who hooked him, Father. After dinner let's go down and weigh him again—with witnesses, and we'll check the scales. Then we can send him to Al Pfleuger in the morning."

Later that night, in front of eight witnesses and with tested scales, four hours after the fish had been caught, he was officially weighed in at 119½ pounds. His girth was thirty-five inches. Now, more than a quarter of a century later, this sailfish is still the largest ever taken in the Atlantic Ocean on rod and reel. The mounted body is on display in the headquarters of the Miami Rod and Reel Club.

The priest had to go back to Miami that night. In the morning there was a great commotion around the house. Ernest came down from his workroom to see what was the cause of the uproar. Pauline and the rest of us had just seen the *Miami Herald*. There on page one, in the center, was a story on the taking of the new Atlantic record sailfish. It had been written by Eye Witness.

"Now who . . ." Ernest mused, read on, and his eyes began to narrow. "Of all the . . . I wanted *him* to take the credit for the catch."

But Ernest had certainly earned it, and the priest had had the last word.

As the season progressed, the fishing improved. Ernest had never before had first-rate equipment and this was the first time he had stayed on the American side of the Gulf Stream during the summer. Al went back to Michigan. Various guests, such as George Leahy of Chicago and John Charles Thomas, the opera singer, came down and had some fine fishing during their stays.

Ernest's morning work continued to please him. He was reluctant to change any part of the formula of his daily life, believing strongly that any change might mean an end to the luck of this "good era" of free-flowing prose.

By the middle of June, he was up to page 147 of the new book, *The Green Hills of Africa*. He had already done three rewrites, he said. The weather was fine, with weeks of steady easterly breezes in between calm spells. It was so cool in the evenings we had to wear sweaters. Though Ernest was feeling wonderful about his writing, he was beginning to feel a certain disenchantment with the fishing. He longed to go back to Africa, though he still suffered from the amoebic dysentery he had picked up there.

"It's a lousy nuisance," he'd say and reach for the bottle of castor oil. The treatment called for numerous small doses of that palate-flattening remedy, during a three-day period following an attack. So he kept a bottle aboard the boat as well as one at home. He'd chase it with either Scotch or brandy but claimed brandy was better. "It slows you down when you've got the trots," he said.

John Dos Passos came for a visit in the spring, and Sidney Franklin came down in mid-July. In between there were times when we went tarpon fishing in the evening with Jim Sullivan, Ernest's solid friend from the early days, who owned a machine shop in Key West, and with Canby and Esther Chambers, two amusing and sensitive Key West friends. Canby was a good magazine writer who had been hit severely by polio. Esther had been with the Red Cross in Europe and now devoted her life to her big Quaker, who made such good jokes though living in and out of a wheel chair. Canby got around very well. "Wheelbarrow me," he'd say and the man nearest would pick up his legs while Canby walked on his hands. In this way he was even able to board the *Pilar* and lower himself into one of the trolling seats.

You could never predict what would happen in a day of fishing the Stream, the reefs, and sometimes the back channels, with

Ernest as captain and fishing guide. He did some beautiful boat maneuvering the Sunday we took Lieutenant Jackson out. Jackson was commandant of the submarine base, as the Navy Yard was known then. He was a fine sportsman. Out in the Stream he got a magnificent strike and lost pounds in minutes fighting the dolphin that had taken the bait. It was a bull dolphin with a forehead that bulged like a cartoon of a Washington bureaucrat, and it weighed more than forty pounds we found when we got back to shore hours later. From the first, the lieutenant knew he had a fish that could pull like a man, and maybe more so. In twenty minutes of fighting, he was panting, aching, and close to slumping out of the chair.

Ever sympathetic toward a game performance, Ernest took a hand. "The boat's going to help you, lieutenant. I'll get ahead of the fish so he'll come right in toward you."

"Ernest, you've got to take the rod. He's going to . . ."

"Nonsense. Just give him the one-two, again and again."

"But I'm absolutely finished, I tell you."

"No you're not. You're going to land him if you just last the next couple of minutes. Look, he's easing our way now."

Ernest had worked the fish with the boat, kidding the lieutenant along in a masterful way to make him feel it was all over, though there was still some time to go. In the next few minutes, we did run so deftly to one side and throttle down so well that I gaffed the big dolphin with more luck than skill on the first try. He was almost six feet long, and had bred recently and thinned to ideal fighting shape.

That day we took a total of eight dolphin, all over twenty-five pounds, along with nine bonita, and some barracuda and cero mackerel. Seven sailfish strikes we missed, but the guests were unused to the slack-line technique.

On the way home, Ernest was garrulous with Scotch, and I sensed that a peculiar kind of boredom was beginning to set in. Something was really eating him and he had to get it off his chest. He loved everything up to a certain point, and then nothing was any good any more. The old longing for Africa would set in and he would begin to realize how little he cared for what had been so important a few hours earlier. Because I took many notes in those days, I'm able to draw on them now.

"Listen, Baron," he began. "We've been learning plenty out here in just the last few months about sailfish. We get them much easier when we're trolling to the westward. That's because they're headed that way. And around these spots"— he indicated three areas on the chart—"we always get strikes. It's a matter of bottom, more than current, once you are out in the Stream. You can't fish the ocean blindly, any more than you would a mountain brook. I think they're headed to the westward to go through the Gulf between Rebecca light and Tortugas, the same way the tankers go to Tampico. We've caught more this summer than the guides did at that famous Florida fishing camp all last winter. It's a better feeding time, and we've begun to shape up as the crew of a real fishing machine." He patted the side of the *Pilar*'s cockpit.

"She sure is," I agreed. "I just hope you don't get discouraged with the crew, or think of something else you'd rather be doing."

"I won't get discouraged with you, Baron, because you're eager and you really give a damn. But a lot of this is just stuff in a bucket compared to Africa. Out there I found what I was after."

"With dysentery," I said.

"Hell with the dysentery. I've got only this one life to live and by Christ I want to go where it interests me. I don't feel any romance for the American scene. It doesn't move me. It's that I just want to make enough dough now so I can go back to Africa. I've worked hard and written some good stories and will again— though last week there was a time when nothing was going well. I can talk about it now it's over. Now I'm going good again and it looks like I'll be a writer yet."

"Maybe you should have had Gertrude Stein aboard to show you how to fix things," I kidded him.

"Oh hell yes," he laughed. "That would have fixed things sure."

He paused for a few moments, then continued, "But I really did learn from that woman. And I learned from Joyce and Ezra at the same time. Gertrude was a fine woman until she went so completely queer. She was damned smart until then. But then she began figuring that anybody who was any good was also queer.

From there she got worse and convinced herself that anybody who was queer must also be good. But before she went way off, I learned a lot from her."

Ernest took a long swallow. "Anderson was another one I learned from, but only for a short time. I learned from D. H. Lawrence how to describe country."

Ernest fell silent for a minute, just listening to the roar of the engines and staring out across the water. Then he said, "But Jeeezus, that book Stein put out last year was full of malicious crap. I was always damned loyal to her until I got kicked out on my backside. Do you think she really believes she taught me how to write those chapter headings for *In Our Time*? Does she think she or Anderson taught me how to write the first and last chapters of *A Farewell to Arms*? Or *Hills Like White Elephants*, or the fiesta part of *The Sun Also Rises*? Oh hell. I talked the book over with her all right. But that was a year after it was written. I didn't even see her between July twenty-first when I started it, and September sixth when it was finished.

"But what really burnt me was when she made out that I was fragile. Dammit, the only bones I ever broke in my life were when I was wounded, and when I fractured my arm that time the Ford turned over out West. These are the scars where they had to cut off the chewed-up meat. The surgeon had to notch the ends of the bones before he could splice them together. Old Gertrude can spot the fragile types, all right."

There was another short silence. Then he added, "And for good measure she called me yellow. But you know . . . I'm still glad I was loyal and kind, even after she stopped being a friend. You could say that last year was not my happiest, what with Stein and Max Eastman in the *New Republic*. But I wrote well anyway. I don't know. Maybe all that's part of why Africa feels so damned attractive right now." Ernest rattled the ice cubes in his empty glass. "Get me another drink, would you, Baron?"

Chapter 8

One morning later that summer, Ernest came down to the boat late. He was with a large, serious young man who looked around warily.

"No fishing today, Baron," Ernest told me. "By the time we'd reach the Stream, the breeze would have a big sea running." He did not seem unhappy about it. He was grinning. "Want you to meet a new shipmate, Arnold Samuelson—this is my kid brother.

"Arnold will be bunking aboard," Ernest continued. "He's come down to learn how to write. Now for Christ's sake keep the boat clean, or I'll throw you both the hell off her."

Arnold had hitchhiked down to ask Ernest to tell him the tricks of the trade. I learned that he had put in some years at a state university in the Middle West, had worked as a harvest hand and on a newspaper, before hitchhiking down to Key West. He figured he had the experience to write well, and if anyone could give him the low-down it was Ernest. In all of Ernest's years of writing, he had never before had a stranger come up to him and say in so many words, "You know how, so how about showing me?"

Arnold was so sincere that Ernest couldn't resist letting him stay. Pauline became fond of him because he was so good-natured. So he became Ernest's only acknowledged pupil. Because of his violin playing, Arnold was promptly nicknamed the "Maestro."

Arnold received a certain sort of fame as the inspiration for Ernest's comic yet valuable piece of advice to young writers published the next year in *Esquire* as "Monologue with the Maestro." The Maestro had never been on a boat before, but in his six months aboard the *Pilar* he learned enough about writing to sell articles about fishing with Ernest.

The first week of Arnold's stay, Ernest wanted to see his reactions and find out what value he might have as a deckhand. So we continued to go fishing. But after the first two days, Arnold had some definite areas of sunburn such as we had had months earlier.

"Come on up to the house, gents," Ernest said the next day. "We'll take a little rest from the sun and do some boxing. Nothing better to keep you in shape for fishing."

Charles Thompson was already there when we arrived. We went to the shady side of the house, and changed sparring partners regularly so that everyone had a turn with everyone else. Arnold had been very strong, but his reflexes weren't quick enough to dodge a number of blows that he saw coming. Charles was fast, as Al was, and Ernest was fast and strong and tricky.

"Come on, come on. Put some drive into them." As he took on each of us Ernest would be full of admonitions, cautions, and swift demonstrations of what he meant. "Come on, hit me. Let's see if you can."

I straightened one out, got through, and was immediately clouted by a right that made everything blur.

"That's to teach you not to punch so hard. And don't smile. You don't have to be a good sport when you box. You only have to be a good opponent. Keep that left up."

Charles was as fast as Ernest, but much more moderate in the blows he landed. We got in several afternoons of good boxing while Arnold gradually got used to the sun.

The gloves were always slippery with sweat, and the last man into his gloves had trouble with the laces. Everyone else was all thumbs, with gloves already on. Then when we were all repeatedly winded, Ernest would let us use the upstairs shower. It may have messed up the household routine, but it was refreshing.

The summer sun beating down in the keys can be fierce, and the *Pilar*'s crew was told to cover up for the day when heading for the Stream. You could wear anything you wanted, as long as your arms and legs were covered. And Ernest would see to it that your face was properly coated with zinc oxide ointment in the first few minutes afloat.

"Over here, like this," Ernest would say and he'd draw a finger of the white ointment down the ridge of his nose, and around the mouth. On anyone with a tan, it was a ready-made witch doctor's dream. The sight of Ernest, bounding about the black *Pilar*'s deck in this make-up, is reliably reported to have given several strangers the shakes. But though these precautions were taken daily, Ernest continued to burn the sensitive ridge of his nose. He had more sizzlability than anyone else. This may have been partly because he could and did order all the rest of us back into the shade from time to time. But he wouldn't take to the shade himself. Nor would he give up fishing long enough for the skin on his nose to reheal properly.

By Bastille Day anniversary, the fourteenth of July, Ernest had more than 200 pages done on the new book and looked forward with tremendous eagerness to getting over to Cuba again. Carlos Gutierrez, who had gaffed for him during the last three years of Cuban fishing, was sending daily bulletins to Key West, via the car ferry that ran from Havana, on the state of the Stream and the marlin catches being made by commercial fishermen.

Arnold, the "Maestro," had made several trips out to the Stream and had proved that he had stamina though he had yet to find his sea legs. Balance is a thing no man starts life with, and balance on the deck of a small boat is an acquired ability that comes only with practice. The tension of the Maestro's arms and legs as he braced himself against the irregular movements of the sea was enough to make any observer's heart go out to him. He was always fearful of another pratfall, or a verbal boner. Yet he was so well-meaning that everyone around liked him and felt a gentle sympathy. He wanted very much to see Cuba, so he went along as sole crew man when Ernest finally headed for Havana on July 18. The mate of the car ferry went as navigator. The seemingly easy trip turned out to have hazards. Twice they overheated each engine through catching Gulf weed in the water cooling intakes. But they finally made it into Havana after nightfall.

A couple of weeks after Ernest left we had an odd visitor at the house in Key West. He was a blond, mature-looking man dressed in a white suit and wearing a bright red sash around his trousers. Lillian Lopez-Mendez, the lovely French wife of the Colombian painter, answered the door when he arrived.

"I'm Richard Halliburton, the adventurer," he said, "and I'd like Mr. Hemingway to tell me about that sunken ship in the quicksands he wrote about. I'm writing for a newspaper syndicate myself now."

Lillian didn't know English well so she called me. I said Ernest was in Havana. Pauline came then and, after introducing herself, explained that Ernest was not expected to return for several weeks but that he could be reached after fishing hours at the Ambos Mundos Hotel on Obispo Street.

"I just wanted to talk with him—get a little local color," Mr. Halliburton said and left. In the next few days he was seen at several places around Key West, always asking questions. On the following Wednesday, when the P & O boat sailed to Havana, Pauline and I were down to see Lillian off. Richard Halliburton was there also, but without the sash. He, too, was sailing to Havana.

We heard later that the famed adventurer had gone immediately to Ernest's hotel. Breathing hard he announced himself over the telephone and added, "I just came over on the boat from Key West with your sister."

"The hell you say," Ernest countered. "My four sisters are all over a thousand miles from here." So Halliburton described Lillian and Pauline, me and Bumby and Patrick and Gigi. Papa was far from happy to hear what a thorough research job had been done on him. He knew Halliburton's background as a writer of "Glorious Adventure" travel books and held some definite opinions about him. So when Halliburton asked to come up for "a private chat before dinner," Ernest bristled.

"I'll be down after a shower—say fifteen minutes. And I'll hear what you have to say at the bar."

After Ernest had cooled off, in more ways than one, he walked down to the lobby. He took the manager, Manolo Asper, aside and pointed out the man gesturing at the bar. "Rent him a room if you must, but not on my floor." Manolo nodded.

Then Ernest went into the bar, clasped his large hand on Halliburton's shoulder, and made a swift announcement to the assembled crowd of friends, fellow fishermen, and lottery-ticket vendors. "Gentlemen," he said in Spanish, "I want you all to meet 'Richard Hollybottom,' the famous American adventurer and —— [he used a particular Spanish word here]. From here on, it's every man for himself!" In the uproar that followed, Ernest managed to duck out. He never heard from Mr. Halliburton again.

A month later, I was sailing along the Cuban coast when the *Pilar* hove into view. Ernest had sighted us from miles away. It was late in the afternoon and after days of slatting around in the Stream while squalls alternately blew and then moved on, leaving us calm but dripping, we were glad to be getting somewhere.

"Stand by for some cold beer," Ernest called. We caught four bottles tossed from boat to boat as we ran along. Then we toasted our arrival in Cuban waters with the good Cristal and shouted news back and forth. The *Pilar* had a marlin aboard, but Ernest had hauled in the lures when he sighted us. I introduced my sailing companion, Jake Klimo.

"Better take a line, Baron," Ernest finally called. "We'll tow you into the harbor or you'll get becalmed under the Morro and spend hours getting in. The wind is fluky in the harbor entrance. We'll show you where to anchor. . . . Hoist your quarantine flag. You can officially enter tomorrow."

We took the line aboard and were soon making knots with a chance to furl sails before ending the day's run. We were later told ours was the smallest boat of foreign registry to enter a Cuban port up to that time.

The next night we had a party aboard the *Pilar*. Jane Mason was there, and I was as promptly overwhelmed by her charms as so many young men before me. I got awfully loaded finishing up her drinks and rushing to fix fresh ones for her so that she would notice me. Unfortunately I was not so touched by the spirits that I missed the amusement with which she and Ernest regarded these efforts. The next morning Ernest was tough but kindly. "You're captain of your own boat in foreign ports now, Baron. You'll have to learn to handle your hangovers or they'll Mickey Finn you and steal your boat further down the coast."

There followed days of fishing and the taking of fine marlin. At lunch time Ernest would run in along the coast, either at Mariel or down Jaruco, and anchor. Then we'd swim before eating and practice drifting underwater down the length of the *Pilar*'s hull in the clear countercurrent. After twenty minutes of this, the sandwiches seemed food for the most fortunate humans alive.

The really big run of billfish didn't begin until the first week of September that year. Then the market fishermen were taking between twenty-five and thirty big marlin a day in their small boats and the prices even dropped in the market.

Ernest performed some highly unusual feats that season. He took a 243-pound marlin in twenty-nine minutes. Then he took a 130-pound striped marlin aboard in just three minutes, bringing the fish in green and still full of fight. "That fish would have taken me nearly an hour a couple of seasons ago," he said. Of the bigger one, he admitted, "It would have taken at least two and a half hours. They were fair hooked. There was nothing wrong with either fish. We just understand more about them, that's all."

Ernest had shown me some of the letters from readers in *Esquire* who doubted the veracity of his own material. I had seen what he was doing and knew that what he wrote was true. "Why are they like that?" I asked.

"They're the people who hear an echo and think they originated the sound," he said. "They hear or read somewhere I'm a phony and it's suddenly a fact in their minds. Like Heywood Broun branding me a phony on boxing. He probably got the idea from reading Gertrude Stein, and liked it. Then it became his idea. I'm getting plenty sick of this branding, and it probably hasn't even run its course as yet." Ernest took another swallow and added, "Young man, the only way I'm a phony is in the sense that every writer of fiction is: I make things up so they'll seem

real. But you really know me, on fishing, on shooting, on boxing.
Do I deliver?"

"Like nobody else."

"And we'll keep it that way, Baron. But I can't worry about
branding and have to get on with my book. This book is a chance
to make some real money and that's good. Because money buys
freedom. I've got a chance to go into business in Tanganyika.
That would give the kids a chance to grow up out there.... You've
got to see it too. I haven't got time to worry about this branding
crap. I've got to keep cracking on that book."

Jake and I wanted to sail to Haiti, and Ernest came down to
see us off. "I'll get our agent to clear you," he said. "Use your
head and keep the ship safe. And remember, keep observing all
the time. This is college, for a writer."

Ernest returned to Key West soon afterward for more provisions
and to make business arrangements. He came back to Havana before the end of September to finish the final spurt of writing on
The Green Hills of Africa manuscript. He had been doing twenty
to twenty-two pages a day toward the end, though his usual production was about five pages daily. His handwritten script ran to
492 pages, and he planned to start another story the next day.

Once the book was finished, not even the afternoon squalls
could keep Ernest from fishing out in the fine run of big marlin
that were moving up the Stream. By the middle of October he had
an infection in his right index finger that was acting like a nasty
case of blood poisoning and had him spooked. It would puff up
tight, then the swelling in the finger would go down and general
swelling would set in. He wrote letters one-handed on the typewriter and they were more comical than ever.

I had written about developments on the eastern end of the
island, where we had run into difficulties with local officials. He,
in turn, wrote local news. He said he was being written about by
Gilbert Seldes in *Esquire*. This was ironic because when Seldes
had been editor of the *Dial* in Europe he had turned down Ernest's
chapters of *In Our Time* and in doing so had advised Ernest to
stick to newspaper work and drop any illusions about becoming
a writer. Ernest had kept that letter of rejection. He figured it

gave him a valuable kick in the slats whenever he needed one. Ernest had some amusing and highly libelous things to say right then. But his hand was hurting severely enough to limit production of anything more than personal letters. He continued to soak it in Epsom salts whenever the inflammation flared again.

A vicious hurricane hit the south coast of Cuba. Before the end of October, Ernest took the *Pilar* back to Key West. He was hard at work helping his friend Luis Quintanilla, the Spanish artist, produce a show of etchings at the Pierre Matisse gallery in New York. The show was scheduled for November. Quintanilla himself was in jail in Madrid, charged with being on the revolutionary committee of the October revolt. Ernest wrote an introduction for the catalogue and got John Dos Passos to write another. Ernest was paying for the show, having already paid to have the prints pulled, because he was convinced they were "bloody marvelous." In writing to all his friends, he explained that he might be expected to be prejudiced, being Quintanilla's pal, but that these were the finest dry points he had ever seen. He also paid the duty on the etchings, and paid for the advertising, and promised to buy fifteen if the show didn't produce sufficient sales. But he was worried about money. From his emergency fund he had made loans to several friends during the spring and summer and none of these had been returned.

A single cold wave reached Key West that fall that actually killed many of the fish, from grunts and snapper to jacks and bonefish, in the shallow water. But it did nothing to spoil the sport fishing at greater depths and out in the Stream. Ernest lured Arnold Gingrich down and together they tied into tuna and sailfish as well as some big barracuda. And Arnold again solved Ernest's immediate financial problems for him.

Ernest took Pauline and the children to Piggott a week before Christmas so that the family could have an old-fashioned celebration there. But in general it was a winter of work and worry. Ernest was wondering how he could help to get Quintanilla off with a light sentence. And he was seriously troubled with amoebic dysentery again. He was working over the book, cutting, tightening, and deciding about serialization. He had offers from both *Scrib-*

ner's and *Cosmopolitan*. Max Perkins came down, but Ernest was feeling miserable with dysentery all the time that he was there. The treatment seemed definitely worse than the disease, with the castor oil, emetine, and other medication. But he told Pauline, in complete sincerity, "I sure don't want to die of any disease that Texas Guinan died of."

The Cuban revolt early in February was a serious one. The government troops took more than 300 people out of the prisons, where they had been held briefly, and shot them. Ernest knew some of the people who were executed and was very glum. My letters from down the island, describing the street fighting, added details and, incidentally, more worries.

Because of the Cuban revolt, Ernest decided to fish in Bimini the coming spring. The big fish were definitely on the south and east side of the Stream, and the British waters were less disturbed by murderous politics. Ernest had heard there was a good hotel, and invited friends to come on down and see what it was like for themselves. Dos Passos was coming. Arnold Gingrich said he would try. The Masons planned to come up from Havana with their boat.

It was as these plans were shaping up that Ernest heard from Zane Grey, who had become in the early thirties the most noted devotee of big-game fishing everywhere. Grey could certainly arouse interest in fishing and had whetted Ernest's own appetite for the sport in early years. But Grey's writing was very general compared to Ernest's pieces in *Esquire*, which contained countless practical tips on how, when, where, and with what tackle to catch the various marvels of the deep.

In his letter, Grey asked Ernest to join him on a gigantic world fishing cruise. He thought they might make a motion picture out of it. Ernest was to furnish his name. Grey would raise the operating money and furnish the boat and thousands of dollars' worth of tackle. Later they could make a series of personal appearances and split a minimum of half a million, he thought.

Ernest considered it one of the most ingenuous offers he had ever received. With some amusement he realized he had Grey worried about the records he had so blandly claimed without first checking to find out if they were authentic. And it strengthened Ernest's belief in the growing need for some kind of international organization to keep track of such things.

Spring came early in 1935. Ernest couldn't wait to get going. By April 7, he had the boat all provisioned, fueled, and lubricated, the cooling pumps checked, vast quantities of extra gear aboard, and everything cleared to leave U. S. waters. So he left.

A few hours later he returned, his lower legs covered with blood, and all his best plans thrown into disorder.

What happened was that Ernest's enthusiasm had overcome his judgment of the needs of the moment. That morning the *Pilar* was to start out on the long run up the keys, and from there to cross the Stream to the Great Bahama Bank. Instead of making time, Ernest was tempted to take it easy and troll while under way.

A shark hit one of the baits, once the boat was well away from port. Fighting the shark and taking it aboard occupied the crew as well as the captain. Like most sharks, this one proved hard to kill. When Ernest drew his Colt Woodsman .22 caliber autoloading pistol the shark was almost wholly in the cockpit and holding still. As he fired at the small spot between its eyes where the brain lay, the shark jerked convulsively, perhaps at some slight movement of the gaff. The shark's head moved out of line. The bullet meant for its brain hit, instead, the half-inch oval strip protecting the cockpit edge and, through simply idiotic bad luck, split into several small pieces of hot lead that ricocheted into the calves of both of Ernest's legs.

These were flesh wounds, but the bulk of the bullet entered his left leg. The accident was no one's fault and was not due to carelessness but to plain bad luck. No one can predict when a shark that is very much alive will wiggle next.

"Dammit," Ernest said. "That's one for the books. Mucking shark gets me and me in charge the whole time."

"What do we do now? You're bleeding quite a lot."

"Smack him with the persuader and put her around for Key West. Let's see how soon we can make it to the Marine Hospital."

Ashore, Dr. Warren at the Marine Hospital gave Ernest

antitetanus and extracted the small bits of lead. But he ordered
Ernest to bed. He did not want to extract the base of the bullet
in Ernest's left leg because of its position.

For three days he had to stay in bed, watching for infection.
During that period of frustration he was very cheered by a letter
from Dinamov announcing that *The Sun Also Rises* had then sold
57,000 copies in Russia, and that *A Farewell to Arms* was just being
serialized in the Russian edition of *International Literature*. The
Russians wanted to translate *The Green Hills of Africa* and said
they would publish anything he sent them.

The Green Hills of Africa had come out in England April 3,
and Ernest received copies of the *Times* and *Sunday Times*, giving
it columns of very favorable comment. "Over there you can write
about the noncompetitive sports and they'll call it literature if
that is what it is. Over here they see the subject matter and say,
'You can't write seriously about stuff like that.' Over here you have
to write about strikes or a social uplift movement or they don't
even know if you can write," he said.

But he was feeling very good. The wounds did not infect. "If
I had to get shot again, it couldn't have been in a better place"
was his stoical reaction. He wrote an amusing piece for *Esquire*,
and headed again for Bimini, determined this time to make the
trip of almost 200 miles without pausing to fish on the way.

In Bimini that spring, Ernest caught the first big unmutilated
tuna that had ever been taken there. They weighed 514 and 610
pounds. He used the technique he had learned while marlin fishing.
By fighting the fish with absolutely no rest, he brought them in
while they were still fast enough to get away from the sharks that
loved to grab great pieces out of the slower fish. As the summer run
continued, Ernest hoped to establish a world record, judging the
fish by weight alone.

One evening in May, just before returning to the United States,
Ernest found himself drawn into a heated argument with a man
whose name he didn't know; it happened on the dock at Bimini.
Before the fight was over, Ben Finney, Howard Lance, Bill Fagan,
and several other fishing captains had come over to join them.

The scene was dramatic. Ernest had come in from a day's good fishing, though he had no big fish to show for his effort. He'd fought something, probably a tuna, that had played deep and given him a tough couple of hours before it was cut off, probably by a shark. Ernest had headed in at sundown. By the time the guests were unloaded, the boat washed down, and gear readied for the coming day, it was dark. On the dock there were only a couple of lights. Occasionally it was brightened by the running lights and searchlights of boats returning from Cat Cay where construction work was going on. Ernest told me about it afterward in great detail. He was still angry.

"Say, aren't you the guy who claims he catches all the fish?" Ernest heard the voice from the darkness but he was unable to see the figure immediately. He was not sure he was the person addressed and he was wary.

Then the voice came again, louder. "Say, aren't you the guy who claims . . ."

"I catch my share." On the dock Ernest could make out a large figure in white shorts.

"Then why don't you bring in the proof? I suppose we're going to have to read all about some monster record you almost brought in today when . . ."

"Look, I don't even know your name, much less who your mother was."

"Leave my mother out of this. Let's just find out if . . ."

"If what? If you ever really had one? Let's ask the boys here."

There was a loud laugh from the circle of men who had come down the docks as the interchange continued. The large figure seemed to set himself. "What I want to know is do you fake those pictures as well as . . ."

"You seem to be an expert on fakery. Maybe you just need another drink. Why don't you run along and get one?"

"Oh no. You brought up the subject of my mother. Now I want satisfaction and I'm going to get it, or I'll shame you off the dock. Someone said that you were yellow and now I'm going to find out." He set himself again, crouching like someone posing for a picture.

"Look," Ernest said, "you don't know me and you don't know

what you're getting into. You're only talking big so that you can repeat what you've just said to me up in New York, in front of your friends. Now that's a lot of ——."

"Trying to get out of it, eh? That's what I figured you'd do. That's just what I figured."

Ernest was up on the dock in three barefoot leaps. His heckler lunged as he came up.

"I figured him for a mouthy drunk," Ernest told me later. "And I clipped him several good ones with my left, but he didn't go down. I couldn't understand it. He was sore and he'd been drinking, but he honestly didn't show it by his reflexes until that instant. Then he dived at me high, grabbing like a sloppy lineman, and seemed to be trying for a low blow. I hit him twice, hard, on the side of the head, and he barely let go. Then I backed off and really got the weight of a pivot swing into the old Sunday punch. He landed, and his ass and head hit the planking at the same time."

Ernest was worried about what he had done. Back in his room at the Compleat Angler he showered and found he had ripped off the tops of two toenails on the dock. He told the friends he met for dinner about the fight, and was even more worried when the word drifted back that the man he had traded words and blows with was reputed to be Joseph Knapp, owner and publisher of *Collier's, Woman's Home Companion, The American* magazine, and others.

"That's what you call limiting your magazine markets," he observed. "That was the first bare-knuckle fight I've had since I was a kid. There must have been sixty people showed up finally—and no purse."

In spite of the wisecracks, Ernest was seriously worried that he might have hurt his opponent's head. At about four the next morning, Mr. Knapp's yacht, *Storm King*, left for Miami to get medical attention for its owner. There, Knapp was very fair about the whole incident. He told Captain Bill Fagan that he was sorry he had spoken out of turn and guessed he'd gotten what he deserved. He outweighed Ernest and had had shoes on, but he was not in good fighting shape, as Ernest was. The Negro band that sang around Bimini had seen it all and that evening they composed a fine song that was often heard in the islands on still nights when the rum began to work and the moon was shining.

Early in June, Ernest flew back to Key West to see Pauline and the children. Pauline had stayed there because Patrick and Gregory were still too young to go everywhere their Papa went, and to supervise some major improvements being made on the house. Then Pauline went to St. Louis to get Bumby, who was out of school and on summer vacation.

Ernest returned to Bimini to fish the rest of the summer. He wrote to Arnold Gingrich, explaining the plane connections in detail. In the following weeks they exchanged many messages through the captain of the pilot boat who ran over from Miami twice a week. Arnold was delayed but finally came to see the fabulous fishing himself.

"One of the things that lured me down was having a chance to hear that song," Arnold said.

Later, Pauline came over with the children and stayed up on the hill. By then Ernest had hooked and fought one huge marlin and had seen the hook pull out when the fish had been worked right up to the boat. He was over twelve feet, Ernest estimated, had made twenty-two jumps high out of the sea, and had run with nearly half a mile of line. Ernest had worked him in during the first twenty-eight minutes. He was using eight-to-ten-pound tuna as trolling baits and having great success. Betting on catches had won him $350 from "the rich boys." But then his skill and luck became accepted facts and there were no more bets.

The week before Ernest's birthday he got into another run of big fish. In four days he took marlin of 330 pounds in twenty-five minutes, 364 pounds in thirty-two minutes, 540 pounds in thirty minutes, and 278 pounds in twenty-two minutes—all fairly hooked and in fighting trim. He caught the biggest fish on his birthday and it ran a wonderful course, jumping eighteen times and twice taking out more than 450 yards of line.

There was plenty of boxing as well as fishing over there—after the Joe Knapp fight.

"Whenever anybody got tight or began to feel dangerous, I'd get called in," he said later. " 'You try him, Cap,' they'd say. I had to fight four times in less than three weeks after that first brawl. We used gloves twice, and two fights were bare-knuckle. I won knockouts in them all. I guess Bimini is about the size place where I could be heavyweight champion. The biggest, toughest islander— a colored boy—took less than a minute, but he didn't know boxing. It was a shame. He was the kind of guy you'd like to see taught and trained."

In Bimini, Ernest and Mike Lerner soon became friends. Mike had come to the island earlier and had caught several big marlin. News of these catches brought many American sportsmen. For a foreign port, Bimini is conveniently close to the U. S. mainland, being just forty-five miles across the Gulf Stream. Ernest invested a few hundred dollars in land there because he liked the place. "Now we own part of the Bahamas," he told me later. "Not much, but a real part."

Before he left, Ernest talked seriously with Mike Lerner and others about the formation of an official group to keep and pass on game-fish records. Later, this group became the nucleus of the International Game Fish Association, under the sponsorship of the American Museum of Natural History, with Francesca LaMonte as its secretary. Miss LaMonte and Ernest became great friends. In his fishing off the Cuban coast, Ernest had already taken ichthyologists from the Philadelphia Academy of Science out to study the habits of marlin in the Gulf Stream. And one species of fish, the *Neomarinthe Hemingwayi*, was named after Ernest, its discoverer.

Ernest planned to go back to Key West the latter part of August. After refitting and taking on new supplies there, he wanted to fish off Havana for three weeks, remembering the wonderful late run of fish there in September the year before. But he had to wait in Bimini for spare parts to arrive because of an alarming increase in the oil consumption of the main engine.

Hurricane season was approaching again, and the best harbors are the most familiar ones, Ernest realized. The weather had turned muggy and he became uneasy. Ernest had developed a good "partridge sense" over the years and suddenly he became very impatient to move on. As soon as the parts arrived, the last week in August,

Ernest made a fast trip across to American waters and ran outside the reef all the way down to Key West. He wanted to make the boat secure against any storm that might be coming, and the submarine base in Key West was a very secure place. His premonition was absolutely right.

On Labor Day that year, a severe hurricane swept in from the east. Ernest had the *Pilar* roped with lines running completely around the hull, and double bridles leading in four directions, so she would not be likely to smash herself against the piers inside the base. Lines parted, but the boat (uninsured, by the way) came through the blow without damage.

When the storm's eye passed on, all communication had been cut between Key West and the mainland. Not until a day later was the damage known. The railroad had been washed right off the trestles for miles. Hundreds of World War I veterans, living in one-story barracks near Indian Key, were drowned as the hurricane and its wall of water swept in between Islamorada and Matecumbe.

Ernest was deeply depressed by the loss of life and general destruction. He wrote bitterly about the lack of sufficient warning by the weather bureau.

Earlier that summer I had gotten my boat out of Cuba and over to Key West. From there I'd gone on up north where I was working as a reporter for the *Chicago Daily News*. Ernest wrote that Charles Thompson had placed my boat up a small creek nearby and that it had come through the storm unharmed. Three years later, while I was vacationing in Key West, we still found G.I. shoes from the drowned veterans washed up in the mangroves on some of the uninhabited keys.

That fall Ernest was invited by friends to go to Kenya for the winter for more shooting. He also wanted to go on to Abyssinia to see and write about the Italian invasion there. He was restless and he was tempted but then he decided against the trip. To a friend he explained that he had already seen the Italians fight once and if he had not cared for it at the age of twenty he didn't see why it should appeal to him at the age of thirty-eight. At the time he was actually thirty-six. For most of his adult life Ernest had been passing as a couple of years older than he actually was, and he was still maintaining the image of a man more mature in years than he really was.

During October and November, Ernest and Dos Passos made two visits to New York, staying as guests of the Gerald Murphys. The Riviera home of the Murphys had for years been an open house for Dos Passos and other serious writers. Except for those trips, Ernest was hard at work in Key West on further chapters of *To Have and Have Not*, and was again working on short stories. It was a good winter of production. By the following April, he had completed several short stories, was on page sixty of a long one, and midway through the novel. Harry Burton of *Cosmopolitan* had come down to Key West to make a very large offer for the serial rights to his forthcoming novel, as well as record prices for his short stories.

On April 24, 1936, the *Pilar* sailed for Havana for the spring fishing. Ernest, always working well in the spring, was after additional material for the novel, as well as a sporting workout. He got more material than he was looking for.

The word "pirate" is still taken seriously by every man afloat. Piracy may be on the wane, but it still exists and it increases in depression times. In Havana that spring, Ernest had his first brush with real pirates.

The *Pilar* had been an object of interest and envy ever since her first visit two years earlier. As the sleek black cruiser became better known and Ernest's circle of friends widened, he was looked upon as one of the wealthy. He had rich friends who owned huge sugar estates. They visited him aboard the boat. Some even began bringing their own yachts around to the main harbor from the Almendares River, close to the yacht clubs where they usually docked. Yachtsmen seemed fair pickings to the poor who lived in Regla, the toughest area in Havana harbor.

Ernest had made friends with all the members of the Pilot's Association, but he couldn't know all the bumboatmen, garbage cleaners, and thieves who prowled the waterfront in rowboats, skiffs, and small launches on the lookout for unwary freighter crews. These water pirates were not averse to murder. They simply refused to specialize, knowing that frequent disappearances often led to investigations that hampered their movements.

"The local thieves are famous for their pride and skill," Ernest would tell visitors. "Last year they held a competition. To cut the story short, the thief who won was given *olés* by his compatriots. He had demonstrated out at the race track that he could steal the shoes off a running horse."

That spring, because of economic pressures, enemies Ernest had made, or his display of too much expensive fishing tackle, the word was out. The word was "Get the *Pilar*. The man who loots her first is the toast of Regla."

The word was broadcast so far that it got to some of Ernest's friends and they tipped him off. He continued to anchor the black, 38-foot fishing machine that gave him such pride only a hundred yards from the San Francisco docks, and well inside the pilot boats.

He knew he couldn't rely on anyone else to do what had to be done. To move the boat would give away the whole show. So for the next few nights he kept watch aboard. After rowing out with a friend in the evening, he had the friend row ashore again with a large sack in the stern of the boat, resembling a figure hunched over and going ashore with him.

The ruse finally worked. One evening after an early dinner ashore, Ernest went quietly aboard and began his silent watch from the cabin below, while his friend rowed down the harbor.

As the hours passed, Ernest waited patiently, listening to the various and familiar harbor sounds. Finally he heard the sound he was expecting. It was the gentle dip-dip of oars approaching. Then the sound stopped. He felt the hull shift under him as the smaller boat came alongside in absolute silence. There was a faint click as he thumbed back the hammer of his .45 Colt pistol. When a dark figure suddenly rose up in the cockpit, clear against the background of café lights ashore, Ernest fired.

The sound of the shot was still ringing in his ears as the figure leaped overboard. Running aft, Ernest played his powerful flashlight over the surface of the water. The only thing in sight was a battered skiff drifting off in the light breeze.

After that the new word went out. "Leave the black fishing boat alone."

That summer the *Pilar* was involved in another piratical action. When Ernest was back in Key West, Archie MacLeish came down for some fishing. One day Ernest and Archie were out fishing with no crew aboard. Ernest regarded Archie as a first-rate poet and a gentleman as well. They had fished together many times and had a number of mutual friends.

But that day the fishing was poor. A discussion of personalities developed and became heated. Ernest reportedly became angry and didn't care to "have just another drink and calm down." An unpleasant tension was created and they decided to continue the discussion on dry land. Ernest then headed for the nearest land, one of the keys between Boca Grande and Snipe Keys. He eased the *Pilar* up in the shallows. Archie went ashore first. In a matter of moments, Ernest had the *Pilar* under way again, headed out.

When he returned to Key West, Ernest was still muttering to himself. Pauline was disturbed to see him in such a ferment. "Where's Archie?" she asked. When she learned that Archie had been marooned, Pauline had no sympathy for Ernest.

"You can't do this, Ernest," she said. "You've got to go back and get him. That's all there is to it. He may be going crazy with the insects, and there's no fresh water on any of those keys."

Ernest argued that Archie might have hailed a passing fishing boat and might already be on his way back to Key West. "I don't care what you say. This has to be cleared up right away." Pauline could and did stand up to him as no one else ever did. As a result Archie reached civilization soon afterward. But the bond of camaraderie between the two men was destroyed.

Later that summer, Ernest returned to Bimini. John Dos Passos and his wife came and enjoyed the fishing thoroughly, though Dos often had work to do and so withdrew from the usual festivities. Ernest's nickname for him was Dos Muttonfish because of his fondness for those succulent members of the snapper family. Ernest's boat was always a popular craft. It couldn't hold all the guests who wanted to come along on any day's outing. The others, and Dos was frequently among them, would then take to the dinghies and enjoy a quiet day's fishing in among the reefs between Piquet rock and the Biminis.

Jane Mason had again brought the *Pelican* up from Havana. Floyd Gibbons of the Hearst newspapers decided to stay all summer because of the amount of fishing news coming from Bimini. Pauline again came over from Key West with the children. By then, Patrick and Gigi were old enough to go out for an occasional day on Papa's boat. Bumby had become an expert fisherman years earlier, but he had a tendency to get seasick, which excluded him from some of the windiest and best fishing days.

The atmosphere aboard the *Pilar* that summer had a curiously memorable quality. Friends there at that time agree on several details. Ernest was often morose, and angry with himself more than with others. There were many temper flare-ups that were unpredictable.

A record player wound by hand was part of the ship's equipment that season. Some of the records that were played repeatedly still haunt members of the guest crew of '36. They included "Experiment," "Stormy Weather," and a Jimmy Durante number about fixing a boa. Then there was "Ill wind, blow away . . ." The songs became such an integral part of life on the *Pilar* that guests and crew members plotted openly for the destruction of the records. Ernest was too vigilant and too fond of the songs to allow the records to be slipped overboard. In the clear harbor water, guests realized, he would probably find them anyway. The disposal system finally chosen was as follows: those detailed to tend the music were to drop the records one by one, then step on each record while bending down to retrieve it while the vessel was under way. Thus poor seamanship could be blamed.

The Bimini native song that year had a catchy tune. Ernest would sing:

> Big fat slob in de harbor; Dat's de night we have fun,
> Bet he ball up his fist, Wid a twist of de wrist, and
> Make like drunk son-of-a-gun.

There were several schools of thought as to whom the song referred. Most people agreed that it was not Ernest, though he was notorious for his willingness to box with anyone. He never fought except in self-defense once the day's drinking had begun. Early one morning, just after sunrise, he and Tom Heeney, the former British heavyweight champion, met by arrangement on the deserted western beach of North Bimini and boxed several rounds with gloves on. It was a friendly workout, with no seconds, points, or referee. Suddenly Ernest looked up. There on the path above was a long line of watchers.

"Listen, Tommy," he said. "We've got to quit now. Here we are giving a free show when any charity would be begging for a chance to pass the hat." Heeney agreed. They shed their gloves and dived in for a swim.

During June and the first half of July, Ernest's fishing luck began to desert him. He had a more appreciative audience than ever. But when the fish were running best, he and the others spent most of their time getting bait. When bait was available, the big marlin and tuna were fickle. When they hung one, the line popped or the fish was cut off by sharks, or a boat full of sight-seers would cut in and foul the lines. These things often happened. Ernest's irritation was evident.

Jane Mason had brought Carlos Gutierrez up from Havana to gaff for Ernest, and Carlos was clearly one of the best in the world. He had a knowledge of fishing that was unexplainable. But in some way, even he finally incurred Ernest's displeasure. Ernest had absolutely no self-pity. He did not regard pity as an admirable quality, and he refused to use it on others. In some instances this turned to a peculiar form of behavior that could best be described as "let's see how much he or she can take." Whether you were an assistant, a crew member, a wife, or a friend, you caught it by the carload. "Papa can be more severe," Robert Capa told me one time when we were talking alone, "than God on a rough day when the whole human race is misbehaving."

Carlos was very close to Ernest emotionally, so his wounds were that much greater. He had fished the south side of the Gulf Stream for more than thirty years in an open boat before Ernest knew him. In this time he had learned most of what there was to know about marlin fishing. He spoke old Spanish, was a fine seaman, an inspired fisherman, and loved the sea as much as he did the people on it.

But that was a bad time in many ways for Ernest. One annoyance was that other boats were taking big fish daily, while his own luck ran to might-have-been wonders. Finally he turned on Carlos, in a burst of self-recrimination neatly missing the target. Feeling for the breaking point where personal pride would be destroyed, he said several things Carlos had never dreamed anyone could say to him. As surely as the hands of a running clock turn full circle, it was Carlos' turn to catch the weight of Ernest's wrath.

At first Carlos couldn't believe his ears. Then his face turned gray under his tan. Finally he began to cry. To make such a man weep by tongue alone and before guests was to destroy his dignity as a man. What was worse, the man who had said those things was his hero. Carlos bent over and wept.

Jane Mason took Carlos back to Havana on her boat. He had been her captain before Ernest had hired him away from her years earlier. A few weeks after their return, Carlos was again unhappy. So great was Ernest's influence that Carlos wanted to return to him. "Don Ernesto," he explained, "understands me as does no one else."

Chapter 9

Ernest had known for months, from the news reports, that conditions were getting rapidly worse in Spain. But the news dispatches of July 18, reporting the revolt of several Spanish generals against their elected government, were more than disquieting. Ernest knew what such men could do if their troops remained loyal. The news of the following days confirmed his judgment.

The Spanish War had begun.

That summer, however, Ernest was deeply committed to his writing schedule. The novel must be finished. He concentrated on getting the book done; but Spain was on his mind at the same time. Those early months of the Spanish War were a time of great production for him. But he managed to read the daily papers avidly, to observe and understand developments as soon as they had taken place. After each day's writing was done he talked endlessly with friends about the war. In December *To Have and Have Not* was in final form. Then he was free to take some positive action about Spain.

In January he signed an agreement with John Wheeler, president of the North American Newspaper Alliance, which represented scores of the biggest daily newspapers in the United States, to act as the news syndicate's war correspondent in Spain during the coming months. He would receive five hundred dollars each for cable dispatches of from 250 to 400 words, and one thousand dollars for mail dispatches of about 1,200 words, with NANA securing exclusive rights for newspaper use.

From the time that contract was signed in January, until March, when he arrived in France ready to cross the border, Ernest was busy calling and writing Washington and New York, rounding up friends and arranging for assistance and permission for various projects.

The first was the making of a documentary film that would show both what life was like in a typical Spanish village before the war and then the extent to which the war disrupted and changed it.

He knew he would have to raise the money for this one himself, and counted heavily on his own ability to file dispatches so colorful and dramatic that editors all over the country would start calling, "More, more!"

He did not plan to stay in Spain very long. His contract called for a two- to three-month visit, and he was to send dispatches either when the news events warranted them or on request from the syndicate. The syndicate reserved the right to limit the cable dispatches, if in the opinion of its executives the developments did not warrant more coverage. Most important, the agreement freed Ernest to write magazine stories and articles, or books.

Ernest concentrated on enlisting the personal services of his friend Sidney Franklin, the bullfighter from Brooklyn who spoke even better Spanish than Ernest did. Franklin had friends and admirers by the millions in Spain. He had both ability and a reputation. But he was so politically naive that when the war broke out his first question to Ernest was, "Which side are we on, Papa?"

Ernest's first big campaign was against the Department of State. He lost the first round when, after weeks of waiting, Mrs. Ruth Shipley, head of the passport division, refused to grant credentials to Sidney Franklin to become an "assistant correspondent" in Ernest's personal coverage of the Spanish War. Ernest advanced the argument that Jack Dempsey had turned newsman overnight in order to have the Dempsey by-line covering fights. He felt that Sidney, though an accomplished novillero who had fought and killed many splendid bulls, seemed particularly well qualified to help cover this conflict, since the coverage would involve no further ring exhibitions but gathering much information and supplies. This was a field in which Sidney Franklin qualified more than anyone.

Ernest was still hopeful that Sidney would be granted official permission to enter Spain when, on March 12, he filed the first of his dispatches from Europe to the syndicate. He told of preparations to fly into Republican Spain and about the friend he had just talked with who had come out of Spain on a very delicate mission, reporting that the more than 100,000 combined German and Italian troops already there were assisting the Insurgents.

His second cable had news of Sidney Franklin's defeat in the lists against bureaucracy. Ernest was undaunted because he knew, as all realists know, that you do not need permission to do many things in this world. You need only to know how to act and to have the guts to act. Permission is a nice thing to have, said Ernest, but it is not necessary in getting on with one's life. Franklin had been refused permission to go to Spain. That was all there was to it. The French government, striving for absolute acceptance of its official neutrality, had also sealed the border against everyone except proven diplomats and newspapermen. Minor officials had told Ernest they had even refused to let pass a Red Cross nurse who wanted to take cases of canned milk to refugee children nearby, and she had come all the way from Madrid.

By March 18, Ernest had flown into Republican Spain. He landed at Barcelona just after a bombing raid; then he continued down the east coast to Alicante, with its African scenery, and finally to Valencia, where fresh meat was still obtainable outside the city and the inhabitants were enthusiastic about the war.

The following week Ernest personally went over the terrain on the Guadalajara front where the Government troops had won over the Italians, their first victory in eight months of fighting against the invaders. In cold rain and snow flurries, he kept moving while under shell fire. He was deeply disturbed by the sight of the dead

Italians who had believed they were being sent to Africa for garrison duty and had instead run into accurate small-arms fire and the antitank guns that took on their so-called invincible mechanized columns.

A week later, Ernest wrote an analysis of the Brihuega battle, where the Guadalajara Italian retreat had begun. He was convinced that it was the biggest Italian defeat since Caporetto in World War I, and described the scene, the weapons used, the scattered and abandoned equipment and papers of the defeated and the dead. Medium tanks had beaten light tanks. Government morale was high.

"One morning I got a letter from some people in Hollywood asking me to do everything possible for Errol Flynn who was coming over to see the war firsthand," Ernest told me later. "I figured he could be valuable in raising money back in America. So when he got to Madrid in late afternoon, I started organizing a grand tour for the following day. I had to get permits, a car, a chauffeur, and gasoline. Had to ask favors to organize it, and I hated asking favors. Favors have to be repaid, and when you're indebted to some people you can't report truly.

"Anyway, got it organized. Then Flynn wants to make the rounds of the bars. Turned out okay. We got back to the hotel by midnight. Had to get lots of rest before heading for the front. Hell. Next morning I was up at six and calling his room. No answer. Went downstairs and they told me Señor Flynn had checked out, get that, checked out. Said he was leaving Madrid. Clerk said he looked fine but seemed in a hurry. The hotel had been shelled but it had been a pretty quiet night.

"I called around and apologized for the change of plans, and waited for word. It came the evening of April 5. Flynn was reported resting comfortably after getting hit on the head by falling plaster in the siege of Madrid."

Ernest hurried into the preparations for making the documentary film. Joris Ivens, who was directing and photographing, had reached Spain, and so had John Ferno, a cameraman engaged for the project. Much of the daily film coverage was being made outside Madrid in the village of Morales, but other scenes were necessary. In order to film actual combat, Ernest took the photographers and their most portable equipment to locations where they could shoot pictures of tanks in action under good lighting conditions. Hank Gorrell of United Press came along. On April 9 they saw the second Republican attack in four days designed to relieve the pressure against University City. Before the day was over, they had all been sniped at repeatedly. Once they found a marvelous observation point with a view of the battle spread out below. But individual bullets kept taking chips out of the woodwork next to them and they hastily moved before the snipers' correction for windage eliminated their group. By the time the light faded they had taken some excellent footage, setting the camera up in a bombed-open third floor of a house where they could observe without being seen.

A few days later they went along on an infantry and tank attack that further helped free the city of Madrid. Ernest sent back stories graphically describing the crackling whisper of small-arms fire, the smell of smoke and ammunition, and the mysterious blossoming of flames as objectives just beyond view through the brush were shelled by the attacking troops.

On April 22, Ernest and several hundred thousand other people had been under bombardment in Madrid for eleven consecutive days. He described the different kinds of explosions, ranging from rifle fire to trench mortars and high explosive artillery, and what each of the missiles did on impact to the buildings and the people.

"When Sidney Franklin finally did manage to turn up in Madrid where we were, everything got much easier," he told me later. "Sidney was the greatest scrounger, organizer, and haggler ever to help hungry people in Republican Spain. He could talk a stranger out of a hatful of eggs like most people can get a light for a cigarette. He was wonderful."

Ernest himself had a talent for providing fresh meat. Borrowing a shotgun from a friend, Ernest used the correspondents' car to drive out to the Pardo front on the other side of the city from the Hotel Florida where he was staying. There in a few hours he bowled over four rabbits and shot a duck, a partridge, and a lone owl that he mistook for a woodcock as it flew through the trees.

"I decided that was meat enough, after what I mistook for a covey of partridges taking off turned out to be a trench mortar shell that landed just over the next ridge," he told me.

Early in May of that year he filed his final dispatch from Madrid and prepared to return to France and then the United States. He had filed nearly a dozen stories, some by mail through the Government censorship. He had also written some magazine pieces; had seen a great deal of the film shot that would be edited into "The Spanish Earth"; and was gathering notes in order personally to do the narration for the film's sound track.

When Ernest reached New York again he was determined to make the most of his time there. He was already laying plans to return to Spain in the fall. He knew how many details would have to be arranged in advance if the trip were to be successful. He wanted to help with the cutting of the film and see that certain sequences were not eliminated. He had to do his own work with the sound track and had to arrange for distribution and showings. The object was to get the maximum exposure for the picture in order to raise funds for ambulances, medical aid, and other assistance for the Spanish Republic and for those who were fighting for its continued existence.

He did everything he could on the film, and also wrote some additional material for the news syndicate to be used in dispatches. He talked things over with Arnold Gingrich by telephone and told him about the new plans. Then he headed for Key West to see Pauline and the children, whom he had been missing fiercely during recent months.

Ernest wrote me just before heading for Bimini late in May. He said Spain had been very instructive and that he had seen the remains of Guadalajara and all of another battle, having gone with the infantry on attacks and filmed one counterattack. In Madrid he had come through nineteen days of really heavy bombardment and the news syndicate had been paying him so much by the dispatch that he figured he'd have to get himself killed by about the fourth dispatch in order for them to get their money's worth. But he was angry over the way he had been limited, pointing out that the syndicate had held him down to filing once a week and that in a single cable he had had to combine two attacks. He described the stuff, however, as all being good sausage material for the old unprintable mill, and said that he was going back again later that summer. He wanted to know how everything was going on the paper, and checked on some personal things.

At that time I had almost completed my second year on the *Chicago Daily News* as a reporter and editor on the weekly regional sections. Soon after I started working for the *News*, I had met Mary Welsh, then assistant society editor. Because the regional sections and the society department were next to each other in the city room, we had frequent opportunities to talk. Mary was a cheerful, petite blonde from Minnesota who kept her stockings nicely pulled up and liked to sit on a desk swinging her legs while she talked. "Gee, it must be wonderful to have a famous brother. Come on, tell us about him," she kidded me.

"Well, he doesn't write any of this regional copy for me. It's every guy for himself."

Mary had read everything of Ernest's that was available and was obviously fascinated by him. "Tell me, what's he really like?" she would ask. I had a small sailboat then and we went sailing in it. After that she jokingly referred to it as "our boat." Our relationship was utterly innocent and based almost entirely on her tremendous fascination with Ernest. Later she went East and worked for the Luce publications. Years afterward in Europe she finally met her hero.

That summer of 1937 was a time of decision for Ernest. He was talking animatedly with friends and acquaintances, doing his best to organize help and raise money for the Spanish Republic. Through his big-game fishing he had met many of the wealthy inheritors of American fortunes. He concentrated on these people, knowing that if they could develop social consciences they could aid the Spanish cause quickly and effectively, through the funds they controlled.

But he ran into disappointments. What seemed so clear-cut to him was murky and full of hidden pitfalls to others. When asked to give medical aid and contribute to alleviate the suffering on both sides of the war, some of his friends would have nothing to do with the idea. Some were afraid that if they gave aid it would assist only the Communists, who were known to be siding with the Spanish Government against the Germans, Italians, and rebel Spanish generals.

"I felt I'd have been betraying my class," one friend told me years later. "Ernest was dark with anger," he said. "Swiftly he arranged to see another friend of mine. There he was given a large donation. From that time on, I felt the friendship we shared had been destroyed."

Some of his friends were as favorable toward the Government side as was Ernest. William B. Leeds, who owned the huge ocean-going yacht *Moana* and was heir to a tin-plate fortune, thought very well of the idea. In Havana that summer, Bill Leeds invited Ernest aboard and they discussed what should be done. Leeds had already decided there must be something useful to society he could do with the *Moana* and had considered outfitting the yacht as a floating hospital and having her stationed in the Galápagos Islands where no medical help was available.

"Let's decide about the yacht later," Ernest said. "Listen, Bill, this is a rough war, very rough, you understand?"

Leeds nodded, and Ernest had the deck to himself. "You can be a colonel over there, Bill. You'll be commanding troops. Here, I'll be your captain. You gents . . . line up over there." Ernest motioned to Thorvald Sanchez, heir to a sugar fortune, Otto Bruce from Piggott, Arkansas, and a couple of other friends who were sitting around listening with rapt attention.

"All right, Bill. Here we are, all lined up. Here are four of your ambulance drivers. We await your orders, mi coronel. Remember, Bill, the unexpected is always happening in time of war. Attention! Now, Bill, the troops await your inspection."

Ernest had the file of volunteers assume a rigid pose while he preened with even more exaggeration. Bill Leeds walked over. On this, his own yacht, he had a crew far larger than this group. But he looked them over with amusement. "Fine-looking troops."

"Right, right, mi coronel." Ernest's saluting hand came up, but in a fist that lifted the new commanding officer and deposited him literally a dozen feet away. Amid the roars and howls of

laughter, Leeds could barely pick himself up. He was helped finally
to a seat and a drink.

"Bill, I told you war was full of the unexpected. Now you know."

Leeds nodded, holding his neck. But he subscribed enough
money to buy a full dozen ambulances, complete with surgical and
emergency equipment, to aid the suffering among the wounded on
both sides. The ambulances never reached Spain. They were
blocked, during shipment, by the American Neutrality Act that
forbade the shipment of equipment of any kind to Spain.

That summer Ernest also made a second contract with the
North American Newspaper Alliance. It was to confirm a verbal
agreement Ernest had made with John Wheeler after his return to
New York in May. The financial terms remained the same but in
the second contract more specific agreement was reached on the
frequency of filing dispatches. Ernest could file several in a short
period if in his opinion the news developments warranted them.
But he was not to be paid more than a thousand dollars in any
one week, no matter how many dispatches he sent. The syndicate
bought exclusive world rights to his dispatches, but freed him
for all kinds of other work. And it was mutually agreed that if the
war should lose its news value by the end of August the coverage
for the following three months would be canceled.

The film's première was held at the White House. Joris Ivens
went down from New York with Ernest to have dinner with the
President before the showing. It went off well and both were house
guests that night.

"They had real fruit in the guest rooms, Baron," he told me
later. "Not the waxy kind like in window displays, but ripe pears
and apples and peaches in a big bowl. I swiped a couple of apples
when I left. They were delicious."

Something else happened that summer that was to have far-
reaching effects on Ernest's career and personal life. While he was
in Key West, Martha Gellhorn, a young writer who had published
one book and was starting to do well in the magazine field, came
down to interview Ernest for a magazine article. Martha was a tall
blonde from St. Louis with extremely good legs, a fine sense of
humor, and the ability to write exceedingly well. She located

Sloppy Joe's bar, saw Ernest's name on one of the bar stools, and
asked if he really came in there as had been rumored.

"He sure do when he's in town," said Skinner, the large, shrewd
Negro who tended bar when Joe Russell, the owner, was absent.
"It's almost three o'clock now. If he's here, he'll be comin' in."

In a matter of minutes, Ernest arrived, took a look around, and
was pleased with the scene. He and Martha were introduced and
were talking like old friends even before the first drink. Ernest liked
the idea of the article and was expansive, considerate, and winsome
in alternate moods.

Martha, in turn, found herself instantly fascinated by Ernest.
He talked as well as he wrote and was wonderfully amusing when
he wanted to be. At the same time he was absolutely dedicated
to the belief that talent in the fine arts was not enough. It must be
used to make the world a better place in which to live, and that
included fighting for human freedom wherever it was threatened.
He had great plans for his next trip to Spain and urged that
Martha go over and see for herself what was happening, if she could
possibly do so. Martha, in her first book, had graphically shown
some instances of man's inhumanity and already shared with
Ernest his belief that a writer should do what he could for human
rights and dignity.

In New York, the middle of August, while preparing for the
trip to Spain, Ernest came to Max Perkins' office at Scribner's
and encountered the writer Max Eastman. Max had written
critically about Ernest's writing attitudes, indicating that there
was an air of "false hair on the chest." His criticism was considered
fair comment as criticism goes in the world of letters. This was the
first time the two men found themselves together in the same
room. Amenities soon changed to obscenities and, while Max Perkins himself withdrew, there was a brief physical exchange of energy
and each of the men was then led off to issue his own statement
to the press. Eastman claimed he had wrestled while Ernest had
boxed, and that he had personally come out ahead. Ernest claimed
he had "disciplined" Eastman and had a book with a bloody
smudge inside as evidence of an impact area. The Perkins office
was a shambles, and the event gave the literary world some juicy

gossip that reverberated in the columns and cocktail parties for some months.

During the summer, while in Bimini, Ernest had made changes and read the final proofs of *To Have and Have Not*, due for publication in the fall. He had used as characters some types that seemed remarkably like recent friends whom he had decided had a definite, if peculiar, value to society, especially as characters in a novel. Once Ernest had taken a dislike to a person, he treated that person as a nurse might treat a fly that had accidentally entered a hospital room.

His new book, the first in which he showed a change from the enjoyment of experience to a justification of his own life, was, he told me, in many ways the most important story he had ever written. Before it, he hadn't cared how life went as long as he could create productively. From this point on, he really gave a damn about other peoples' lives.

That summer he had addressed the League of American Writers at Carnegie Hall. He made what he described as "the only political address I ever intend to make," and told what he had seen in Spain, how it had affected him, and what he intended to do about Fascism everywhere.

The speech was serious and it put him on record. Ernest was always at his best once he had made a difficult decision. From then on, he was committed to implementing his beliefs. At the end of summer, when he was again back in New York, ready for Spain and a more lengthy stay, he had privately raised some $40,000 in advances from his publisher and other sources, which he donated for medical aid to the Government of Spain.

Ernest did some serious convivial drinking before he sailed. Talking with John Wheeler, he said he would do the syndicate one article and not charge for it, so pleased was he to be again representing dozens of the largest daily papers in the country, including the *New York Times*. His dispatches would again be running in the columns of his old alma mater, the *Kansas City Star*. And he would have a chance to learn more, as the war continued, about the extraordinary effect it was having on the lives of all his friends and acquaintances in Spain.

Ernest's first dispatch on his second visit was filed from the Aragon front, where he had a chance to talk with the tough, trained Americans who had survived the first year of the conflict. He noted that the wounded, the cowards, and the romantics had all been cleared away, leaving the good, dedicated fighters. In the time that Ernest had been back, these men had captured Cuenca and Belchite, using Indian fighting tactics that were again proving their value to infantry in the field. He went over the ground at Belchite with Robert Merriman, a former University of California professor who was a staff officer in the 15th Brigade and who had led the assault on an ancient fortification there. The stink of death was so strong there afterward that the burial squad members wore gas masks while doing their work.

Then Ernest concentrated on making an analysis of the Aragon front where a stalemate had developed. So simply did he present the aims of both sides in the war that even readers with absolutely no battle knowledge were able to understand the various military possibilities.

A week later his report was an essay on a rebel strong point, the Mansueto of Teruel, which rose out of the plain like a great ship on the sea. It was a natural fortress that had held against centuries of attacks and had been in rebel hands since the war's beginning. He sensed that it would have a historic importance before the war's end.

Ernest's experiences of the war and what he knew of it could best be presented as a play, he decided. The fact that he had never written a play before did not bother him. He was a master of dialogue. He had been a dramatist all his life, seeking turning points and crises as other men seek security and social status. He set to work drafting a series of acts, while continuing to advise and assist in filming additional footage in the village outside Madrid.

His romantic life took on a sudden upsurge when Martha Gellhorn arrived in the capital with full status as a correspondent. Martha and Ernest gravitated toward each other naturally. They were both romantics, determined to make their contribution in a fight against tyranny. Each held the other in high esteem. They both stayed at the Hotel Florida where literally all correspondents stayed. By combining forces on the food, entertainment, and companionship front, Ernest made his room one of the few places (though he changed its location from time to time) where friends and strangers could get a drink, sometimes a snack, and even a meal. They could hear good music played on the portable, hand-wound record player, while listening to typewriter keys clicking out the phrases and sentences that would be read later throughout the world. Ernest worked on his own material, worked over Martha's; she in turn copied out his material, and they combined their thinking and sometimes their phrases in magazine pieces under one by-line or the other.

By then Ernest had also come to know all the correspondents within sight or sound of his own headquarters. He became the firm friend of Herbert Matthews of the *New York Times*, and Sefton Delmer of the *London Daily Express*. When they visited the Brunete front together early in October, they used Delmer's open Ford "staff car." This vehicle was reasonable on gas consumption and was decorated with flags that made it vaguely resemble a diplomatic vehicle.

The resemblance of Delmer's "staff car" to the real thing became an almost deadly liability when the three merry word-magicians went down an approach road one afternoon near Brunete and promptly found themselves not only observed, but believed to be of great importance by the rebel forces.

"They think it's a super staff car," Ernest said, as they heard and then felt the first of a serious number of six-inch shells come in where they'd been only moments before. The vehicle survived, having been moved over a ridge where the bursts were ineffective. The three, whom Ernest characterized as looking like a bishop (Delmer), Savonarola (Matthews), and a cheerful Wallace Beery (himself) also survived only by moving in a sprightly manner way the hell off the road.

Ernest pointed out, as had not been done before, that the present war was being fought over an 800-mile front that ran the length of the country. Between the fortified towns that had withstood sieges since the Middle Ages, the front was a very fluid thing.

Towns had to be attacked obliquely, passed, encircled, infiltrated, and overrun before the front really shifted. And the men and armament on both sides were equal to the task only when concentrated, so wonderfully had the medieval defenses against enemies been organized.

In late September, Ernest, Herbert Matthews, and Martha Gellhorn made an adventurous trip through the northern mountains to study this "lost" front. They were the first American correspondents permitted to make a survey of conditions there. In preparation, they bought blankets and a sleeping bag, and carried what food they could. Using the truck as a base, they visited the higher positions in the mountains by horseback. They camped out and cooked for themselves while moving about in this rough terrain, and bought whatever bread and wine peasants could occasionally spare.

"Ernest and Martha were wonderful traveling companions," Herbert Matthews told me later. "She and I used to call him 'Scrooby.' By nightfall we had always found something to drink. But even while we were camping, Ernest enjoyed the soft luxury of pajamas, whenever he could."

That fall Ernest was a beaver. He polished off pieces for *Esquire*, advised on film footage, wrote some wonderful scenes for the play, *The Fifth Column*, and captured several hearts among the inhabitants of Madrid. The most perceptive, outgoing, and enraptured was that of Martha Gellhorn. They came to mean as much to each other as people could who were living daily with death in a heroic atmosphere and doing creative work in the fine arts.

Pauline somehow knew or sensed from Ernest's letters that the old relationship no longer existed. Ernest was still as strong a Catholic as she was, and Patrick and Gregory had been brought up in the tenets of that faith in no uncertain manner. Their marriage was subject to the stresses of this peculiar Spanish War, in which elements from many countries—Russia, Czechoslovakia, Hungary, Yugoslavia, Germany, Italy, and North Africa—were passionately taking part. By mid-1937 Spain was fairly divided into two parts. Each had much to be said for and against it. In America the liberal-minded readers and writers were overwhelmingly for

the Spanish Republic in its fight against Fascist elements backed
by Hitler, Mussolini, and Franco.

Pauline determined to fight for what she had, and hoped to hold.
Early in December she planned to go to Paris for Christmas, and
there have Ernest join her. The trip was a rough one, with December storms. But Pauline arrived with plenty of will power and a
determination to preserve their marriage.

Ernest had been so busy that he had not filed a cable dispatch
for more than two months. But on December 19, after observing
the Republican attack on Teruel for three days, he beat out a dispatch full of high hopes, describing the situation. By then the
Government troops had the city almost within their grasp, beating
off the winter weather as well as the enemy. While the outside
world awaited an offensive by General Franco, the Government
forces had taken the initiative and were making astonishing headway in zero weather with high winds and snow flurries on a plateau
of 4,000 feet elevation.

On December 23, Ernest graphically described the fall of Teruel,
freeing the Valencia-Barcelona road from possible severance and
providing Madrid with greater security than it had enjoyed in the
past. Together with Herbert Matthews, Ernest had worked his way
forward to where no noncombatants should have ever been, amid
high explosive bombardment that sounded like great forces tearing
huge bolts of silk as the shells ripped in fast and burst.

They had seen an easy-moving group of light foot-troops approach and then pass, so loaded with explosives it would have
given an insurance man the shakes. Quickly obtaining swift permission from an officer to follow them, Ernest, Matthews, and
Delmer tagged along behind the young dynamiters who were literally blowing their way into the city. The red flashes and black bil-
lows of their bombs and grenades were the only markers the writers
had as they reached the high ground and the shops and bars of
the city itself.

Soon after, Ernest made arrangements to fly out of Spain and
arrived in Paris in time for the Christmas celebration. After some
days of visiting and sight-seeing, he and Pauline returned to New

York, then back to Key West, leaving a trail of friends, acquaintances, business people, and sympathizers who knew the difficult time that was at hand.

Ernest had a great amount of work still to be completed and he had, in a sense, left a part of himself in Spain. He knew he had to go back. But he was unwilling to discuss it with anyone. He felt so strongly about it that he avoided all talk of future plans.

The winter weather would limit both sides to patrols and raids during the coming months, he realized. But he had vast and only partly matured projects under way in Spain. He was beginning to keep his own counsel at last, like a good general unable to trust, or unsure of the value of, his advisers. And like most such historical figures, he was making important gains without any debate whatsoever. He was reaching a new plateau.

While Ernest was in Spain in the fall of 1937, he had shown some sharp pangs of remorse, even recalling the look of his garden in Key West in a dispatch that described the devastation of shelling and the strange feeling that had come over him as he looked at a field of swaying blue flowers which had sprung up soon after high explosives and incendiaries had cleared the surface of all living things.

He had experienced tragedy at firsthand and vicariously through innumerable friendships. When he went to visit the home of his friend Luis Quintanilla, the great Spanish painter, he was appalled. Several members of Luis' family had survived. But the family house was a shell. All the fine paintings that had taken years to produce were destroyed. Shreds of them hung on the partial walls of several rooms. In one corner he saw several large leather bindings. He went over eagerly, thinking that at least some of the books were still intact. He touched one. And then another. They fell apart. A smoldering fire had reduced them to ashes.

Robert Capa had come to Spain via central Europe as a photographer. He went where Ernest went, drank what Ernest drank, made jokes that made Ernest laugh, and generally proved himself one hell of a fine fellow. And he had at last found *the* girl. Capa was in love. For that short, swarthy, independent, openhearted Voltaire with the Leica around his neck ever to fall in love seemed about as unlikely as for Al Capone to retire to a monastery.

When Capa did something, however, the world knew about it. His girl, Gerda, was a gentle, honey-colored creature who brought out the magnificent best in this Hungarian artist with the lens. To Roberto she was the most precious person in existence. On the way up to see a Republican attack, Capa's girl was standing on the running board of a correspondent's car which had stalled. Friendly armor was passing on the road where the car was stalled. Suddenly a Republican tank, misjudging distance by mere inches, sheared off the edge of the car, killing the girl instantly. Ernest took care of the melancholy details, and helped bring Capa through the shattering experience.

When a wave of arrests swept Valencia, Ernest found that his good friend, Professor Robles, had been picked up, tried in haste, and executed. John Dos Passos arrived soon afterward and searched for the man, fearing some harm might have come to him because of his views. It took days—and they were agonizing days—before Ernest could be absolutely certain of his information. Then he had to confront Dos with the news. The event and the delay in getting facts, and the enormity of the execution of a good and innocent man, was another of the gut-wrenching wounds that worked on Ernest. It disturbed him far more than the deaths of thousands of men he did not know on both sides of the conflict.

Ernest could smile at fat señoras breaking into a run for cover from the strafing planes. But his eyes showed the horror when he saw children lying dead. Ira Wolfert told me how Ernest choked up and said, "God, those small, white faces—like stepped-on flowers. They're so innocent and pure, and forever thrown away."

When telling me about it the following spring, Ernest also spoke of the funnier aspects of the war. He told me about meeting Hungarian General Lukacz of the 12th International Brigade for the first time. "He held a big banquet for me, Baron," Ernest laughed, "but I damned near choked trying to keep a straight face. The real honored guests were the prettiest girls in the village. He'd invited them too. That was the closest I ever came to being a solicitor."

And one night he went to see a Marlene Dietrich movie in Madrid. Just at the moment when Marlene was to be shot as a Mata Hari, a shell landed right outside. The whole building shook, but Ernest said the patrons kept their seats and roared with laughter at the perfect timing.

The early spring of 1938, Ernest worked intensely while he was in Key West, revising *The Fifth Column* and, thinking beyond it, he began to feel that there must be a great novel buried in the treachery, courage, and sacrifice that he had seen during recent months in Spain.

Fishing was still wonderful in Key West waters. But now Ernest's heart was not in it. He kept the *Pilar* in Key West, refusing to take the time and effort to go to either Bimini or Havana where not only bigger fish were to be found, but also the yachts and the owners of yachts who controlled some of America's greatest fortunes. In other years Ernest had shown them how to get a kick out of life through fishing and marine research. But in 1938, he didn't give a damn. He was preoccupied with doing everything he could to help the people of Republican Spain; he was concerned with the great need for help.

In March I visited Key West. Ernest seemed curiously relieved to have the chance to talk again. We had written and phoned each other, but we had also been out of contact occasionally because of time and distance. I had sent him clippings of some of the best stories I'd done for the Chicago paper, and he in turn sent me carbons of some of the articles he had been writing under pressure for other papers.

The fall before, our sister Sunny and I had jointly taken the responsibility of digging out family pictures and records for a research team *Time* magazine had sent out to Oak Park. They were preparing a cover story on Ernest and his latest book. Because we did not confer with Ernest, I knew we were wide open to his severe discipline. A truthful explanation of the way the *Time* team had gone about its work, the urgency, and our mutual decision finally to co-operate with *Time*, seemed the best action possible. Luckily Ernest was forgiving and realistic.

"Christ, Baron, you did the best you could. They had you, in the old journalistic way, with that 'We'll get it from the neighbors if you don't give.' Hell. I'm not sore. One of the pictures wasn't me, though. They probably have an entirely different staff doing picture captions. What about that book review?"

I explained that the Chicago paper, through its literary editor, had persuaded me to review *To Have and Have Not*. Ernest was disturbed and I couldn't understand why. "It was a good review," I pointed out, "nicely positioned, two-column box."

"Sure it was good. And it was honest," Ernest said. "But nobody would have expected it to be honest. Because it was you doing it, they would have figured you were partial. So don't ever get conned into reviewing another book of mine. You're a pro now. So feel it and act it for the rest of your life. A pro doesn't get sucked in. Give these guys an inch and they'll unprintable you right on Main Street at high noon. And for laughs, that kind of laughs you can get by scratching your butt when you come on stage."

Ernest pushed the horseradish-catsup sauce closer to me. "Have some more shrimp, kid. They're good with the beer." We ate the shrimp and drank the beer, feeling content in the warm sun of a clear spring day. Then Ernest went on, "A pro writes the stuff that will give himself a lift, and that expresses the truth as he knows it. Of course you have to avoid libel suits," he laughed. "But you've got to level with your audience or the readers won't respect you. If it's something you can't level on, you keep silent. It's either level or shut up, whether it's reporting or fiction. The greater the truth, the greater its value. There are damned few things you feel you need to keep silent about—maybe about what's bothering your mother, or your president, or your church. But let's face it. I've managed to level on every one of those, by word or by action. If it hadn't been me, it would have been somebody else. That old crap about Murder Will Out still goes for the Truth, understand? And it's a damned fine thing that it does. Any statement to the contrary is the old ballroom bananos."

In the next few days we talked a lot, went fishing once, went swimming often, and hoisted a number of tall glasses. Ernest was then drinking fifteen to seventeen Scotch-and-sodas over the course of a day. He was holding them remarkably well. Gustav Regler, a German writer, and his wife were staying as house guests before taking an apartment. Gustav had an awesome shrapnel wound in his back; you could put both your fists in it without filling the gap. He had been hit early in the Spanish War and was alive only because of superb surgical care.

Ernest was breaking in a new houseboy then and kept him on the run, bringing drinks for all comers. "It's good for him," he'd explain. "Got to learn to deliver in a hurry if he's going to last."

The houseboy, named Luis, was light, fast on his feet, and had excellent balance. "We'll see how he does with the gloves," Ernest said one afternoon. In a matter of moments we were struggling again with laces and, in swim trunks, Luis wearing a borrowed pair, we were all set. Luis' dexterity with his long arms and his nimble footwork won Ernest's admiration. "Look at him hit, Baron. That kid's job is safe with me as long as he can feint like that."

Young Gregory and Patrick were taking life in stride. One evening just at dusk, the cocktail party around the pool was breaking up to move into the house. There had been a lot of kidding with the boys about werewolves. The sunset colors hadn't yet faded but darkness was moving in swiftly. Gregory's sneakers had been tossed into the pool during some horseplay about an hour earlier. Ernest had suggested the confident seven-year-old get them out right after they had splashed and sunk. As the group walked up to the porch, Ernest checked on the retrieve and found it hadn't been made. He reissued the order.

Gigi glanced back at the pool in the darkening shadows. "I'll get them first thing in the morning, Papa."

"Patrick," Ernest called, "bring me the werewolf-attractor oil."

"Never mind, Papa. I'm getting the sneakers now," Gigi said and trotted back. We heard a loud splash and, before everyone was seated on the porch, Gigi returned, dripping but displaying the soggy shoes.

One morning a friend of the family, who had been asked to take young Patrick on an errand, went out to the garage to start the Ford roadster for the trip. Patrick squirmed as the starter was pressed and dutifully rotated the engine without kicking off. When the family friend finally gave it a rest, Patrick had some sage advice:

"Why not hit the side with your hand and call it a dirty yellow basket? That always helps when Papa tries to start it in the morning."

That was the way it went, but it abruptly ended one morning with a long-distance phone call. Ernest took it in the front hall, then shouted for a pencil and paper. I rushed them to him.

"They've started a drive, you say? This may be the drive to the sea. It would cut off all the rest of the country if they seal the border. Sure I'll go again. There's a plane out of here this afternoon. No, I'll see you when I get up there. Goodbye."

Pauline was very quiet. Then she said, "What do you want me to do to help?"

"Pack my cold clothes, and warm clothes too. Poor Old Mama." Ernest's look of angry eagerness changed to one of hurt. "Oh damn! Things were going so well, I should have known it would bust wide open." Then the hurt look was gone and he brushed past Pauline, still talking to her. "It'll be mountain fighting and I'll need cold clothes for that, but the summer's coming on. I don't want to get my damned throat in an uproar, not with the price of Scotch at that many pesetas per gargle. The spring thaw has got everybody ready to end the war in a month. . . . Come out here, Baron, I want to talk with you."

We went out back and had a quick one out of the bottle without dirtying any glasses. "Listen," he said, "I can get you a captaincy in the Lincoln Brigade if you want to come. It might straighten a lot of things out for you and at least you'll learn a hell of a lot. This war's got to wind up, because the big one is coming fast. How about it?"

I explained that I couldn't go because of finances: I had a wife and young son to think about. I don't mind admitting that I was strongly tempted.

"Come on out to the airport then and see me off. And look, you guys stay down here as long as you can and keep Poor Old Mama feeling good." He went to phone Arnold Gingrich then. Ernest was very excited about getting going. A couple of hours later when the plane took off for Miami, Ernest's bags had been packed with all the spare clothes he would need, and the public send-off was a cheerful one.

Pauline was feeling miserable. It was a relief to everyone when Jay Allen's wife and son came down for a visit. Allen was in Spain as a correspondent for the *Chicago Tribune* before the war began and was still there when it started. They did a lot for Pauline's morale.

Ernest's third European trip during the Spanish War was a crucial one. He was in a hurry to reach the territory he'd left only three months earlier. He knew how much might have happened in that time.

Ernest did not need to renew his contract with the news syndicate. His credentials and passport were still in order. Finding that more news coverage was wanted, he crossed the Atlantic by boat and flew into Republican Spain by the now-familiar route, stopping at Barcelona. There he filed his first dispatch of the new series, April 3, after the breakthrough at Gandesa. He described the refugees going through on the roads under airplane strafing, though pink almond blossoms covered the sunlit hills nearby.

Ernest then concentrated on the experiences of American members of the Lincoln-Washington Battalion which had been surrounded on a hilltop outside Gandesa. The Americans in their flight had moved with extreme caution. Their objective was to swim the Ebro River to safety, and a chance to fight again. They had made their way through the Fascist lines at night. Some literally stepped on the hands of Fascist troops resting in the pitch blackness.

Working his way up the Ebro valley to check on whether or not Tortosa had been taken at the end of the first week in April, Ernest found the town badly bombed but with its bridges and roads intact. The Franco forces were making very slow headway in their drive to the sea, and Government morale was excellent. Later that week he personally checked the entire front between the Mediterranean and the Pyrenees, and found that the great danger of a successful Fascist drive was in the north. There the mountains gave the Government troops such a feeling of security they were not fighting as hard as they could. Ernest was scornful of the Italian infantry; they were brought up to a new area, he said, only after it had been thoroughly pounded and overrun by armored units. This procedure was taking the time that the Navarrese and Moors never needed.

At Tortosa on April 15, Ernest witnessed the Fascist bombing of the Barcelona-Valencia road by scores of planes. The city disappeared in a haze of yellow dust. When they could see it again, he and his friends managed to get through on an emergency bridge. He reported feeling like a mountaineer exploring craters on the moon.

Down at the Ebro delta, the new spring crop of frogs filled the ditches. There Ernest picked and munched on wild onions while he watched preparations for the coming battle as the Fascist forces pressed their way to the sea.

Ernest interviewed James Lardner, the twenty-three-year-old correspondent of the *New York Herald Tribune* in Barcelona that spring. James, one of the sons of the late Ring Lardner, had just enlisted in the International Brigade. He felt that there were enough newspapermen in Spain, but that the Loyalist side needed all the artillerymen it could get. Several months later James was killed.

Entering Lérida on foot while the old city was one-third occupied by Fascist forces, Ernest described his feelings, and those of others who moved about while covered by enemy machine guns. The town's importance lay in its control of roads leading into Catalonia, and the Loyalist troops holding the major part of it were fighting defensively. They hoped that rains would raise the Segre River level and make the city more secure against armored attack.

A week later Ernest visited Castellón to the southward and saw the wonderful underground defense made by the city dwellers

against air attack from Italian bombers. Four hundred big bombs
dropped the day before his visit had killed only three people. He
went to Alicante and Valencia again and was astonished at the
amount of good food still available and selling for the equivalent
of thirty cents a meal. Shipping from all over the world still
crowded these seaports.

In Madrid on May 10, Ernest filed his final news dispatch of
the war. He was very pleased to see his old friends in the capital,
and to note the excellent defensive positions that had been developed during the months of stalemate on this front. The morale
of Loyalist troops, officers, sappers, and civilians was still excellent.
They seemed honestly more content to be fighting their own separate war than to be lumped with the defenders of other regional
cities. The food situation was critical, and had been for some
time. But there was plenty of ammunition to withstand a further
siege. Though diplomats at that time were certain the war would
end in a month or so, Ernest felt that it might well go on for
another year. History proved that his estimate was accurate.

Before flying out of Spain again, Ernest first went through all
his things and destroyed many of his papers, personal and professional.

"I'd gathered so much information, some of it very hard to get,
that I'd have been a prize catch if our plane had been forced
down on the Rebel side," he told me later. "It hurt like the devil
to destroy my own notes."

Once out of the country, Ernest and Martha, who had again
met in Spain, headed for Paris and a few days of fun before
sailing to New York to face the realities of civilian existence all
over again. In Paris one day they were introduced to a young man
named Tom Bennett who had just made his way out of Republican Spain after being thrice wounded a year earlier. Bennett
was a former Federal employee who had gone to Spain on his
own to see what he could do, and had joined the Lincoln Battalion early in the war. He had been to Europe before, had met
Somerset Maugham, and had been hoping, for almost ten years,
to meet Ernest. He said it had smacked him harder than the bullets when he was taken to the hospital and another patient said,

"You should have been here yesterday. Ernest Hemingway was here."

When they finally met in Brentano's bookstore in Paris, Ernest said, "Listen, kid, you need to get home and get those legs tended to. You broke?"

Tom, dressed in an ill-fitting uniform, nodded.

"Here. Go to the shop around the corner and get some clothes." Ernest handed him money. "And meet me here at three in the afternoon, day after tomorrow. You're going home with us. Got a place to stay until then?"

Tom said that he felt warm inside for the first time in months. Two days later, he came early, waited half an hour, and was beginning to sweat when Ernest and Martha walked in. Ernest beckoned. "The cab's waiting. Get your gear. You can stand going tourist class? Good. You can come up to our cabins every day."

The trip home, Tom remembers, was a happy blur. There was the kind of drinking anyone would have wanted after seeing and learning about that particular war. But as the *Normandie* neared New York, Ernest became more preoccupied, then gloomy. By the time the ship docked, Ernest was keeping to himself, truculent, and his statements to reporters were subdued. He made no predictions and excused himself as quickly as possible.

Ernest headed directly for Key West, tired from the tension more than from the activity. He knew he had some good stories and that the sooner he wrote them the better he would feel. But this reasoning didn't work out. Ernest was moody and torn by conflicting feelings. Pauline was so glad to have him back safely that for a time it seemed they would be able to work everything out smoothly again.

Ernest was thoroughly involved with getting *The Fifth Column* produced. He ran into one difficulty after another. Instead of easing out to the Bahamas or cutting over to Havana, where he often found it possible to relax and increase production, he stayed in Key West through June and July so as to be able to communicate easily with people in New York. At the end of July he drove with Pauline, Patrick, and Gregory out to Cooke City, Montana, where he could find friendly ranch life and a complete change of scene. But a month there was enough to clarify his feelings. By the end of August he was heading back to Europe again on the *Normandie*. He was determined to return to Spain.

In a letter that summer, he told me how my boat was; and how one play producer had died after he had already signed a contract and how another one had developed money troubles. He said he had completed some new stories but was going to go over them again before sending them off for publication.

I had sent him some work I had done in Michigan and had asked his advice. Ernest very kindly said that because we were brothers he was not honestly the right person to judge my stuff. While he had enjoyed reading it, he felt it was a kind of five-finger exercise with too much reporting and not enough creating. He suggested that on the next one I should really invent as well as remember and that inventing was probably what had me stalled. This sure sounded easy, he admitted, but I was to stick with it. And he enclosed a hundred dollars and wished me great luck. To me the advice was much more valuable than money.

The fourth time Ernest went over, he stayed for a time in Paris, working. Ever since his second trip he had been thinking out a big book, a novel that he sensed and wanted to know all about before he began to write it. When I asked him about it two years later in Havana, he had most of the book done and didn't mind talking about it. He knew then what a gut-wrencher he had let flow from his mind. His research had taken him into little-known parts of Spain, and out to Montana again, to get the feeling of the place from where a sympathetic, idealistic young man might come. Now he had it and was studying, learning, and listening for other characters and scenes. His taste was as great as his creative talent. Taste kept the talent from being wasted on unworthy projects.

When he did get back to Spain, still with credentials and able to fulfill magazine commitments, the war was definitely going against the Republican side. Ernest missed the most exciting part of the battle of the Ebro in the humid August heat, but he was there when it came to an end. The Ebro front was the last hope of the Republican cause. It temporarily worried the Fascists, but when it began to cave in it took the Republican hopes with it. By October, Negrin, Premier of the Spanish Republic, was convinced that all available troops could not stem the flow of Fascist invaders.

In mid-November, Ernest and Herbert Matthews were with Vincent Sheean on the west bank of the Ebro, just before that front collapsed. The air held an autumn mist that obscured details and at one point Sheean asked a stranger where the front lay; "wasn't it right over there?"

"Holy unprintable," Ernest said, "Jimmy, your sense of direction is missing. There are the lines back there." The party proceeded successfully. A few days later they were among the last to recross the Ebro as the Fascist advance continued. Ernest saw the war drawing to an end, and left Spain for the last time without filing further news dispatches. The news syndicate felt there was little interest being shown by readers in America.

Chapter 10

Ernest was carrying a heavy load of misery when he returned to Key West. He was having difficulty with his own personal code of ethics. He had finally decided that he needed to make a clean break with Pauline, and with the Catholic Church. Neither move would be an easy one. As Ernest once said, "Once you've really loved someone, you never stop . . . completely."

It did not ease his problems when our mother came down to Key West for a visit. She was on a self-appointed good-will mission. Ernest knew it and would have nothing to do with it. He got her a suite at the Casa Marina Hotel, had her come over to the house frequently, and kept his own counsel. He knew the spot any son is in when explaining to a parent that his previous wisdom has been open to criticism. And he had taken enough censure during the time of his first divorce to avoid all future encounters. In between spells of watching worriedly and saying little, Mother busied herself with her paints and easel, producing some fine, realistic seascapes.

After Mother left, Ernest took the *Pilar* to Havana and began writing *For Whom the Bell Tolls*. He got the same room on the fourth-floor northeast corner from Manolo Asper, owner of the Hotel Ambos Mundos. Starting at first light, he worked to midday whenever possible.

Late in May, after several months of concentrated work, Ernest wrote Mother from Havana to explain the headaches he had been through while trying to locate a clipping he had mentioned to her during her visit. It related to an ancestor, William Edward Miller, who had written a great many of the hymns in the Episcopal Hymnal, and of course Mother, with her intense love of music and fascination with family genealogy, was eager to see it. It had been sent to him in Spain a year and a half earlier by the editor of a British paper in—he thought he had finally remembered the name of the town—Doncaster. Ernest assured Mother that he would wire me in New York, where I was working on *Country Home* magazine, so that I could look up the name of the paper, just as soon as he could be sure it was Doncaster he had heard from. The clipping had reached him in Madrid just before the battle of Teruel, and he had been too busy at the moment to reply. Then he had destroyed everything before flying out of the country. Ernest added that he was working well, was on page 212 of a new novel, and that Pauline and the children were fine too. They had gone to New York that spring because infantile paralysis had broken out in Key West. Pauline took an apartment on the upper East Side where Gigi and Patrick enjoyed shooting at pigeons on nearby roof tops with an air rifle.

Martha came down to Havana and Ernest continued to work well on the book. During her visit, the two located a fine, high piece of land six miles east of the city, just back of Cojimar where there had once been an ancient watchtower, or vigía. A sprawling, one-story house was in one corner. The place had an air about it and a marvelous view. They bought the nineteen acres, kept the old name of Finca La Vigía, and proceeded to refurbish the entire grounds.

The summer of 1939 Ernest's predictions on the coming big war came true. He read all the dispatches as they were released. And he kept working in the face of continuous distractions, ranging from guests to political problems. That winter Martha went to Finland to do some magazine pieces for *Collier's* on the Russo-Finnish War.

In December, *Country Home* magazine discontinued publication. I headed south to Key West for a month's cruising. There I met a young Englishman, Tony Jenkinson, whom Ernest had told about me the week before. Tony had a title, a bank account, and a naval intelligence assignment. He needed someone who liked sailing, could navigate, and wanted to do something adventurous. Two months later we had a second boat which we had taken to Havana and we were in business, sniffing out possible and actual refueling depots for Nazi submarines in the western Caribbean.

We outfitted with final stores in Havana. There, Ernest was his most considerate self. We had many dinners together. He and Martha came out on the schooner with us. And Ernest lent us Gregorio, his captain, to check rigging replacements. We went to Comparsas with Allen Grover, of *Time* magazine, and his wife. And we were there when Ernest played host to Charles Scribner, his publisher. For this occasion he got a haircut, wore a necktie, and ordered the champagne iced in advance. Ernest was very ingenuous about the responsibilities of a writer to his publisher. "Mind you, I wouldn't give an unprintable for all the others, but Charlie is the exception," he explained. And he ordered me to get a haircut too.

Ernest knew all the Basque pelota players. Champions like Guillermo, Piston, and the Ibarluccea brothers would come out to the house afternoons and play tennis with calculated, deadly accurate strokes. By watching them play, Ernest knew which of them was in top form. Then if he could not come down himself, he would send Tony and me notes saying which to bet on at that night's jai-alai game. We won good, useful money, night after night, based on Ernest's personal form sheets. Ernest himself was too tired after dinner to do more than go to bed. He had to be up early the next day feeling out the paragraphs that would make readers of *For Whom the Bell Tolls* cry.

"'Watch their arms,'" he'd say when we played tennis against these champions. "You can't see their eyes. But if you watch you can see whether their arms are behind or on time in stroking. You can expect the ball either where it will be returnable, or where you couldn't make it by tomorrow afternoon even if you were on the Australian Davis Cup team." We'd play until we were all streaming with sweat and then we'd cool off with showers and wonderful drinks by the poolside. Martha would join us in the drinks and swimming. When she surfaced from the clear water, laughing and reaching for her drink, Ernest would grin, "That's my mermaid. What a woman that one is."

Martha was enchanting. She told me wondrous things about Finland, about the fighting she had seen in the miserable weather, and she showed me the hunting knives that had been given her. Her mother came down to visit. A generation older she too had charm. Martha had real brains, beauty, and the body of a Circe. I was delighted that she was about to become my favorite third sister-in-law, though I gave full honors to the first two.

About Spain, Ernest had become evasive though still intense. "So damned much went on there, Baron, it will take years to get it out. I wish you could have come, though your luck might have run out, like it did for Lardner's kid and for so many other young guys. You're shrewder now, but don't forget, you need luck. And you need a feeling of unease at what you're going to be doing. Whenever that feeling grows, take evasive action. I'll give you a good Mauser pistol with a shoulder stock and plenty of ammo, in case anyone catches up with you. I'll lend you my Winchester pump gun too. But get it back to me or don't bother to come back yourself, understand? Learn how to use the Mauser and you can clean the deck of a submarine with one clip. But keep the extra clip loaded at all times. It fires just like your Colt Woodsman. I took it off one of the Republic's battle police before the war ended. It's in perfect shape."

Five months later, when I came through Havana on my way back to the United States, I had left the boat in Panama. Ernest was very proud of my navigation, but he was disappointed that Tony and I had not had more violent contact with the enemy. We had been in touch. However, the showdowns had been

Ernest with a large rainbow trout and a small brother; the trout weighed 8 pounds 5 ounces.

Ernest with pack and trout rod ready to leave for a few days on foot in northern Michigan.

Ernest in Italy, wearing Bersaglieri helmet and equipment.

The young lieutenant walking with a cane after being wounded.

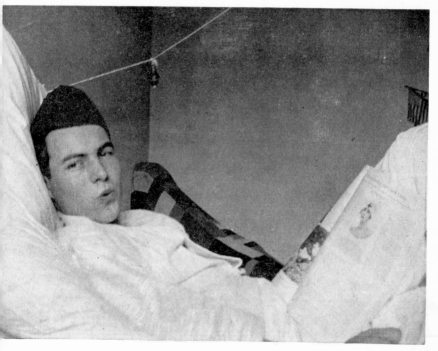

Ernest whistled whenever in pain. Here he is in the base hospital in Milan, after being wounded, July 1918.

Nurse Agnes von Kurowsky in Italy, 1918.

"Aggie" and Lieutenant Hemingway outside an Italian hospital, 1918.

Ernest taking an airing in Milan before returning to America, October 1918.

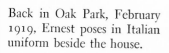

Back in Oak Park, February 1919, Ernest poses in Italian uniform beside the house.

Ernest with some fine trout and a corncob pipe after a fishing trip, 1920.

Bride and groom at Horton's Bay, Michigan, September 1921: Hadley Richardson and Ernest.

Family group in Oak Park after Ernest's first marriage: Father, Leicester, Madelaine, Hadley, Ernest, Mother, Carol, and Marcelline.

Hadley and Bumby in Paris, spring 1924.

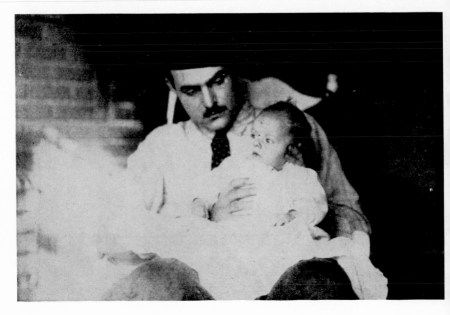

Ernest holding his first son, John Hadley Nicanor Hemingway, Paris, 1924.

Kid brother and big brother: Leicester and Ernest, Christmas visit, 1923.

Mother and Dad when visiting Ernest and Pauline Pfeiffer in
Key West, spring 1928.

Gregory and Patrick Hemingway
n a Key West garden, 1932.

Ernest resting beside large elkhorn trophies after a hunt in Montana, 1932.

A good sailfish caught aboard Captain Josey Russell's *Anita;*
Ernest lifts the dorsal fin.

Pauline and Ernest aboard the *Anita* with a large sailfish taken
off the Cuban coast, 1933.

Ernest and Pauline hold up the huge wings of a greater bustard shot
while on safari, 1933.

Charles Thompson and Ernest with fine pair of oryx trophies on the Serengetti plain, 1934.

A gun bearer displays eight feet of snake, Tanganyika, 1934.

Michael Lerner, Ernest, and Hedley Doty on the dock at Bimini, 1937.

Mike and Ernest shooting sharks in Bimini harbor one windy day, 1937; Mr. Cooke observes from the rear.

Ernest and Martha Gellhorn at Sun Valley lodge, 1940.
Photo by Robert Capa—Magnum.

Ernest and son Gregory, age nine, resting during a duck shoot in
Idaho, 1940. Photo by Robert Capa—Magnum.

Ernest and Taylor Williams after a morning with the ducks near
Sun Valley, 1940. Photo by Robert Capa—Magnum.

Ernest and Martha aboard schooner in Havana harbor, 1940, while working on *For Whom the Bell Tolls*. Photo by Leicester Hemingway.

Ernest and Mary Welsh on the flying bridge of the *Pilar* after World War II. Photo by George Leavens—Photo Researchers.

avoided, in the interests of continued espionage. But that's another story.

Ernest had some legal problems with our mother at that point. He wrote her about the proper procedure, and he thanked her for her wish that the coming book might have something constructive in it. He did this with a straight face. Then he gave me some papers to take back to Florida to have executed before authorities and assured me he would execute the rest at the Consulate. We went out drinking and fishing and hangovering just for the wonderful release that came of his winding up new projects. For Ernest was at last finishing *For Whom the Bell Tolls*. He told me he had worked on it steadily for fifteen unprintable months. "It's a ballwracker, Baron. An honest-to-Christ-ballwracker."

We took Ralph Ingersoll, a former publisher of *Fortune*, out fishing before leaving for the United States. The fishing was less than great. We picked up fine tuna after we came out of Havana harbor, and very little else in a half day's trolling. The boat felt good again. Ernest was full of talk, expansive thoughts and gestures—his old free-flowing self. Ingersoll had come down to talk about a new paper he wanted to start in New York. Ernest was for it and full of ideas.

A few weeks later all three of us were in New York. By then I was working for *PM*, the newly formed paper. Ralph Ingersoll was daily visiting Ernest in the Barclay Hotel, where headquarters had been established while various business arrangements were completed.

Within a few months the situation had changed completely. Ernest and Ralph were no longer confiding in each other. I was no longer on the paper. But I left with my Caribbean information intact and was able shortly thereafter to use it for a series of syndicated newspaper articles and for the *Reader's Digest*.

Early in November 1940, Ernest's divorce from Pauline became final. Pauline was as gracious and considerate as any human being could be. She wrote a wonderful letter to Mother saying that she was certain the news had been a blow to her, as it had been to Pauline's own parents, and that she was sorry. But she said Mother would always be a mother to her. She was convinced that under

the circumstances it had been the best thing to do for all concerned, and that she was glad it was over. The heart of another,
she said, was a dark forest, and she then observed that people
could only do what they could and "really considering what they
have to contend with in this world, it is amazing that they do as
well as they do." She urged Mother to come down again to see
her and her sons, Patrick and Gregory, and to visit me and my
wife and sons, Jake and Peter, who were also in Key West. She
reported everyone strong and healthy and said I was writing well.
The letter expressed the kind of feeling which Ernest had long
searched for in others.

Two weeks after the divorce Ernest and Martha were married
by a justice of the peace in Cheyenne, Wyoming.

While vacationing at Sun Valley that fall, Ernest and Martha
had completed the sale of film rights for *For Whom the Bell Tolls*.
It went to Paramount for $150,000, then a record sum. The sale
was made possible by Donald Friede, who had been an editor at
Boni and Liveright back in the twenties and was then head of the
story department for the Myron Selznick agency in Hollywood.
He had personally helped get Ernest's first book published in the
United States. At that time Donald had done his best to help Ernest, but had been overruled by Horace Liveright. Ernest assured
Donald later in Paris that he would make it up to him. Donald
devised a plan to sell the book's film rights for a higher price than
Maurice Speiser, Ernest's lawyer and acting agent, thought could
be gotten for it. He also devised the clause whereby the film company agreed to pay Ernest a certain bonus sum for every hard-cover
copy of the book sold. After a wonderful day of drinking and reading, Ernest and Martha let Friede phone Speiser, who then approved the idea. Friede's successful formula netted everyone money
and pleased Ernest enormously. In New York, later, he showed
friends the check which he carried around for several days just
enjoying the thrill of having it in his billfold.

Ernest wanted Ingrid Bergman to play Maria and Gary Cooper
to play Robert Jordan in the film. Ingrid at that time was under
contract to Myron Selznick's brother David, and when Ernest

heard this he was delighted. He knew Coop would do everything possible to arrange his own freedom for the role. They were friends who had shot many birds together, and for years Ernest had been an admirer of Cooper's acting style.

In the spring of 1941, Ernest and Martha flew to San Francisco and from there to Honolulu, Midway, Wake, Guam, Manila, Hong Kong, and Singapore. They also went inland to see what had happened to China since the fighting had forced the relocation of the government's headquarters. As guests of Generalissimo and Madame Chiang Kai-shek, they moved about within the permissible areas, and floated down the Yangtze River like a pair of Connecticut Yankees in a Mandarin's Court. Ernest enjoyed the situation enormously.

Covering the British defenses in the Far East, as well as the American preparations for a defensive war, Ernest filed a series of dispatches to *PM*. He talked with British military officers, coolies, the members of exclusive clubs, and foreign adventurers, trying to bring into focus their assessments of things to come. In this, he was both lucky and astute. He predicted the war would come during the following six months and that the attack would come from Japan, against British and American bases throughout the Pacific and southeast Asia.

Heading home across the United States, Ernest was very tired. Absently, he fished a flask out of his pocket and had a few sips of what he told me later was Chinese vodka. Noting this, the stewardess asked the plane's captain to come back with her, possibly to quiet a disorderly person.

The captain approached and looked down at Ernest.

"Why, you old son of a medicine man. It's Ernie himself."

"Hi, kid. Weren't you ferrying big ones for Bernt Balchen?"

"Sure, but he's on something else now. Where you in from?"

"Kunming."

"Listen, wouldn't you like to come visit up front? Come on. It isn't every year we get a passenger like you."

"No thanks, kid. I'll just nap here."

"Okay, but we'd be honored. And for your information, Miss

So-and-so, this is how you tell a tired traveler from a rummy. The tired traveler, sometimes world famous, generally carries a dented flask. And Ernie, if you'd like any mix to drink that with, Miss So-and-so will be glad to get it for you."

By July, Ernest and Martha were back in Havana. Joe Russell came over from Key West for an operation. He was in good shape during the surgery. Ernest saw him safely out of the anesthesia and expected him to make a rapid recovery. But the second day, Josey suddenly hemorrhaged. Before transfusions could be given, he died.

Ernest wrote me about it. Josey's death had hit him very hard. Then Ernest gave me a long piece of advice on working for intelligence, telling me who had said what in Washington and what I was to do about it. He was full of admonitions, warning me about certain people, telling me in whom I could have complete faith. He said that when we had a chance to talk again, he would teach me plenty.

After the United States entered the war, Ernest and I continued for more than a year writing through the censorship between this country and Cuba. I was in radio intelligence stationed in Washington for two years before I was finally sent overseas. Ernest wrote Mother that I would probably come back from England with an accent that could be ladled with a soupspoon. That's the only one of his predictions I know of that turned out completely wrong, but it was merely a remark to cheer our mother.

Ernest also said that the last news of himself he had seen in the press was that he had just been spotted riding around in a Chinese junk somewhere in the Yellow Sea. And he said he was terribly afraid Richard Halliburton had been mistaken for him. Answering Mother's birthday congratulations, he said he had not supposed he would ever reach the age of 44. He wanted to give Mother plenty of credit for having started this whole thing, but said if she had any suggestions for how he could get through the next 44 years, he wished she would send them along.

Two years passed before we had a chance to see each other again. I was in England in the spring of 1943, a year before Ernest arrived, but Martha got there as a war correspondent for *Collier's* about six months after I did. I wangled out of the soft job doing radio intelligence work at the Embassy, and into an army uniform as a member of a documentary film unit. Martha loaned me twenty pounds before she headed back over to the Mediterranean front in the spring of 1944. Soon after, Ernest came bounding into town. He had been made chief of *Collier's* European Bureau, a real tribute to Joe Knapp's fair and forgiving nature after the fight they had had in Bimini years earlier. As *Collier's* chief of correspondents, Ernest would approve expense accounts, including Martha's.

There was a lot of catching up to do when Ernest finally arrived in London, six weeks before the invasion of Normandy. He sounded mighty cheerful when I called him at the Dorchester Hotel just after he had checked in. "Come on over, Baron, soon as you can. I'll meet you down at the bar in ten minutes."

I reached the small bar downstairs in his hotel in seven minutes flat and was just ordering a beer when Ernest walked up, resplendent in a full beard and his correspondent's uniform. "Ho, Stein, you're looking good," I said.

"You too, kid," he grinned and punched me on the shoulder lightly. He was effusive. "Those bucket seats on the Lancaster bomber were for the birds, but we beat them here, the birds, I mean. The ones we saw over Newfoundland and Ireland. Damn. Have you ever seen such a green island as Ireland from the air? I flew over with the RAF and those citizens really knew the course. Beats standing in line for a priority on the civilian airlines. Here—what are you drinking?" He saw the beer being poured. "Bartender, save that beer. Another time it may save a life. But right now, us brothers are going to have a few mouthfuls of Scotland's most noted product. Baron, don't you agree?"

"I'm backing you, Stein. How long's it been since the Floridita?"

"Too long," he said. "And hell's own number of things later."

We got our whiskies, touched glasses in a silent toast, and drank. Then Ernest went on in a quieter, calm voice. "Got something to show you. Promise not to tell anyone? *Anyone*, you understand?"

I nodded. Ernest took another swallow, unbuttoned his tunic enough to reach into a shirt pocket, and handed me a well-used envelope. I opened it and suddenly knew how good a man can feel about a job that is over, when it has been using all his nervous tension for a long time.

It was quiet there in the small bar of the Dorchester. Most people were upstairs dressing for the evening. Ernest finished his drink and had another as I read down the black sheet with the small white letters. It was a photostat of a letter on a Department of State letterhead. Beyond "The United States of America," I read the name of the Embassy, the salutation, and the involved, two-paragraph statement by Spruille Braden, the Ambassador to Cuba who was the personal representative of the President.

In summary, it stated that the bearer, Ernest Hemingway, had, over a lengthy period of time, performed hazardous and valuable operations in the prosecution of the sea war against Nazi Germany that were of a highly confidential nature. The undersigned was highly cognizant of the value of these . . . and grateful for the manner in which they had been performed.

"Jeeeeeezus, man, you've done it again."

"Listen, Baron," Ernest began, "it wasn't the time, or the danger. That was the best part, truly. But those unprintable underlings had me feeling my temper a couple of times."

"What was the first time?" I'd been a straight man for years, but never a more eager one than at that moment.

"When they made me sign that memo receipt. It was for thirty-two thousand dollars and it covered only the radio equipment. We had good stuff to listen with, stuff so sensitive you could get bearings if you could keep the boat from swinging. We even heard weak signals from out in the Atlantic."

"Who was the crew? What equipment did you have?"

"That was the best part. I worked it out like you and Tony did. The most everybody could handle and we stowed it so it wouldn't show. During most of the time we had a full crew—nine, counting me. You wouldn't have known her. The *Pilar* has new engines now. We had the best crew we could get. Mr. Gigi and Patrick the mouse. And Gregorio. But he's got six kids. I used to have those three stay ashore while we were operating out of a definite spot like Cay Sal and Cayo Confites—remember your old hangout? We had Patche and another pelota player, a sergeant in the marine guard at the Embassy, and some local boys. They were pros from the very start. Some Cuban boats had been sunk damned close, you know."

I knew. I reminded him about the Colombians and the schooners that had been machine-gunned, with survivors getting back weeks later. They were people we knew.

"That's what we hoped for, having one come alongside like that."

"Would you have been able to get them?"

"Nobody knows for sure. That was bad luck. But you should have seen what we carried, and our defenses. One of the local boys came to me and said, 'Papa, I don't feel good without some armor for the boat. Why not carry armor? Then if the Germans shoot straight at us when we close in, we won't be full of holes. I can't sleep good just thinking we ought to have some armor.' So then I found some steel plate. We had one section that would have stopped or deflected anything but a five-inch deck gun, and maybe that. It was so damned heavy when it was stowed, we ran trimmed down by the head. She didn't respond well and felt logy. Plenty of our value was being lost in weight. We had to be maneuverable. But I carried the armor anyway. The kid had been talking for the whole crew, I figured. Finally the boy came to me. 'Papa, I don't sleep so well knowing we are heavy in the water forward.' So we took off the armor and she was a real boat again."

"What kind of damage could you do?" New drinks were in our hands.

"Plenty. Besides small arms, we had machine guns, bazookas, and something big to put the chill on a Kraut conning tower. We had a bomb with a short fuse and handles. We kept it topside, below the canvas spray shield, unlashed and ready to fling. The idea was to keep nosing around where we heard them talking. Eventually one would surface and order us alongside. Then Patche and his pal would arm the bomb, grab the handles, and, as we came abreast of the sub's conning tower, we figured to clean her decks with our guns while the pelota players flung the bomb over the lip of the conning tower. It would either blast the watertight hatch off or go down the hatch and explode in the periscope control area. Either way we'd then have a live one that couldn't dive. You know . . . all her code books, armament, and the crew as prisoners for intelligence to use against the rest of the Kraut fleet everywhere."

"But no contact?"

"None close in. We came awfully near though. We could hear them talking out by Cay Sal and both east and west of the city, down the coast. I found myself remembering plenty of Kraut and they used slang even, talking with each other. The one we located for certain was bombed by a plane the day after we were called in. The pilot said he was certain that he got it, but it didn't satisfy the *Pilar*'s crew. We got whistled in like dogs that had found game but couldn't stay to see it bagged."

"How long were you at it? Didn't Marty yelp?"

Ernest considered that a moment. "She was busy being a female correspondent. Here. One time we were out for ninety days straight, with me making trips into Nuevitas by lancha for supplies. Hey, your old boat is still running down there. I saw her. Another time we were out a hundred and three days. That's how I got this unprintable skin cancer crut. Too much sunburn on same places. Doctor advised skipping the shave for several weeks. By then, had beard. I like it, so make cracks at your peril. Let's have another drink."

The situation had me entranced but I knew he'd pulled the shutters temporarily. We talked about what our kids were doing, when we'd seen them last, and where they were. Then we checked through members of the family and their health, had another Scotch, and began naming friends and their activities. Finally I sensed he was ready to go back to the original subject.

"What would you have done if you were captured?" I asked.

"That was a delicate point. I'd considered it carefully," he said,

"And finally we drafted a letter of marque, like in the old days. It's back there in the house now. Stated vessel's crew were of various nationalities, but acting in the national interest on authorized basis. That way we hoped to have some status and not be executed should luck swing against us. Because luck swings both ways."

Before we parted, Ernest got my promise to come to the hotel the next day as soon as I was free. He had to see some people in the morning, but there would be many errands and I could help. We'd take a walk, he said. He wanted to get the layout of the city. I was surprised to learn that he had never been to England before.

The next afternoon Ernest was his old self, stimulating and full of energy. "Big morning, checking damned documents and thinking out coverage with Bill Courtney and Joe Deering," he said. "Dammit, I wish Marty would show up. She's somewhere in Italy. I sent a radio message yesterday. No answer. C'mon, kid. Let's walk. You can show me where things are, without making it a Cook's tour."

We headed down the edge of Hyde Park, then past the Palace down Pall Mall and over to Piccadilly Circus and then Bond Street, talking all the way. "Damn," he would say admiringly, from time to time. "This is a rich country. Look at that, Baron. Even after the big bombing raids, these buildings stand up well. And the clubs and homes. Such quiet taste. The dough they have, they know enough not to show. I even like the stores. Let's walk around by Hardy's. I want to see the place I've been buying fishing tackle from for all these years."

We walked all afternoon. When we got back to the hotel there was a message from Capa, and Ernest was off for the evening.

I saw Capa the next day. "Papa's got troubles," he grinned. "That bloody beard scares off all the girls."

"I've got an idea," I said, remembering the old Chicago days. "Introduce him to Mary Welsh. I saw her the other day talking to Bill Walton. He'll know where she can be reached."

"Ha," Robert laughed, "I can reach anybody."

In a couple of days, Ernest was feeling personally admired again, and life was very pleasant around him.

"Come to our house. It's a party for Papa tonight," Capa said a few days after Ernest's arrival. It was a time of great uncertainty. Only general officers knew how close D-Day was, and one of them had already been sent back to the States for talking too loud. London was a beehive with all the frantic, often aimless activity. There were always parties by correspondents or officers and the most popular party game seemed to be the making of fascinating, guarded hints to pretty girls. Everyone knew something about everyone else. For journalism is a fairly limited, crafty occupation. Those who had survived a few years of it were seasoned observers, versed in sources, indications, and an ability to write hunch stories. The coming attack was to be the show of shows. It would either wrap up the war in Europe or be one of history's great fiascoes, the gathering observers said.

At Robert Capa's apartment that night there was a general air of seriousness that soon disappeared with the diversity of the drinks. Capa was a master at organizing, scrounging, and liberating. In this city full of rules and regulations, he had organized a supply of the finest bottles from various officers' messes in the city and nearby.

There were descriptions of great dispatches, anecdotes of the times that fantastic pictures had been caught, recitals of inoculations, drawings of strange equipment and discussions of units that had odd missions, and comparisons of stories yet to be written.

Ernest was several years beyond all of this, having already sweated through privations, horrors, and tensions in the Spanish War and World War I. "Come on out to the kitchen, Baron. Let's do some boxing, or talk about old times or find Roberto or something." We filed out, refilled our glasses, and got to talking about friends in New York, Washington, and Key West and what they were doing.

"Remember the time you brought that nice couple over to Cuba in your sailboat, and that other one, and how I chewed you out for moving them into the Finca. Why the hell didn't you tell me the girl had gotten her skull fractured? Why didn't you tell me that?"

"I didn't get the chance," I said. We had been over it all before. He'd flown into a rage when he found out I'd brought
strangers to his house and, when he finally paused for breath and
I had the chance to explain that it was an emergency, he'd been
furious with himself for bawling me out and so he'd taken that
out on me too. I hated to remember that and now that Ernest
had brought it up again, I guess my feelings showed. "Oh damn,"
he said with a rueful grin. "That's the same look you gave me
when I was giving you real fine hell for shooting the guinea fowl,
and I ended up giving you a lot of shirts to make you feel better.
I don't know what to do about you, kid."

I changed the subject fast. "Remember how shocked that officer was when you told him about the snipers' school you'd organized in Madrid?"

"Oh boy, I remember."

"And remember how you fooled those officious roadblock officers by telling them you had 'the coronel' riding in the back
seat, coming home from dove shooting?"

Ernest roared with laughter and gave me a glancing punch on
the shoulder. "Remember that secret police guy who didn't want
to give up his gun when I told him I'd take it away, said 'Try and
get it' and I did."

"Sure," I said. "And remember the two yachtsmen who came in
the Floridita bar that other night and busted glasses on my head
to see if I was Hemingway—meaning you?"

"Right. I heard about it from the waiters the next day, and
how you'd dusted the bits off you onto them. Remember the time
we sighted the killer whales and you wanted to fire the Mannlicher
at them and I told you to let departing whales blow?"

We got to going back over so many times, and the weird things
that had happened, that the time, the drinks, and gradually the
other guests began drifting out. Suddenly it was very late.

"That's the good thing about alcohol," Ernest said. "It ruins
your time sense. If you can pick the times of destruction, you've
got a very happy life ahead. . . . Come on, kid, let's box. We need
some action."

We put down our glasses and sparred for a while, trading

stomach punches and practicing tensing up, and we let the others who had come in hit us in the gut. It's surprising how much defense you can produce with tense abdominal muscles. And no stranger ever taps you as hard as you would hit yourself, on a bet.

Capa's girl was named Pinky. She was a Belgian girl who had escaped; she was freckled, charming, and an engaging hostess. "Reason I call her Pinky," said Roberto, "is because she tastes like strawberries. Honest. Kiss her yourself and see." He was absolutely right.

"Miss Pinky, my daughter," Ernest said, "you are a treasure. You are the kind we seek. You are something beyond words."

Pinky was taken aback. She blushed.

"Now you do this," Capa said. "She's my girl. Don't make her blush. Get your own girl."

We sparred some more. A good doctor stayed out in the kitchen with us. His name was Peter and he was simpático, Ernest felt. He wanted to talk more about things of the past and how things had been. "Easy and lucky," he summed them up. "Easy because that's the way it goes best, and lucky or we wouldn't have made it this far and we wouldn't be here now."

The night was almost over and there was a singing in my ears. We all were intent on clearing the apartment and went around saying, "Shhhh, shhhh," and out in the foyer we called "Good night" in loud voices to signal our leaving. Suddenly we were out in the foggy night air. Peter and his girl and Ernest headed around the corner. "I'll drive you to the Dorch," Peter said to Ernest. "You can't get a cab this time of night. Not even a general could."

I called a last farewell in what seemed much too loud a voice on those early morning streets, as they headed around the corner. I faintly heard a car start up as I went on down the block to my own billet nearby. It was after three o'clock of a cloudy morning.

I had slept less than three hours before first call. Out of the sack, dressing, shaving, and on the move, I was out of the billet, the last house next to a singular bomb crater in Knightsbridge, within ten minutes. In the early morning air, I shed the last of a hangover and in twenty minutes had reached Ernest's hotel on

foot. I rang. No answer on the house phone. I went up. As I
walked down the hall to his pale green suite, it was absolutely
silent. He liked having people check on him. I knocked. No answer. I tried the door. It opened. But neither bed had been disturbed. It was like the story of Goldilocks, except nobody was
home and nobody would be for a long time. As I came out, Capa
came down the hall.

"Papa had an accident right after they left this morning. Where
were you?"

"I said good night and went to get some sleep. Where's Papa?
Is he badly hurt?"

"Not bad, just cut. He's in the hospital right near here. They
phoned me just awhile ago and I came over to see if anyone was
here. Let's go see him."

We moved swiftly then. At the hospital in Knightsbridge past
which I had just walked, the night shift was still on. The day staff
hadn't taken over yet. No guard was at the door. No permission
was needed to enter. There was only a sleepy admission attendant
who looked up the numbers. We went upstairs to the room where
Ernest lay, half propped up. The top of his scalp was split not
quite half open, pink and gaping. A bandage ran like a halo around
his head below the wound. Below it twinkled those birdlike eyes,
taking in everything.

"Hi, Baron. You missed a great ride in the London air. Seen the
papers yet?"

"What happened?"

"Hit a water tank right down the block. Peter's legs are bad.
His girl is all cut up. I'm the lucky one. They'll operate on each
of us, soon as the doctor comes. I need some stitching done. But
have you seen the papers?"

"No . . . why?"

"Some reporter came to the desk. Thought he had a story. I want
to see what the press says. Those bloody unprintable . . ." He was
like a great bear who had just had a meat cleaver removed from
his skull. He was hurt, yes. But he was far more thoroughly en-
raged and nothing was going to stop him at that point. It was
a poor time to say it had all been an accident. Ernest had suddenly

been thrown from the back seat clear into the car's windshield. What infuriated him was realizing he was going to be in bed at such a crucial time.

". . . so get me the papers, will you, Baron? Don't worry about me. I'll be out of here and in bed at the hotel as fast as possible. I just need a mending job. But try and wangle some leave from your outfit, if you can. There's so damned much to do, I'll need somebody reliable around the joint."

Later that day the administrative officer of our film unit gave me the word. Jock Lawrence of Hollywood was the Public Relations Officer for SHAEF. He got me placed on detached service so I could be Ernest's orderly while he was on the mend. Jock Lawrence was as considerate as he was generous and helpful to everyone working on news coverage in the area.

That morning none of us in London realized what bulletins had gone out in the day's news. A British dispatch had reported Ernest Hemingway killed in a blackout accident in London. With wartime censorship in effect, an error that could have been corrected in a minute during peacetime became an all-day job of correction in May 1944. In the meantime, early staff members on major newspapers elsewhere were preparing obituaries for the first time in Ernest's life. It took time for the major wire services to straighten out the report. While that was being done, people in far-off places were mourning the loss of Mr. Papa, the spokesman for a generation that liked to think of itself as lost.

In Italy, *Stars and Stripes* carried the report of Ernest's accidental death in blacked-out London. Bumby was stationed there as a lieutenant in Military Police. When he read the news he promptly went out on a bender of serious proportions.

Back in the Middle West, our mother heard the report and was shocked but did not believe it. "I hadn't felt anything the night before, so it just wasn't right, I knew. I have that psychic ability, you know," she told me after the war. Mother calmly insisted to sympathizers that it simply had not happened; and then the correction came through, admitting he had merely suffered a head injury and was doing well, though hospitalized.

The next few days passed in a whirl. Martha came back from the Mediterranean area. The situation called for diplomacy. Once sewn up, Ernest's head was giving him hell, but he didn't want to admit it. And when Marty came to visit, there were words bandied about. These were followed by notes to be delivered. I was the messenger. It was a bad spot to be in because I felt a definite loyalty to each of them and hated to hear things that rankled.

As soon as possible, Ernest left the hospital and got into bed at the Dorchester. He was grouchy as a bear with sore toenails. Though ordered to stay away from alcohol, he was pouring himself whisky only five days after the accident, and growling to himself whenever room service was slow, or if my errands took unduly long. He read a lot of newspapers, but without seeming to care how contrived the bits of news were.

It was just a week after the crash, but Ernest was dressed and ready to get some exercise when I reached his suite in the morning.

"How's the head actually feeling?"

"It's working all right, kid. It throbs pretty good. Took my pulse this morning just by listening. The way it feels, you ought to be able to hear it right from where you're standing. . . . Come on, let's walk. I want to see some of the RAF types today."

No human being ever talked Ernest out of an idea. He either tried it or discarded it himself. That was how it was when, through friends, he managed to get permission to go along on first one, then two, low-level missions in Mosquito fighter bombers against "targets of opportunity" in occupied France.

He made the first flight only ten days after the accident, and when he told me what had been arranged I did a kid brother's level best to slow him down, pointing out that sudden changes of altitude could bring on bleeding and that as the son of a physician he knew he ought to wait until the stitches were removed.

"Skip all that, will you, Baron?"

"It's been skipped because you're in charge. But you should wait."

"This is when they're flying these missions. They run into all kinds of interesting things. You know me, kid. I'll be back." Then he went down the hall. He said he wanted to ask the maid for some small gift, for luck. He came back with a champagne cork.

The next afternoon Ernest was up in his suite feeling jubilant. "It was great, Baron. I felt terrific as we came back." He had seen a lot of country, had been in some fast action, and the plane had not been hit or knocked down, or set afire, or forced into a scrambled landing. Best of all, his head wound hadn't hemorrhaged. It was a fantastic chance he'd taken. He had his own reasons, call them reactions, for taking those chances. Any logical man would have stayed in bed, listening to the arterial throbbing while the ice packs melted on his brow. I realized Ernest had found a drastic cure for the blues that had been trying to set in. Looking out the window, he said in a sad, quiet voice, "She only came to see me twice while I was laid up and hurting here. What a way for a wife to be. . . ."

From then on, whenever anyone asked about Martha, Ernest would explain briefly, "She's here, too, right now. But this isn't her area. She was assigned to the Mediterranean theater of operations. And it's quite a show. Down there, I mean."

Each of them tried to put personal feelings aside when it came to business. They were, no matter what their personal problems, each capable of delivering great value in their publishable dispatches. Yet Martha was obliged to regard Ernest as a news bureau chief, an official who would look over and authorize her expense accounts. "He's worse than the government," Marty told me by way of summing up Ernest's attitude.

"I've tried talking to him, Baron," she said one afternoon. "He refuses to understand. Will you please see what you can do?" Ernest was busy getting information from someone else in the next room at the time. I waited and then, when all was clear, said what needed to be said. Ernest was immovable. He knew where he stood, where everyone else was positioned, and he had no interest in shifting his stance, as wrestlers say.

Then one day things really began moving. "Get over to this supply place and draw me some equipment, Baron. Here's the list."

Ernest was already thinking of something else as I read down through web-belting, canteen, haversack, helmet and liner, wool cap underliner, correspondent's note case, first-aid pouch, gas mask, plastic poncho for gas attack, and other things.

"Hey, Stein," I said. "You want this right away?"

He nodded.

"The supply place at the PX is mobbed right now. I came by there this morning. Could bring you my own gear as far as possible. I can always replace it later. It would have my serial number, though."

"That's okay. It's fine with me."

So Ernest went through the formal part of World War II with equipment lettered "Hemingway 10601462" on the reverse of everything.

In the weeks before D-Day there had been a campaign strange to the practiced observers in the public relations field. Throughout London the correspondents were literally being given the pitch. Young publicity-conscious officers were telling them why they should join the such-and-such group during the invasion. The public at home was full of curiosity and every outfit was conscious of home-town news.

Ernest had been approached by several outfits. One that he liked considerably, because of its leaders, was the 4th Infantry. The major general in charge was Raymond Barton, an intelligent Southerner with a bushy mustache, who loved his men and his assignments, whatever they might turn out to be. He had made gentlemen out of clods and riflemen of ditchdiggers. The 4th Infantry Division had Theodore Roosevelt, Jr., a man of thought as well as action, as one of its three brigadiers. He was a New York editor with guts, stamina, and ability and had just come through the North African Campaigns with the kind of record most officers dreamed of. General Roosevelt's aide-de-camp was Captain Marcus B. Stevenson, son of the then Governor of Texas. Stevie knew Ernest was the combat correspondent he wanted, the one person the men in the outfit would respect. Stevie outlined a campaign, carried it out, and won the interest and decision. Ernest would go in with the 4th, wherever it went. The publicity siege was over.

A great scurrying movement spread over the staging areas the first weekend in June. There was a lot of talk, but it was all small talk. Ernest headed down the coast where he would load aboard the attack transport *Dorothea Fox*. I went with another unit to Scotland where we boarded the cruiser *Southampton*. With hundreds of thousands of other Allied troops, we crossed the Channel the evening of June 5.

D-Day was up to everybody's expectations. As the greatest show on earth began, most persons were too nervous to enjoy the grandstand seats. Once aboard his assault boat, Ernest identified the mine-swept Channel to the south for the lieutenant in command, while the spume and spray sifted down over the company. He went ashore under heavy fire in a 36-foot LCVP, through antitank obstacles on Fox Green Beach. Behind, to the north and east, the U.S. battleship *Texas* fired salvo after salvo over the landing craft. A great flash of white licked out at every salvo. The 16-inch guns of the *Texas* accounted for a number of objectives off the Cherbourg peninsula. From the distance I watched her down the line of ships.

Ernest told me afterward, "She looked huge and formidable. It was comforting to feel that big battlewagon whooshing those hunks of stuff inland and well over us. We figured somebody could always call in and ask them to blast a little closer, even though the rebound might be down our necks. She was *our* navy, and never felt so good before, even in a newsreel with bugle calls."

I asked him about the enemy planes down his way. "No aircraft worth mentioning. I figured we must have fighter cover for hundreds of miles to group surface targets that way. We even reached our coastal area on time." Ernest was pleased. "As far as my eyes could see, ships were behind us and spread out on both sides. Going into the beach was easy. There between Easy Red and Fox Green, the lousy cliffs west of Thionville stared down at us—it was the Krauts there doing the staring. Once we waded ashore, they began doing their stuff. But whole platoons of our guys would flop into the sand, thinking that was cover. They'd just lie there while heavy metal whistled over. They didn't seem to realize they were being observed and that the Germans were shortening the range every minute they stayed down. I looked where we'd come from. It was creeping closer and closer.

"There was a lieutenant near me. 'Come on, boy,' I said, 'they'll zero in here in a minute.' He shook his head. So I said, 'You mother unprintable unmentionable, undoable, let's get up the beach to where we can shoot back,' and I kicked him squarely in the butt as I got going forward. That got action. He could have let me have it with the Tommy gun, but instead he followed with his men and we moved further in. Those gents who stayed back in the sand won't ever move again."

I told him of my own luck down the coast, and then asked, "How did Marty make out?"

"She did everything possible to make the landing," Ernest said, giving her full credit. "Went over on a hospital ship. Got good human interest stuff. They refused to let her ashore because she didn't have accreditation to this area. A damned shame. She got good stuff, though, and then came back here. What about Shaw? Was he with you?"

"Irwin? Not him. He'd cooked up a super private deal to go in with Commandos. Then they didn't go. He never landed or saw our kind of action the whole week."

"Tough luck," Ernest grinned. "But don't underestimate him. He's fast."

Some British reporters came to see Ernest then, hearing he'd returned. The questions came thick and fast. I was typing clean copy for a dispatch Ernest wanted to send off by radio and I needed to keep the pages moving, no matter how interesting the drinking and laughter became. Right then anyone who could type and concentrate was in demand. Having a brother and a sister-in-law with officer status, this Private Hemingway was one of the luckiest and busiest enlisted men in the army. I knew that what I was running through was a pleasure compared to KP duty. It lasted longer too.

"Come on over, Baron," Ernest called. "I admire your concentration in this setup. But I want you to meet these gentlemen from the London press. Friends, my kid brother, Leicester, like the Square. But he's shaping up and rounding off, a little more all the time." There was appreciative laughter. I refilled glasses and brought in more club soda.

"Goddammit, my head still hurts," Ernest observed. "What any wound needs is a good stiff drink. . . . Make a note of it, Baron. Future historians will one day realize that alcohol has been one of the most profound contributions to the prosecution of any war known to man."

Glasses were raised and clinked to this.

"Does your own family know you are safely back from the beachhead?" one of the reporters asked.

"Write to our mother, Baron," Ernest directed, as though in answer. "Tell her we're safe and had an easy time, like we always do." He winked broadly. "Gentlemen, I've got too much to do right now getting ready to go back again where the fighting is heavy at this moment."

That week the first buzz bombs came over London. Their targets were unpredictable and senseless. One would hit a vacant lot in the suburbs. The next would plop into the Thames. A third would come down on a small hotel, or a barracks, scattering parts of both buildings and people over acres of nearby areas. For several days the flying bombs were an official secret. When they were finally admitted to be "pilotless aircraft," the evidence of their destructive power was so formidable that it convinced the most skeptical citizens that Hitler had developed a really nasty weapon. The swift, buzzing drone would approach in the still air. Then as the engine stopped, everyone would almost stop breathing. The "Blam!" of the explosion, however near, was a relief. If it hadn't blown you into the air, it had been a clean miss.

"There's no way to figure where the next one will come down," Ernest told Ira Wolfert. "From now on, we'll all be able to sleep better on the Normandy beachhead than anywhere in London town."

Correspondents who had planned to stay in London, with its easy access to the telegraph office and filing facilities, made arrangements to cross the Channel where the battle against the Wehrmacht was going better all the time.

Ernest had another chance to go flying on a combat sortie and took it. He went over in a Mitchell B-25 bomber to hunt out and bomb the new buzz-bomb launching sites. He flew with Wing Commander Lynn and had some great luck in hitting targets and being missed by heavy flak.

Ernest was itching to be over on the Continent. All other members of *Collier's* staff were there covering specific operations. He wanted to report the actions of ground troops again himself.

My film outfit, traveling with vehicles, took two weeks to reach France. Buzz bombs were hitting the port of Southampton, from which we sailed, they fell every half hour or less, and a nor'-wester had injured the emergency harbor built off the French coast. When we finally got ashore again it was like being on a conducted tour. Paths were laid out, with signposts everywhere, and there was the debris of many advancing troops ahead of us.

It took hours to de-waterproof the vehicles. More time was spent locating headquarters and we finally arrived where we'd been assigned, among the hedgerows and weird trees in a field near Ste.-Mère-Eglise in Normandy. When the outfit was settled, we began working out of liberated territory and checking in with Allied Press Headquarters. There a group of correspondents had just arrived. Among them was Ernest.

"Hi, Baron. What good things have you been covering?"

"Flying-bomb launching sites, glider landing areas, uses of wrecked gliders by occupying troops, burial of the dead of all classes. You know what. How was it with you?"

"Plenty buzz bombs. But if you're in a good spot, why worry? How would you like to come talk with some fighter pilots?"

It was a great chance to learn about another part of the war. Ernest said to try and come over for the press briefing the next day.

He would have the transport. When I came, I brought him part of a camouflaged green-and-brown silk parachute. We'd found that pieces of these drop cloths worn around the neck were good to keep out the dust of Normandy roads.

Ernest fingered the cloth. "Poor guy," he said. "I hope they got him clean or that he got away."

"I think he made it. There were some supply chutes nearby and the farmers hadn't found them yet. They were back of a mine field. I was careful, reaching them."

"Ah, good. He must have made it then. Try and get here again tomorrow, eh?"

I was able to reach the press camp two days later. Ernest was just shoving off. "Jump in, kid. The commanding officer at this field is a friend. He's Charlie Wertenbaker's brother, so be polite, for Christ's sake. Remember the Air Force isn't like the unprintable Signal Corps." Then he laughed to take the sting away.

At the airstrip, Thunderbolts were taking off and landing with great regularity. The strip was less than a mile from where my outfit was bivouacked, but our commander had said there would be no visiting. So none of us ever officially went there during our stay in Normandy.

Colonel Wertenbaker was a tall, easygoing flier who had a tight schedule of dive-bombing and ground support during daylight hours. He ate when he got a chance and invited us. In the mess tent everyone was polite. Clean linen covered the tables and the food was excellent.

"Does the Air Force always live like this, sir?"

"Oh yes. Things get better when we're more settled. The front's only three miles from here and we may get pushed somwhat. But if we do have to evacuate it will be in a hurry. We've moved swiftly before."

"General, do you personally check the day's operations from the air?" Ernest asked.

"Why yes. Would you care to come along one day?"

So Ernest arranged to be over the next morning. He had a chance to look around and get the feel of how it was done from a two-seater Thunderbolt right over the lines. The experience made an excellent magazine piece. Later I asked him, "Why did you always address him as General, when he was wearing eagles?"

"Always call a colonel a general. That's what he's intent on becoming and he will think well of you for knowing what's on his mind. When you've learned that, you know something about war."

The hedgerow fighting in Normandy continued, though the 4th Division had long since cleaned up the Cotentin Peninsula. Nazi resistance was very effective in containing the beachhead. Ernest continued to check on the progress of the 4th, but he wanted to learn about everything else he could before the breakthrough that experienced observers predicted would come.

On Bastille Day, the first French holiday since the Allied landings, the liberated area really celebrated. By then the French were convinced no Nazi counterattack could drive the Allies back into the sea, so they let go after four long years of oppression. Parts of our film unit were covering celebrations by American generals. The unit I worked with was shooting the reopening of Cherbourg Cathedral. In misty rain, and later hot sun, we got a great deal of footage, including the Archbishop's entrance into the Cathedral while the bells pealed and the crowd cheered.

When we had most of the film shot for the day, a gentleman from the OWI came up and began examining our gear and equipment. He wore an officer's uniform, but without insignia. He didn't introduce himself, or ask our names. Clearly trying to impress all of us, he sledge-hammered in the idea that he and his outfit were winning the war.

"Without information, the American people would refuse to support the war effort. So we give it to them, and man, do they eat it up. You should see the reports we get on the reception of our material by the home front." Somebody snickered.

"You probably got into this thing early and helped build it up, didn't you?" one of us asked, dead-pan.

"Oh yes, I was in right from '42 when it started. We fellows with foreign experience were needed, you know. Too bad the expatriates, Hemingway and those others, are too busy lolling around the

Caribbean and Hollywood to come back to France now. They could be useful to us. . . . Get away, you boys," he said to some kids who were playing skip rope with a recording wire. It happened to be ours. The man's English was affected; his French was impeccable, though the accent was lousy.

Irwin Shaw spoke up. "What do you think is the trouble with these dissolute expatriates?"

"Dissolution is their trouble. You hit it there. They're sunk in degradation. They've abandoned their country and *this* country, which gave them their greatest stimulation, at a time when everyone is needed to free La Belle France from the Nazi oppressor."

"Where did you get so much inside track?" someone asked.

"Oh, I used to live here. For years, you know. That's where I got my background. What's yours?"

"None of us have any," Shaw said. "C'mon, Hemingway, let's go tell your brother where us dissolute enlisted men get off. We probably weren't even supposed to come over on D-Day, making things safe for the OWI."

The man turned away. His reddened ears stood out from under his jaunty officer's dress cap like bright twin spinnakers on a sailboat running downwind after a lost race.

The next ten days were a time of waiting. Our units were sent to the wrong places and there were other mix-ups, as in any campaign.

Finally the day we'd been waiting for actually arrived. We'd heard of it ever since the rumor first started around. "There's going to be a hell of a bombing, all in one place, right south of us. It will chew things up and the stalled infantry can jump off. Then the armor will get going and we'll tag along and shoot liberation stuff—we hope."

I checked with Ernest and found he was going to move out with the 4th Division, whatever its fortunes. General Roosevelt had died weeks earlier, during the peninsular campaign. But Ernest liked General Barton and the general thought well of him.

The morning of the big bombardment we were up early, having

been wakened by the warming engines of the fighter planes over at the airstrip. I had watched those planes coming in after sunset many nights, and on their first flights out; and I had developed an affection for them. "All planes are mechanical," Ernest had told me, "but the way men handle them they become alive, like boats under stress of weather."

The flights that morning were like those of migrating birds, high and in good company. They came over in nines, twenty-sevens, and in converging formations. The sun glinted on their wings and they made a thunder that shook the ground where we stood in the field. Once the bombing started, the taut canvas of our pup tents quivered, though we were several miles from the impact area. Planes came over in waves. They thundered on, shaking their eggs as in some gigantic fertility rite, and disappeared in the distance. The bombing continued until nearly noon. By midafternoon we had the word. The breakthrough was a success. Some nervous bombardiers had dumped their loads too early and killed General Mc-Nair and others back of the bomb line. But men on foot were moving through, and armor was ready to run as far and as fast as the Nazis could be shown the error of their ways.

The next day there was no permission yet for photographers or correspondents to go up. We waited days. Shaw somehow managed to get permission to take two cameramen out on patrol. When he got back, Ivan Moffet and I helped him go through three of the bottles he'd brought back. He was loaded with information and wonderful film, and needed to relax. Then word came that the whole unit could take off and catch everything filmable. We stowed gear in a hurry and left caretakers to bring up what was left to the chateau that was our next base camp before Paris.

On the theory that someone might catch something that would otherwise be missed, the outfit broke into smaller units and more cameras were issued.

From the breakthrough three miles west of St.-Lô, we began spotting shell craters. We'd been up there before, but only shelling and infantry probing had been going on. Now there was an area of shell craters for a solid two miles. The rich soil of Normandy looked like the surface of the moon through a telescope.

There were land mines planted along the streets of the previously German-held towns south of the breakthrough. As our vehicles came through, some land mines exploded. They must have had time fuses, for the buildings nearby were empty and gutted. Seconds after we went over one spot, it erupted. Three vehicles were wrecked and several men were blown to pieces; others writhed in their last agony. There wasn't anything on earth we could do for them. We swung around, shot some film, and moved on. The advancing armor was up ahead chasing the Nazi columns in full retreat.

Ernest's foresight and good judgment in rejoining the 4th Infantry Division were amply borne out by his luck and skill in literally commanding a unit on reconnaissance patrol ahead of the outfit. He was guided unerringly by his inborn partridge sense. The partridge is a bird seldom shot because it seems to sense what is coming long before it arrives.

Ernest was there when the combat troops of the different regiments jumped off after the hole had been made for them by air power. He had been with one regiment when it drove in close pursuit of the attack. He had been through a rugged counterattack by Nazi tanks that threatened to wipe the unit right out of its wooded positions between Villedieu and Avranches. General "Lightning Joe" Collins, the 8th Corps commander, commended the entire 4th Division "for its great contribution."

By then in hot pursuit again, driving to and beyond St.-Pois, Ernest realized that this outfit might actually be the one that would reach and take Paris, ahead of everyone else. "I always keep a pin on the map for old Ernie Hemingway," General Barton said when asked by correspondents what was going on. "Ernie is way out in front," the General explained, and added that he was the kind of war correspondent you dreamed of having with you, or even nearby, when a combat outfit was taking territory. He sniffed around for intelligence data, usually found it, and passed it back successfully.

When it arrived it was just what a great agent would come up with, and it was accurate. What more could anyone want?

There were several things Ernest wanted then, and they were commodities that were in short supply, like sleep, relaxation, and a hot bath. Ernest's jeep had acquired first two, and then three, young members of the French Forces of the Interior. They were Jean Decamp, a former Pathé news cameraman, and Marcel and Richard, younger men who had amazing records in the Resistance. Another young man, also named Richard, who joined the jeep as it went through St.-Pois, was wounded later and dropped out. These combat buffs rode behind Ernest, with Red Pelky from upstate New York as driver. Red's first name was Archie but he hated it. He was comical and full of guts.

The first week in August Ernest had gone much farther than he should have. The 4th Division had to fight off a counterattack by General von Kluge who was heading his crack panzer divisions down west. All three regiments were thrown into a slaughter. Battalions were reduced to two hundred men. By August 12, the counterattack was stopped, near Mortain, and from then on the Nazi retreat was historic, a rout.

The 4th Division and the French 2nd Armored Division were in the clear for the race to Paris. By then Ernest was up at Rambouillet. He slowed to a halt, realizing the need for reinforcements and the necessity to learn enemy strength in the area.

"I had Jean and Richard bring in the locals who knew what was going on," Ernest told me in Paris the week afterward. "Marcel was in charge of prisoners. Red and I kept our headquarters operating in the Hotel du Grand Vineur, which had a splendid wine cellar. When locals came in with the true gen, I debriefed them and made notes. We had maps that were invaluable."

His personal intelligence system was extremely accurate. "Send these men out on their bicycles on all side roads. I want them to check personally every patch of woods," Ernest told Jean. "We need to know where all enemy tanks are, how many, what kind, and their situations and ammo supplies, if possible. Tell them I want no estimated reports. They are not to tell me about tanks unless they've actually gone up and touched them with their hands."

Ernest soon had the background and details of the local picture. Working with these young Resistance fighters was as natural to him as writing short, lucid sentences. He'd been running his own private resistance movement all his life.

When they rode along they sang:

> Dix bis Avenue des Gobelins,
> Dix BIS Avenue des GOBELINS,
> DIX BIS AVENUE DES GOBELINS,
> THAT'S WHERE MY BUMBY LIVES.

This was the song Ernest had taught his young son years before in Paris in case the boy ever got lost.

Colonel David Bruce, commander of all OSS forces in Northern Europe, showed up in Rambouillet while the intelligence network was operating. He and Ernest had many mutual friends and they instantly joined forces on the problem at hand. It was a combat operation; but without its success, Bruce would never be able to use Paris and its network of communications for his future efforts.

"The colonel was in command," Ernest told me, "but he let me complete what I'd started, because it was bringing in fantastic results. Those locals were enormously reliable, the way people should behave under stress knowing that they may be counter-attacked and liquidated at any moment. Besides, I was working for their side too, you could honestly say. And they trusted me in a way that was touching."

Then he told me about the deserters from the Wehrmacht, and the local girls, and the obstreperous prisoner they'd put to peeling potatoes in the hotel kitchen, after removing his pants so that he couldn't get away. He described the dinner they'd had with General Leclerc's chief of staff and the Allied intelligence agent from the area. They'd sketched drawings, given Leclerc's chief their maps, soothed his feelings, and felt full of virtue.

But General Leclerc had a very low opinion of all civilians, and correspondents were in a special category of their own, very possibly below civilians. Ernest was specifically forbidden to accompany the Leclerc column, which had been chosen by Allied headquarters to liberate Paris.

Ernest then moved out of sight. Nobody saw him go. He just disappeared.

"I still have that champagne cork the maid gave me at the Dorchester before I went flying," he told me later. "Such things have no monetary value. They're priceless. She said it would bring me luck, and who do you see before you? The luckiest guy I know!" He laughed.

By driving a few blocks away, Ernest and the FFI boys in the rear seat advanced parallel to one of Leclerc's columns to the edge of Versailles. Then they took a series of side roads while the Leclerc units were held up by some serious resistance that evening.

On August 25, the City of Light was in an uproar. The 4th Division had come up swiftly. Headquarters got what sleep it could, only twelve miles south of the city. By morning, the 8th and 22nd Regiments crossed the Seine, and the 12th Regiment advanced up the Boulevard d'Orléans, before the infantrymen were picked up on the shoulders of Parisians and literally carried forward through the city. They rode commandeered trucks. They had drinks pressed on them. They fired occasionally, as occasion required. By noon the 3rd Battalion of the 12th Regiment reached Notre Dame Cathedral.

When the Eiffel Tower showed clearly against the horizon that Friday, Ernest's feelings rose and memories came flooding back. "That's Paname," he mused aloud.

"What did you say, Papa?" Red Pelky was interested as he took in the curves and possible firing points toward which they were speeding.

"That's Paname, the name for Paris for those who love her very much."

Their jeep soon joined elements of the 4th Division that swept in, liberating the first city that Ernest had ever loved. Ernest checked on Sylvia Beach and found that she was in fine shape, and then he directed Red over to the Place de la Concorde and to the Ritz Hotel. They piled out, cocked their weapons, and swept through the hotel cellars, taking two prisoners and noting an excellent supply of brandy. Then they cleaned out the upper floors. Ernest picked himself a suite, posted guards, checked over the staff, and then settled back, ready and free to handle whatever situations might arise. There were many. In the main, they were delightful. There were alarums, excursions, welcomes to late arrivals, chases of the Milice, the calming down of a mob that wanted to cut off the hair of the many local girls who had been fraternizing with the Nazis. And there was some drinking to be done.

I didn't reach Paris until Sunday evening, coming in with the first convoy of food for the city since the Liberation. By then Irwin Shaw's unit was already there with Capa and many correspondents. They had taken over the Hotel Scribe. I checked in with Ernest as soon as possible and found him still excited.

"Our friends came through in good shape, Baron. As far as we know none of the press people got hurt coming here. The Krauts are still in full retreat. I checked with Division, and until they reach the homeland, this ought to be a piece of cake, as the RAF types say." Ernest grinned. "Bloody unprintable job of getting info about the opposition," he added. Then he told me about the intelligence work.

"What happened to Leclerc?" I asked.

"He was damned rude," Ernest said. "Told us to unprintable, so we did. And beat him into this burg. But speaking of the old ballroom bananos, I had fun with one gent, a very serious type who came up with Leclerc's chief of staff. He was a veritable boy, but with rank. So he could talk down to me. He was studying this," Ernest touched his head wound, "and he said, 'Whatever kept you from failing to rise from captain? With your age you must have had experience. I thought our American friends were most generous with their promotions.' "

" 'My friend, it is for a very simple reason. I neither learned to read nor write,' I said. You should have seen his face. First he wouldn't believe it. Then he did. Then he was sore at being taken in, but not quite sure. It was the works." Ernest shook with laughter.

Then he went on, "But I tell you, Baron, General Barton said I did good. You know what a lift that gives." He patted himself over the heart, then abruptly changed the subject. "You seen the catacombs yet? No? Hell, there hasn't been time. But I'll bet there are more guys down there, waiting to be taken prisoner. We'll check it later. These Nazis are like rabbits, once you get real close. They freeze with expectation."

Ernest poured us another drink. "Here's to the city that's like no other, in all this world." We clinked glasses and felt the warmth descend.

When Capa arrived, Ernest was into a second bottle. "Hola, Roberto. This place is the best by far. You like the Scribe? That's not enough reason. Here everything is organized as it should be. Plenty elbow room. Look." He waggled his elbows and then switched to the old fighter's stance. "We take on everybody. We take prisoners out of cellar, where they slowly drink up supplies, like big mice on liquid diet. . . . Don't you want to stay here?" He asked the last in Spanish.

"Thank you but no," Capa said. "They'll start charging, sooner or later. At that point my money would disappear. But let's eat together tonight." So it was arranged. We had a fine dinner uptown at a small hotel.

Very soon the friendliness among the press people was gone. The correspondents were showing off again and whatever ability they had to help each other had been smothered in compliments, credits, and an almost visible desire to climb to the top of the heap. Ernest refused to compete and declared no contest existed as far as he himself was concerned. I heard all this and a lot more in the next few days. Several correspondents arrived late and the bickering began.

"How did Hemingway get here first, when we had to wait?"

With the jealousy and envy common to competitors, they decided to see what trouble they could create for Ernest. He was soon informed that he had been placed under investigation for possible revocation of his status as correspondent. He knew he faced possible removal from the area at a fascinating time.

Mary Welsh, looking very chic and self-contained, was among the earliest to arrive in Paris. A few days later Martha arrived. Then I again carried notes between Martha, who stayed at a small hotel uptown, and Ernest at the Ritz. On the way back from delivering a note one day, I saw the OWI gentleman from Cherbourg. He stared, went white, and looked quickly the other way.

Typing clean copy on dispatches for both Martha and Ernest, locating carbon paper, finding out about available cars, and running errands kept me busy after hours. But I enjoyed working for both of them. By day I was still working for the Signal Corps, and my own unit was after a Presidential Citation.

One of Martha's dispatches had been memorable. I told Ernest about it, thinking he would be pleased things were going well with her. He always tried to be absolutely fair as far as writing went.

"Let her get all that out of her system for now," he growled. "There will be a damn sight more to come. She can't seem to realize what's going on." The political spot he found himself in was bothering him more than anyone realized.

That first week of the liberation of Paris had all of the excitement of an adventure film. Incredible rumors drifted around. There was sporadic shooting in various parts of the city. German sympathizers still sniped intermittently from strategic buildings. The shots sounded like tire punctures.

Every night, Ernest, Mary, Capa, Marcel Duhamel, Red Pelky, and I went out for dinner in a new place. Marcel, who was Ernest's translator in France, knew where the food was. The second night he took us to a small restaurant on the Rue de Seine where Pablo Picasso ate frequently. Pablo and Ernest saw each other from a distance of about twenty feet.

"Pablito!"

"Ernesto!" The abrazos were complete. Tears streamed from the eyes of these old friends. Then there was a lot of fascinating talk while we enjoyed the red wine and fresh lamb. The next afternoon, we went over to where Picasso lived. He showed us what he was doing, led us through his studio, and he and Ernest talked rapidly and incessantly. He had a wonderful place to work.

"Your connecting corridor is like the deck of a ship bowling along in the trades, at about a thirty-degree angle," Ernest said.

"Yes, when I start out toward my work, I have to keep moving toward it or I slide downhill." Picasso laughed.

He showed us the bicycle handle bars he had used as a surrealistic representation of the horns of a large animal, and pointed out how you could use other items from daily life within a design to make a grand composition.

When Ernest checked and found that the investigation of his activities was likely to be a drawn-out affair, he promptly headed off to catch up with the 4th Division. He reasoned that if he stuck with the outfit a little longer he would know a lot about this war, and the outcome of the investigation would not matter.

He rejoined the 4th in Belgium before the attack on the Siegfried line, and was there when the 105mm. tank destroyers with their great shocking power were used to blast in the entrance doors of the concrete blockhouses.

"Those wump guns were the answer," he told me later. "The Krauts still alive would come staggering out. They were dazed, unable to see or hear, blood streaming from nostrils and ears from the shock-wave pressure."

In a few weeks, Ernest went back to Paris to check on the political machinations there. The investigation was still dragging on. He re-engaged his suite at the Ritz and life picked up. Mary had a suite directly above his and the Ritz became a social spot with lots of daily visitors. Within a few days, however, Ernest was again missing his friends in the Division, in the 22nd Regiment especially, and the excitement of combat action. Again, he hurried to the front.

John Groth, the artist, reached Paris about that time. He wanted to visit the front and picked the 4th Division as the territory to see it through. Hearing that Ernest was back, he asked if he might go to where he was. Stevie was still the PRO and arranged transportation to Regiment, Battalion, and Company headquarters. But

Ernest was not there. Groth had to make his way on foot to the farmhouse Ernest had staked out for himself near Blialf.

"It was wonderful to come upon Ernest in his element," John said. "He had the big farmhouse completely barricaded and fortified. The valley just to the east was filled with the enemy. In daylight we controlled the area. But at night it was disputed territory. Patrols probed around every night and Ernest was ready for them. He had worked out alternate plans of action for enfilading fire and all the other things that could possibly happen before morning.

"The night I got there we had an enormous supper, did considerable laughing and drinking. We mainly talked about the formative years of *Esquire* and the old Chicago days. When I decided to turn in, he said, 'Take these with you when you go up to bed,' and handed me all the grenades I could comfortably carry. 'If anybody works in close to the house, ease your window up, pull the pin, and drop one of these outside. I'll be right downstairs here, checking on things.' His advice gave me more insomnia that night than any other I've ever had."

Ernest had many chances to find out what life was like in a holding position that fall. He rode around on a liberated motorcycle behind John Kimbrough of Special Services, checking and investigating. Sometimes they liberated serious quantities of cognac and schnapps while checking for illegal arms and hidden members of the Wehrmacht.

In another month he had to return to Paris to see how the investigation of him was coming along. On that return trip he carried a load of friends on temporary leave, including Captain Boughton and Joe O'Keefe. As they went through the great battlefields of World War I, Ernest pointed out features of the terrain and lectured on what had happened, who had been bogged down, and with what. By the time he reached the Ritz he had a bad cold, starting in the throat again.

I checked in, learned that the investigation was stalled, and began the round of errands. In a short time the cold cleared up, and the investigation was suddenly completed. Ernest was cleared of

ever having borne arms or taken part in combat, actions pro-
hibited to correspondents by the Geneva Convention.

With Jimmy Cannon and me, he attended the opening of the
bicycle races one afternoon in the crisp fall air. We rode over to
the Vélodrome in an open carriage, drank from Ernest's silver hip
flask, and had a wonderful time feeling the civilian life return
to the city.

"Good word, Baron," he told me. "Bumby's transferred to the
OSS. He may be working out of our area soon."

Ernest returned to the 4th again and saw the beginning of the
incredibly difficult, deadly frontal attack on Hürtgen forest on
November 16. The late fall rains, cold and penetrating, had already begun. In the steep hills and thick woods west of Cologne,
the Nazis had mined and wired every usable pathway. The fire-
breaks were filled with tank traps and machine-gun nests. The
crests were gun emplacements. It took five days to move a half
mile forward and the losses were fantastic. Cutting logs and digging
holes were the two activities of every waking hour when the troops
were not firing, shivering and blowing on their hands to warm
them, or lying wounded, hoping to be evacuated. Successive lines of
resistance, with constant artillery fire making tree bursts that shattered the pines and sprayed the men beneath, were what lay ahead.
By the 27th, the 22nd Regiment took Grosshau, and only one more
strip of deadly forest lay ahead. Other regiments joined in this push
through the last main line of resistance and broke through after
three incredibly difficult days. By December 3, the 22nd was withdrawn to Luxemburg as another outfit was shoved into the gap.
The other regiments were withdrawn the following week.

Ernest came back to Paris that time with an infection that did
not respond to the best medical treatment. He was coughing up
blood freely. After getting rid of half a cup of the stuff, he'd rasp,
"Just a little discharge, Baron," with a tired, almost rueful grin.
He had something worse than pneumonia. His face was pale beneath the beard. He had a high fever; breathing was difficult. For

once, even he had a conviction that bed rest would be good. His doctor was excellent. And Ernest paid attention to him.

"Must get you on detached service again, Baron. Have a lot of work to do, and need somebody. . . . Mary can't be here half the time. All right if I put in the word?"

I said it was and Ernest arranged it over the phone. For a week he was seriously sick. Then he was definitely on the mend, had stopped spitting blood, and, though still running a temperature, was ready to take on the universe again. We talked out dozens of subjects, including the doctor, the family, our hopes and worries, and the women of the universe.

The work he had for me was a long and tedious copying job.

"Cripes," I said when I was into it. "This is dynamite. You sure you want it?"

"Absolutely. That's why I needed someone like you that I could trust completely."

Ernest really laid off drinking for almost a week. Then as he started getting better he said, "I miss the gastric remorse, Baron. The doctor can't be serious about taking a healthy kid like me off the water of life. Call room service and get us up some *fine*."

I did, and used the rough French I'd learned since landing in Normandy.

"Je SUIS," he corrected. "Goddammit, we can cut our mother tongue to useful bits. Everybody knows you know English. But when using a foreign tongue, speak grammatically!"

Ernest was still regretting how little time there had been to see Marlene Dietrich during a recent entertainment she had given for combat troops in a rest area near where the 4th Division was fighting yard by yard.

"Marlene's voice was as fantastically throaty as ever, Baron. And the stomping and yelling whenever she did a number was ten times the volume for any night club act she's ever done. When you hear her sing, the Kraut makes up for everything you've ever missed in life. It was almost like when we met on that French ship coming back from the Spanish War. When I see her, she always seems a kind of talisman."

Mary got back again, and Ernest's morale picked up. She soon had to leave but he kept on gaining. Through Marcel Duhamel, who appointed himself social secretary, the backlog of callers, well-wishers, and true aficionados built up. For the first few days, Ernest had been too sick to be tough with anybody. When he began getting better, he was propped up in that big white bed, in the ornate gold-and-white room. There he held court afternoons and evenings. Those he wanted to see, he saw. Others were told, with considerable truth, that he was too sick for visitors and probably would be until after Christmas.

The callers varied from visiting Americans to the reigning local literary lions. Andy Graves, one of the most amusing, was Ivan Moffat's uncle. Andy was in his late seventies, had an absolutely blue tip to his nose, presumably from serious quantities of brandy that he had taken in over the years. Andy had lived in Paris the past twenty-four years, since cornering the American corn market one day after World War I. His profits had been astronomical.

"I don't know how much money I made that day, Ernest," he mused. "I've never bothered to count it in all the years since." Andy had owned the original Yale bulldog and was full of stories about Paris life during the German occupation. "The most delightful countess lived right across from my apartment. She's younger than I am."

"Tell us youngsters something, Andy," Ernest said. "Is it true what Socrates said about men your age?"

"Absolutely," Andy laughed. "Thrice a week is quite enough, and thoroughly worth living for."

Another afternoon Marcel came in. He was excited. "Sartre wants very much to meet you. So does his girl."

"All right," Ernest decided. "Tell them to come about eight. The Baron will still be here. He can be bartender."

Sartre came on time. He was a short man with myopic eyes and a friendly laugh. His girl, Castor, better known as Simone de Beauvoir, was taller, darker, and more likable. We started on champagne. About the third bottle, Castor wanted to know how seriously ill Ernest really was.

"I'm this sick . . . healthy as hell, see?" Ernest kicked back half the bedclothes, flexed a well-muscled leg, and grinned. In the next hour, he insisted repeatedly that he was feeling tremendous. He sat up straight, made good jokes, and spoke scornfully of his compatriots who were keeping the home fires burning while the eastern edge of France, down in the Vosges, still needed liberation, and the Krauts needed to have their ears permanently boxed for having debased civilization as we knew it.

I refilled glasses beyond the sixth bottle before having a nightcap and returning to my barracks up by the Etoile.

"How did it go last night?" I asked the next morning.

"Fine," Ernest yawned. "We sent him home soon after you left. We talked all night. That Castor is fascinating."

Years later, when her book *The Second Sex* was published, Ernest commented to friends that he was disappointed in the book and thought she could have done much better.

When André Malraux came to Paris, Ernest immediately invited him up. "Come have a drink," he said on the phone. "I'm not sick. They just say I am." André wore the uniform of a colonel in the French army. He had been a flier, and a flying officer, in the Spanish War. Now he commanded infantry.

"Mon vieux," he began. Then they were off, both talking at the same time. I opened new chilled bottles, filled and rinsed glasses, opened more bottles, and listened as rhetoric flowed. André had a command of the language that would have awed a Marseillaise fishwife. Ernest spoke well and eloquently, using slang that was fun for me to try to follow.

With pantomime, Ernest told about the pompous Nazi officer they'd taken prisoner after entering the city. When he had demanded his rights as a prisoner of war, the members of Ernest's local FFI unit had been so taken aback by the effrontery of his choice of words, they had removed his pants and marched him up the Avenue de la Grande-Armée to the Etoile. "It destroyed his dignity very effectively," Ernest said.

Malraux had been on the southern front as a Resistance leader in the FFI. The Gestapo had captured him before the invasion and they were preparing to torture him when he pulled his gigantic bluff. "Listen. I know your superiors and they respect me," he told them. "If they hear of anything being done to me, you will each be executed, one by one." It worked. He was treated as an honored prisoner of war, and later managed to escape.

A great many bottles were uncorked that night. The two men sluiced down amazing quantities of the fermented grape. I went out twice to get some air while they discussed the war. André was commanding troops near Strasbourg. Ernest went into the problems of the line to the north. It was very late when the drinking and talking finally slowed down.

When the big Nazi counterattack came against the northern front on December 16, it took several hours for word to filter back. Then there was sudden strict censorship. Few people in Paris realized that the Battle of the Bulge had begun. Ernest had enough facts to know the seriousness of the situation.

"There's been a complete breakthrough, kid. Got to go back up right away. This thing could cost us the works. Their armor is pouring in. They're taking no prisoners."

He was putting in calls about transport and a few minutes later told me, "General Red O'Hare is sending a jeep over for me. Load these clips. Wipe every cartridge clean. We may have a bad time getting up there. The Germans have infiltrated with guys in G.I. uniforms. Jeep coming in fifteen minutes. Try to get up there yourself, and look me up at the 4th. Now look after yourself, will you, Baron? Good luck, kid."

In the first week, the Nazi counterattack slowed. But it had done fantastic damage. The 4th, from its position on the eastern edge of Luxemburg, fought well. It was after Christmas when I got there, on detached service as aide and cameraman with William Wyler, an Air Force colonel who knew how to shoot documentary films as well as Hollywood epics. For more than a week I was able to join Ernest and the 4th Division during its time of pressure, and then relaxation, as the Nazi attack was blunted and then fell back.

Ernest was at home with the 4th Division. General Barton was transferred right after Christmas because of sickness. But his suc-

cessor, General Blakely, was a calm and competent officer who had
handled division artillery for many months.

While in Luxemburg, Ernest had taken a hotel room across from
the hospital, locked himself in, and poured out the makings of dispatches and great fiction. He came out to relax with good pals like
Kurt Show, who had been General Roosevelt's driver, Pelky, Kimbrough, Jean, Marcel, Reg Denny of the *New York Times*, Hank
Gorrell of United Press, Jimmy Cannon of *Stars and Stripes*, and
Jerome Salinger, who was a good CIC man with the division.
Ernest was the dominant figure. He loved to tell stories, drink,
and listen. The different companies and battalions were fighting
all night as well as day. In many instances they were cut off. All
anyone could do was wait and either move up to them or hear
about their last moments.

When Ernest greeted me at his hotel, he was effusive. "I'm in
another belle epoch," he announced. That was the term he used
to describe those times when he was writing very well. "And you,
Baron, you are at the right place and on time."

"Is it still bad?"

"That's the wrong word. Wonderful is more accurate. I'll show
you the positions. How long have you got? I'll take you on patrol,
and I'll show you, point by point, where the Germans came from
and what we did and how everything is now. This has been a time
from which to learn, if ever men could learn."

We did all of those things, our boots squeaking on the snow as
we tramped through the trees, down into valleys, and up along
the ridges, Ernest explaining, the entire time, the actions that had
taken place in each area. He was experiencing a pure, unadulterated
delight in living.

"My chest doesn't bother me any more. Dry air is a help." He
breathed in deeply to demonstrate. It was very cold, but he loved
it. The snow and high-pressure areas made us feel good. We skied
and sang off key, and we had plenty of food and drink as well.

"Marty was just up here," Ernest confided at one point. "Didn't
go good. She's a real woman, but . . . Well, she insisted on speaking
French, thinking this was gaining us privacy. I let her go on be-

cause she didn't ask. But Buck"—Ernest motioned toward the
Regimental Colonel—"has all the military classics in French. He
knows the tongue well."

We went on patrols. Some afternoons we went back to a fine
hotel in Luxemburg where the 5th Air Force had press headquarters. There, with Bill Dwyer, Joe O'Keefe, and Captains Stevenson
and Boulton, we frequently savored lovely distillates. After spending a considerable time in open jeeps, heads hunched down and
hands slowly freezing despite the mittens, we wallowed in the
warmth of cheerful surroundings late in the day, the drinks like
dreams in thin glasses.

Ernest had become scrupulous on forays into town. To his driver,
or to me, if I were along, he would entrust his pistol. "Hold it
until we leave. That way I know I'll get it back," he'd say. He had
learned a depressing lesson back in Paris. Other correspondents,
unless they were genuinely friends, were out to get him.

The day I left, Ernest said, "Dammit, I miss Willy Walton. We
did some useful stuff for the 4th back there." He gave me a message to give to Walton in case I saw him first. Then Colonel Wyler
and I worked our way into Bastogne while it was fighting free,
and checked out the fighting in the far south, along the Swiss
border. We got wonderful film and didn't reach Paris for another
month. When we got in, I phoned the Ritz.

"Come over, Baron. Lots of news." Ernest sounded distraught.
When I got to the hotel he told me, "Bumby's been captured. He
was on an OSS mission and got hit and picked up by the Krauts.
We may be able to pull a snatch job and get him back. I'm getting
more information."

He kept pacing the floor and slamming his right fist into his
left palm. What had him in this impotent rage was that he didn't
know if Bumby would be treated as a prisoner of war or as an
enemy agent. Ernest was determined to try to get his son back.
But so far he had not even been able to find out how far to the rear
Bumby had been taken.

A week went by with no new information. Ernest entertained
officers from the 3rd Division, in whose territory Bumby had been

captured. He also entertained officers from the 4th, where he'd spent most of his time during the war.

Ernest talked well, with great reasoning ability, about the way the war might go with the coming spring weather. Mary was pensive, sensing his own mood. When asked about her own writing she was definite. "For some time I've been working on a long thing about truth," she said.

More time passed. My transfer came through, and I went off to the 4th Division. Word often came through from officers who had had leave to visit Paris. Ernest was still there. Then finally the good word arrived. Through the International Red Cross, Ernest learned that Bumby was officially a prisoner of war. He relaxed.

Marlene Dietrich had returned to Paris from her many front-line visits, and in an intimate talk with Mary and Ernest convinced Mary that she should try and make a life with him, despite his uninhibited behavior. Ernest, feeling pretty good, had fired his pistol into the toilet. This action had upset Mary, and Marlene says she took some time to quiet down. "You two need each other, and it will be good for you," Marlene said. Ernest and Mary made up, and went on from there.

By March, Ernest knew how the war would come out. He headed back for New York. He wanted to write. He had had his firsthand view of the war, and he said that it made sense. He said that World War I had made no sense to him at all. Twenty years after the Spanish War, he said, the more he read and remembered about that one, the less he understood any of it. But World War II made sense.

Chapter 11

In Havana after the war, Ernest wrote steadily. In December 1945 he and Martha were divorced. In March 1946 he married Mary Welsh. The Finca and the *Pilar* required a great deal of attention in those early postwar months. He built the tower workroom, and outfitted the boat again. Then he got back to his routine of writing in the early hours. Then came fishing, swimming, drinking, eating, and sleeping until production time the next day. He described his work habits to columnists Leonard Lyons and Earl Wilson. In turn, they described them to the world. And he was absolutely honest in his advice to writers, urging them to read the best works available; to try to see, feel, and know as much as possible about their subject; and always to stop the day's writing at the point where the writer knew what was coming next—so that the next day's work would start easily.

Ernest sent urgent letters of invitation to his friends to come visit him. He admitted he missed the old feeling of having the outfit with him, and the free flow of stimulating conversation after each day's work. He used these personal letters as a further release of energy. As the world situation became tense through growing Russian truculence, Ernest wrote Buck Lanham, former colonel of the 22nd Infantry Regiment, that if the Russians really got tough and pulled a surprise invasion of the United States, the only sensible thing would be to take to the hills and crank up the resistance. He was in favor of human freedom at all times. And he was willing to get out and personally fight for it. When the first organized opposition to President Trujillo of the Dominican Republic developed in Cuba, Ernest addressed the troops who were planning to invade that dictatorship to the east. Then the invasion was called off, after massing at Cayo Confites.

The Cuban government was very unstable at the time. Ernest's house was searched for weapons, and a large number were found. "Before the trial was to take place we had the judge out to the house for dinner," he told me later. "Bumby volunteered the information that the guns actually belonged to him. The judge wanted to know what Bumby did for a living. I said, 'He's an industrialist.' He was, you know. He was making very fine trout flies, tying them by hand. The judge was impressed that such a young gent was an industrialist." Later, the charges were dropped.

I was working on a magazine in New York and began writing a novel about the war. Ernest was very interested and suggested that I send him what I was doing as the book progressed. Whenever I finished a good chunk, I sent it along to him. He kept the manuscript for a long while. Then he wrote saying how useless it was to offer alibis for not replying, especially when I was biting on that kind of nail, but that he had been working with everything he had on each new day's production. He was always intending to reply, then putting it off to do his own writing. He enumerated the problems he faced, including a chance to sell "Fifty Grand" for that exact amount. But he said that taxes would take more than four-fifths, and that he didn't want to let the property go for what he'd get after taxes. He was then in process of working something out with Mark Hellinger so he would come out ahead if a picture were made, instead of chopping up individual stories, which was like chopping up fine, hand-crafted things just to keep a stove going.

Ernest felt he couldn't lend me any money at the time but that I should let him know if I was seriously hurting. I had great credit with him, he said, because of past actions and present production. He took the manuscript of my novel apart, piece by piece. He pointed out what was no good, and the sections that were N.B.F.G. Then he pointed out the good parts, the excellent parts, and the section he thought splendid and said he wished to hell he had written that himself. He went into detail on the parts that needed further development. The lack of integration bothered him, and he thought it might go better as a collection of short stories on a single theme. He was delighted with the feelings that came across, but was concerned with some "half-written material." He felt that was clearly better than overwriting, but that it still was not written as it should be. He thought I could invent more than was already there, and urged me to try because in those times, he said, even a great war book could miss. In closing he said he had not yet expressed his excited feelings and wanted to talk personally instead of developing points and sounding like an amateur Henry James. He asked me to let him know what I thought about doing it as a collection of short stories, and signed the letter with affection.

That summer we had a chance to meet and talk out at the Finca. Mary was away visiting her folks. Patrick was very sick. Ernest was caring for him and asked me to stay over a week so that we could talk. It was a time of strain, of evaluation, and of loneliness.

"Goddammit, Baron, there have been so many brain-pickers down here lately. They all want to do magazine pieces or get ideas or find out what their thoughts are worth. It's a cheerful thing to see somebody with plans of his own. Stick around. We need to fill the air and let the thoughts fall where they may."

I had planned to stay about three days and said I didn't know if I could be free for a week.

"A bloody week won't ruin you. Patricio will appreciate it and we've got to get him eating and on the mend. And we need to talk. I'll tell you how to pick them in the quinielas. I'll tell you what's worth reading, and how to write from imagination as well as from what you know. I'll tell you about women. . . . What do you want to know?"

It wasn't feasible to leave the house long enough to go fishing.

But other things were possible. We swam, shot doves, boxed, drank, ate, read, talked, and Ernest got tired enough to sleep, which was what he really needed to do.

By then, Ernest had an annex for the big house. It had three bedrooms and was on a lower level, down the drive. Taylor Williams and I stayed in the annex. Ernest kept a second library there. We talked about a possible book, discussed the family, sorted out values and experiences, and agreed on developments. The guests during the past two years had ranged from multiple members of the Gianfranco family to reputed escapees from Devil's Island, though the penal colony had been closed since early in World War II.

A friend came out from town one afternoon. He wanted to discuss a private cockfight.

"How many fighting chickens you have now, Ernesto?"

"Seven, in good shape."

"How about making up a new group entry? Say you lend my friend your three best birds, and group them with my friend's best four. Then both of you would have a combined force of seven entries. You could take on any competitors, and win. Isn't it a great idea?"

"Chico," Ernest said, "would you lend someone your wife?"

Beyond cockfighting, for which he had a passion, Ernest was as blithe in his social life as he was serious about his writing. He delighted in afternoon and evening visitors, but refused to admit any callers before noon.

"If our mother came out at the wrong time of day I'd send her back to town, kid. You know that. Now if you citizens keep quiet in the morning, you're damned welcome. Read, eat, or take off like South American Indians through the rain forest. Only our folks were from further north. The Edmunds side of the family had some real Indian blood, you know."

"Truly?" I laughed.

"Damned right. Everybody always sat on the information. But you know how we all took orders. In our tribe everybody was chiefs."

Ernest talked without inhibition. "You know, Baron, I've been married three and a half times, really. Of them all, Pauline was the best wife any man could have."

The next year when I came through Cuba on the way north from doing a fishing survey in Jamaica, Ernest was more cheerful, and just as candid. During the survey I'd boated a record white marlin. When he asked for all the details, I gave them to him, and admitted that the fish should not be submitted as a record because I'd had to help the angler get it aboard.

"It's your tough luck, being my kid brother, Baron. Being a vice-president of the Game Fish Association, I pass on records. Naturally, I have to be harder on you than on anyone else. So don't get your hopes up about ever winning any. That doesn't have to keep you from being a damned fine writer or fisherman, or keep this fish from being the largest white marlin ever taken on rod and reel."

On the good life, Ernest was just as explicit. Winston Guest was down at the Finca then. So was George Brown, the famous trainer who had boxed with the great fighters of the past, and had a perfect nose to prove the excellence of his timing and footwork.

"Wolfie's shooting beautifully, both at the Club and out in the field," Ernest said. "You'll have to see him in action to believe it. He needs his brandy glasses to correct his vision. But when he gets on the second bottle of brandy, he's sensational. Like George here, with the gloves. It always feels good to see the best in action."

Ernest missed Marlene Dietrich. "Hell, Baron, my spiritual life is always in good hands as long as Don Andres is around. But Marlene—there's a woman who could cheer a man going to the gallows, much less a gent just lonely for a feeling, a vision, or maybe a voice that goes with it. I'll write the Kraut again and try and get her to come down for a visit. She'd be wonderful to see beside the pool and remember old times with, and Miss Mary likes her fine."

Ernest was writing well, and not showing his work around. He kept the production flowing, in between head wounds, automobile accidents, and jarring concussions. When his postwar profits from foreign rights built up to good proportions, he and Mary took a trip to Europe. He wanted to see northern Italy again, where he had worked so well and had been so pleased with life in his first years overseas. While duck shooting in the marshes near Venice, he got a bit of shell wadding blown into his eye by the wind, and a serious infection developed. It looked for a time as though it could cost him his sight, and perhaps his life. But many millions of units of penicillin later, he came out of the experience. And he had the manuscript of *Across the River and Into the Trees* on paper. It had been written with urgency. But Ernest thought it excellent and was annoyed by the critical barbs that followed its serialization in *Cosmopolitan*. Of this book he said to a friend, "There is in it a true and lovely girl."

After the eye infection had healed, Ernest wrote Marlene offering to do a wonderful Dietrich scenario based on the search for the Holy Grail, in which there would be an innocent German girl who had to find her way through whole countries of unpleasant people. He said she was not to feel too cocky about a happy outcome for the story, for they were both to remember Ingrid, who had herself been burned at the stake in full armor and with the handles on, yet all she had gotten out of it was Rossellini. Ernest said he loved Marlene very much, as she damned well knew, and that someday maybe he would write a story about both of them and then they could live happily forever.

Before returning to Cuba, Ernest was thoroughly examined by an excellent European doctor. He was told he had cirrhosis of the liver and given advice on what he could do, or else consider himself in the final ten years of his life. Ernest had defied the predictions of so many well-wishers in his time that he felt honor-bound to disregard the advice.

When our mother died in 1951, he was again working well, and the prospect of facing an emotional situation was disturbing to his composure. When he learned about the funeral arrangements, he sent one of our sisters a note and money, asking that she take everyone to dinner in his name, and tend to everything else that was necessary.

While working on his own serious writing, Ernest continued

writing wonderful letters. He wrote Marlene Dietrich, telling her that he and she were the last two innocents in this world, and that she was a talisman to him. He urged her never to lose touch, and said that in the material he was writing he was putting in all the love that he never did anything about, and that if he could ever be of any use or obey her orders, he would, because he was a Kraut too, she was to know, even if only by contact.

The following year, he was persuaded by Leland Hayward to publish *The Old Man and the Sea*, first in *Life* magazine and then as a book. Ernest was deeply pleased with the professional way the book's publication was handled; he knew he had written a memorable story, with power and value beyond anything he'd ever done. It won him a Pulitzer Prize, which gratified him enormously.

After the book was published, someone wrote a magazine interview with him that made him furious—because the interview had never taken place. Local fishermen accused him unfairly, and he had to explain to many writing friends that he had given no such interview, that the story was a fraud. He said that he had created *The Old Man and the Sea* out of years on the water, and from his knowledge of dozens of fishermen.

With plenty of production behind him, Ernest headed for Europe again, and re-entered Spain for the first time since the closing weeks of the Spanish War. He wasn't mobbed or framed, as he thought might happen. From Spain, Ernest and Mary went down to British East Africa for another hunt with Philip Percival. Ernest wanted to find out about the feelings of a hunter on foot, at night, in good leopard country. He was working up to this by substituting as a game ranger in one area, and killing some marauding lions in grass fifteen feet high with poor visibility and excellent chances of a surprise attack.

One lion tore away from a thrown spear and was in a killing rage when Ernest shot it at close quarters. He dressed out the big cat's shoulder bones and false collar bones and saved them for a boy who played guitar at the Floridita, back in Havana.

Wanting to see Victoria Falls, Ernest and Mary chartered a four-seater Cessna monoplane with Roy Marsh, an American pilot, to take them there and into the back country. Near the falls,

Marsh encountered a flock of ibis. Diving to avoid them, he hit an abandoned telephone line and crash-landed nearby.

They were considerably shaken by the impact. The most injured physically was Mary, who cracked two ribs. After a rough night on the ground near the plane, with elephants taking a disturbing interest in them, the party hailed a passing launch on the river nearby, and reached Butiaba. There they chartered another plane. On take-off, it crashed and burned, shocking them all severely. By then a search plane had spotted their first plane and reported no signs of life. The world press was informed of this and obituaries flowed freely. Ernest had been almost fatally shaken up in the second crash. His internal organs had been wrenched out of place, his spine was injured, and he was bleeding from every orifice when he reached medical aid at Nairobi by car. The doctor there explained that by all medical logic he could easily have died during the night. In not dying, he stood a fair chance of recovery. During the next few days he was able to read the many choice obituaries of himself while resting in bed. He ignored the pain to savor the experience.

After the crashes, Ernest and Mary returned to Cuba by way of Europe. Ernest was still hurting and the intensity and depth of the pain were real. He said he could take his mind off of it sometimes while he worked, but night was the worst time for that kind of pain.

Writing Marlene, Ernest urged her to come to Cuba and visit the Finca, promising not to make bad gallows jokes or to let her read his obituaries. He said the waves of pain at times were rougher than rough, but that at those times he would think about her and then for a while he did not hurt at all. He said he wished they had more contact, for there was always a part of him that stopped aching when he put his arms around her.

In 1954 he was awarded the Nobel Prize for literature. He made no speeches, except over the Cuban TV network. After remarking on how much pleasure it would have given him to see Isak Dinesen, Bernard Berenson, or Carl Sandburg receive it, he calmed down and accepted the award with humility. His doctor refused to let him go to Sweden for the award. Ernest refused to send Mary, so the American Ambassador made the formal acceptance. The medal and money reached Ernest in due time. He gave the medal to the shrine of the Virgen de Cobre in eastern Cuba, remarking that nobody ever really had a thing until it was given away.

In the years between Ernest's African crashes and his revisiting Europe, I had repeatedly written him without getting any indication of his having received the mail. I had published a novel, remarried, and done some things that logically would have interested him. It was during this time that Ernest asked mutual friends he saw, such as John Groth, and others to whom he wrote, particularly Harvey Breit, why he didn't hear from me and what news did they have. Finally a letter I sent to Spain reached him, and in a return letter he rehashed personal and public events, the business of writing, and other matters. He had been infuriated with a single line concerning a certain character in my novel. I recalled his advice to me at the Finca after the war:

"Never hesitate to call a spade a dirty unprintable shovel. And regarding unsympathetic characters, blast the unprintables with everything you have and let them dare to sue. Good guys we level on also, but more gently. Nothing is worth a damn but the truth as you know it, feel it, and create it in fiction. Nobody ever sued me in England over *The Sun Also Rises*. Yet the characters in it had very real origins. Some went around pleasuring themselves with identification and being literarily angry for some time. So slip it to them, every one. If a writer cannot do with words what a cartoonist or artist does with lines, he should write political speeches where the premium is on volume without insight."

During the fall of 1955, Ernest worked with Spencer Tracy in Cuba making most of the sequences for the film of *The Old Man and the Sea*. Ernest, Spencer, and Leland Hayward had agreed that they would each share a third of the picture's gross in return for their roles as writer, star, and producer. But there were countless delays in shooting parts of the script. The camera crews were excellent, but Hurricanes Hilda and Ione bitched the schedule with gale winds and ground swells that halted all activity. On good days Ernest spent eight to nine hours on the *Pilar*'s flying bridge, maneuvering the vessel for the camera crews. Then he would stagger ashore to be rubbed down by George Brown before having his evening meal—and all the sleep possible for the coming day.

Before the main Cuban body of the picture was finished on September 15, Ernest was almost sick with frustration. He declared that he was a writer and had to be faithful to his trade. He had to continue working in his one-man fiction factory, no matter how absorbing the film work might become. He made up for the time out to some extent during the winter that followed. By the next spring, another camera crew journeyed with him to Peru, where it was hoped a giant marlin could be taken and used for the final scenes.

In the first fourteen solid days of fishing there were no marlin strikes. Then in the next two weeks, six fish hit the baits and four of these were boated. They were big marlin by any standards. They ran fourteen feet and over. But they were not huge, and the picture needed one such fish. It was finally necessary to resort to Hollywood magic to obtain the desired effect. It took something out of Ernest when that decision was made.

Throughout the fifties, in letters to Harvey Breit, in conversations with friends, and in comments while enjoying the sports he loved, Ernest threw away more shrewd observations than most men make in a lifetime.

His interests were unlimited. He followed the entire world around him, through the newspapers, magazines, and books that flowed in from the farthest corners of everywhere. Visitors, invitations, and distractions came in from everywhere too. Through it all, Ernest worked steadily. In letters to Harvey Breit he noted that one of the problems of the working writer in Cuba was to be in his best form early in the morning, and to get the work done by midday before sweat streaked down the arms, ruining the paper. On boxing, Ernest made predictions of coming matches that proved to be two-thirds correct. In one prediction-making mood he bet that crime would win over Kefauver, Eisenhower over Truman, and income tax over Hemingway.

When Charles Fenton published a book, *The Apprenticeship*

of Ernest Hemingway, Ernest commented that Charlie had been nosing around like a real FBI man, but had missed such facts as that the Hemingways had Indian blood on the Edmunds side, that when Lewis and Clark went out West they found a man named Hancock who had been there for years, and that one of our uncles had been decorated by Sun Yat-sen while a Protestant medical missionary in China.

On Southerners, Ernest had succinct advice. He felt that the rule should be never to trust anybody with a Southern accent unless he was a Negro. On novel writing, he advised having the kind of self-confidence a structural steel worker had, especially when you reached the level of about the seventy-second floor. Ernest said there had been some wonderful men in the recent human past. These included Cervantes, Cellini, and the Elizabethans, and among contemporary writers he had affection for George Orwell, Edwin Balmer, Edwin Fuller, John Peale Bishop, and Owen Wister, as well as Dos Passos and MacLeish.

Harvey Breit refused to ask Ernest to write an introduction to his book of interviews with writers, *The Writer Observed,* though he had been strongly urged to do so. He felt such a request would be an imposition. When Ernest heard about it, he wrote Harvey a wonderful letter, suggesting that the honor should go to his senior colleague, William Faulkner. He said he would personally pay Faulkner $350 to write one introduction while he, for no financial consideration at all, would write a rival introduction based on an interview with the Deity, which he was almost certain he could obtain, once he explained the circumstances and the high honor being afforded Him of appearing in there with Dr. Faulkner.

In 1956, shortly after Harvey's son Sebastian was born, Ernest and Mary were guests of the Breits in New York for a week. Ernest was godfather to the boy. Ernest said afterward that it was the only time he had ever been in New York when he had been free and had fun being there.

Writing Marlene Dietrich, Ernest talked of the new work he was doing. He said it was much better than the great poem on war he had written during that bad winter of the Ardennes offensive, which he wanted her to have, if he ever ceased being around, and which he had already placed in a safety deposit box for her. He said Marlene would always have him with her wherever she was, since he believed in her without reservations, and nobody loved her as he did.

By the following year, even thoughts of New York were less pleasant. Ernest was no longer excited, even by the prospect of seeing the great paintings in the Metropolitan. He felt that there was something wrong with the city itself. Though he didn't know exactly what was wrong with it, he felt that George Brown might be the only person in it who would survive.

Life in Cuba was beginning to become something less than comfortable. At one point Ernest was challenged to a duel by a British columnist working on a Havana paper. Ernest considered the challenge for a short time, and then dismissed it. The columnist's version of this well-publicized incident indicated that Mary had insulted him because he'd said he would not care to eat the meat of a carnivore.

Ernest would eat any kind of meat. His taste in food was simple. During Mary's absences, he claimed he could get along very well on sandwiches—peanut butter and onion, creamed cheese and onion, corned beef and onion—as long as he had plenty of dry red wine. During one such absence, however, Sinbad Dunabettia, one of the *Pilar*'s wartime crew, was Ernest's guest. He preferred more elaborate meals. Ernest said he was damned if he would write and cook too. That was how he discovered, with amazement, that Mary's maid could not cook. He claimed he thought cooking was something anyone could do, since even Bumby had learned to cook in prison camp. But he admitted the trouble with Bumby's recipes seemed to be that they were all based on cracker crumbs or stale bread.

Another low point of his life in Cuba came when Blackdog was killed. Much has been written about Ernest's enormous fondness for cats. He claimed they were superior to people of unknown quality. "A cat has absolute emotional honesty, Baron," he told me once. "Male or female, a cat will show you how it feels about you. People hide their feelings for various reasons, but cats never do." But one of his favorite postwar friends was Blackdog.

That black springer spaniel lived in the house and regarded himself as a watchdog's watchdog, just as Ernest was a writer's writer. Over the years he came to love Ernest as more than a master. He regarded him as the center of existence. He quietly mourned when Ernest went on trips. He ate well only when the master was in residence. When Ernest slept, Blackdog guarded the entrance door. When Ernest swam, Blackdog waited beside the pool. When Ernest went to the tower workroom, Blackdog climbed the steps and waited to come down with him. Ernest said Blackdog had learned the relationship between typing and food, for Ernest always worked first and ate afterward. He said he sometimes fooled the dog by typing a letter in the afternoon.

By the mid-fifties, Blackdog's eyesight was failing. He had learned to track lizards by smell instead of sight. In a letter to Harvey Breit, Ernest confided that Blackdog had suffered a wonderful near miss recently. A lizard had been on a chair, and Blackie had tracked him expertly with his nose on the yellow tiles, while the lizard admired him. Finally Blackie located the chair but still had not seen the lizard on its arm. Ernest told him to look up and he would see the lizard. Just as Blackdog looked up, the lizard leaped clear over him, but the dog made a beautiful snap at him in midair. This, Ernest said, was the classical type of near miss that the establishment specialized in.

Blackdog was still deadly on moths and flies because of their steady movement. It was frozen motion that baffled his tired eyes. He hated the police and military, but Ernest said he worried about the dog's inability to distinguish between the Salvation Army and the Guardia Rural.

As the Castro guerrilla warfare spread in eastern Cuba, life in and near Havana became more tense. A nocturnal search for arms out at the Finca resulted in a show of loyalty by Blackdog. For this he was struck in the skull by a rifle butt and killed instantly. Ignoring the urgent advice of everyone, Ernest went into Havana and formally lodged a protest against the member of the search party who had wantonly struck and killed his faithful dog. The protest was duly noted by the Batista government. Though no action was taken, Ernest maintained enormous public respect. Before Fidel's revolutionary movement took over Cuba, Ernest did everything he could to aid it.

He was hunting in the northwestern United States at the time of Castro's triumphant overthrow of the Cuban government. When he returned, he reactivated the annual spring marlin tournaments he had organized in 1951 and continued for several years until political conditions grew intolerable. The spring of Fidel's triumph, Ernest officially presented the bearded dictator with a trophy and was quoted as saying, "You may be new at fishing, but you're a *lucky* fisherman." It was common knowledge during the tournament that Dr. Castro had one of the insular champions aboard his boat and the champion had been observed hooking a fish and then passing the rod to someone else. After the tournament, Ernest had a bad taste in his mouth. He knew he had been used.

That summer he and Mary went to Spain. They had an exciting time following the many competing corridas between Domínguín and Ordóñez. Previously, Ernest had thought tremendously well of Domínguín and had come to know him and Walter Chiari when they were both squiring Ava Gardner around. He thought well of Ava too. In one of his letters to Harvey Breit Ernest declared that Ava certainly had the body and he certainly had the morale.

But Ernest was finding that morale was not enough. He instigated and prosecuted battles of insults with other journalists. And in reporting and writing the Domínguín-Ordóñez season, which he published in sections as "The Dangerous Summer" in *Life*, he was again writing as a journalist. His agreement with *Life* stated this, but some readers criticized the material for not being literature.

Ernest headed for New York in October. Once there he dipped down to Havana for only two days before going out to Sun Valley for the fall hunting season. He was not feeling well but kept telling himself that everything was all right.

That winter Mary had a nasty accident which shattered her right arm. It kept her near medical care until the end of January. When she was able to travel, she and Ernest went down to

Havana again. I talked to him by telephone before he left Idaho and he seemed very cheerful, though slow on answers.

Much of what Ernest had known in Cuba had undergone change. Fidel's decrees were shaking the economy, the foreign colony, and the existing business structure. In the spring he left Cuba with thirty-two pieces of luggage and quietly headed for Idaho.

Ernest's weight had dropped to 173 by fall. His answers were coming with great effort and hesitation, no matter whose questions he addressed. When Leslie Fiedler and Seymour Betsky from Montana State University drove to Ketchum to interview him, they were taken aback by Ernest's appearance, behavior, and loss of confidence in his words.

In November, Ernest went to the Mayo Clinic with his own doctor from Ketchum, signed himself in under the doctor's name, and became for a time George Xavier at the St. Mary's Hospital of the Mayo Clinic. When word reached the public that Ernest was there, a bulletin was released stating that he was under treatment for an unidentified ailment. Later releases stated it was hypertension. There Marlene Dietrich was able to reach him by telephone, and he talked slowly, but clearly, about his condition.

"I'm able to keep the blood pressure within limits, Daughter," he told Marlene, "but it's very lonely sometimes and the weight is a separate problem. It's so wonderful just to hear your voice." While in the hospital, Ernest received fifteen electroshock treatments. He was released after Christmas and he returned to Sun Valley.

Before entering the Mayo Clinic, Ernest's blood pressure had been 220/125 and he had a mild form of diabetes mellitus that was confirmed during his stay. He hoped to maintain his weight at 175 with diet and exercise. After leaving the Clinic his blood pressure was considerably lower. On February 15, 1961, the last reading he had was 138/80; however, tests at the Clinic had uncovered the possibility that Ernest might have hemochromatosis, a very rare disease that could bring an end to the functioning of various organs.

By March, Ernest was again feeling depressed. One day that

April, a lively party was in progress in Harvey Breit's apartment in New York. George Plimpton, who had done a recorded interview with Ernest that was published in *The Paris Review*, was there; also there was A. E. Hotchner, who had adapted some of Ernest's stories and books for TV. So was George Brown, Ernest's sparring partner, conditioner, and friend of more than a generation. They put through a phone call to Ernest and each of the men took a turn talking with him, trying to cheer him up. But Ernest's answers came haltingly and with obvious difficulty. Afterward there was great disagreement as to how he had sounded. One claimed he was fine, just fine. The others felt he had sounded awful.

Soon after, Ernest took a plane back to the Mayo Clinic. There he admitted himself under his own name, and had ten more electroshock treatments. Temporarily he seemed more alert, less withdrawn, less depressed. He wrote calm, pleasant, and lucid letters in longhand, and showed awareness of political as well as domestic problems. He swam in the pool frequently.

In the last week of June, he was released. By then he was down to a gaunt 155 pounds. That week Mary phoned George Brown in New York and asked him to come out and drive them to Sun Valley. A new Buick was rented, and the trip West was made in five days. The daily runs often ended shortly after noon when a picnic lunch, prepared by Mary, was served. Ernest ate sparingly. He watched the road a great deal; he was concerned about reaching each appointed destination—seemed worried about the gas supply, the tires, and the road, and followed their progress constantly on a large map which he carried.

When they finally reached Ketchum, Ernest seemed relieved. Saturday night George, Mary, and Ernest went into town and had dinner at the Christiania Inn. It was a quiet meal and Ernest seemed preoccupied. He had lost so much weight he seemed frail, some of those who were there said.

He had been deeply distressed by the deaths of his good friends Gary Cooper and George Vanderbilt. And a letter he had written to our parents more than forty years earlier may have come to mind. Ernest had written the family in 1918, after being wounded, that dying was a very simple thing, for he had looked at death and he knew. He said that it was undoubtedly better to die in the happy period of youth, going out in a blaze of light, rather than having one's body worn out and old, and illusions shattered.

And then, what has been called "the incredible accident" took place, the explosive period ending the career of this century's greatest American writer.

The next morning, around seven, he took the final positive action of his life. Like a samurai who felt dishonored by the word or deed of another, Ernest felt his own body had betrayed him. Rather than allow it to betray him further, he, who had given what he once described as the gift of death to so many living creatures in his lifetime, loaded the weapon he held and then leaned forward as he placed the stock of his favorite shotgun on the floor of the foyer, and found a way to trip the cocked hammers of the gun.

This book was set in

Electra and Janson types by

Harry Sweetman Typesetting Corporation.

It was printed and bound at the press of

The World Publishing Company.

Design is by Larry Kamp.